The Future of Democracy

Ronald M. Glassman

The Future of Democracy

 Springer

Ronald M. Glassman
NYU School of Professional Studies
Stern College of Yeshiva University
New York, NY, USA

ISBN 978-3-030-16110-1   ISBN 978-3-030-16111-8   (eBook)
https://doi.org/10.1007/978-3-030-16111-8

This Springer imprint is published by the registered company Springer Nature Switzerland AG.
The registered company address is: Gewerbestrasse 11, 6330 Cham, Switzerland

This book is dedicated to my wife, Urania, whose love of American democracy is as luminous as the legacy of her ancient Greek ancestors.

Preface

In the latter part of the twentieth century, there was a "third wave" of democracies emerging in the world. Spain went democratic, and when the Soviet Union broke up, the Eastern European countries went democratic. So, too, did South Korea, Hong Kong, Taiwan, and Singapore. It looked as if the whole world was moving toward advanced capitalism and democracy.

Yet, here we are in the twenty-first century wherein a countertrend is occurring. Authoritarian regimes are overturning democracies: Putin has overridden Russia's democratic constitution; Xi has declared himself president for life and is actively surveilling China's citizens; democracy has collapsed in Venezuela and has been overthrown in the Middle East. Even Western Europe is threatened by new fascist movements. And the USA, the great beacon of democracy, has its president, Donald Trump, criticizing the Free Press and encouraging his supporters to commit acts of violence.

Can democracy survive in the modern world? Will Russia and China ever go democratic? Will the new global communications networks destroy democracy or enhance it?

This book focuses on the processes that serve to stabilize and expand democracy: the link between advanced capitalism and democracy is described, emphasizing *contract law* and *the separation of the economy from state control*; the positive influence of the *scientific worldview in enhancing legal-rational authority* is also emphasized; and Aristotle's theory of the *majority middle class* as stabilizing democracy is applied to the contemporary situation.

Further, the "cyber world" is analyzed: Will computer hacking and extremist blogs undermine democracy? Can the global Internet enhance democratic participation in the electoral process? Will AI make democracy irrelevant?

In the face of the rise of neofascism, Russian hacking, and Chinese totalitarianism, this book attempts to take an *optimistic view*, for it is possible that global capitalism, global science, and the emerging well-educated global new middle class can still prevail in engendering *a democratic ethos*, wherein human rights are accepted as inalienable, and state power is limited by constitutional law.

The history of the world is not just a history of kings and dictators. It is also the history of tribal democracy, such as that of the Iroquois League and the Vikings, the city-state democracies of Ancient Greece and the Phoenician cities, and the nation-state democracies of post-feudal Europe.

This book describes the face-to-face democracies of the past in order to give us a better perspective on the high-tech democracies of the future.

New York, NY, USA   Ronald M. Glassman

Acknowledgments

I would like to thank the many scholars who have encouraged me in my work on the origins and the future of democracy. Special thanks go to Professors Nico Stehr of Germany and Wilbert Van Vree of the Netherlands. Their suggestions made this volume more comprehensive and more focused.

I would also like to thank my friends: Stephen Cantor, Gus Davis, Ira Glasser, Lawrence and Carolyn Raphael, George Rappaport, and Gerald Scorse for their continuing dialogue with me and enthusiastic encouragement.

Thanks also to Hendrikje Tuerlings and Esther Otten of Springer Publishers for their ongoing logistical support.

And lastly, to my wife, Urania, without whom this volume would never have seen the light of day – her comments and her editing made this a better book.

Ronald M. Glassman

Introduction

Mixed Messages in the Middle of the Twenty-First Century

Just a few short years ago, Francis Fukuyama, in his work on "the end of history,"[1] theorized that the world's nations were all moving toward one model of society: free market capitalism and representative democracy with constitutional law.

The prediction seemed correct. After all, the Soviet Union had broken apart, and many of the newly independent nations moved joyously toward democratic government. The Czech Republic, Poland, and the Baltic states all established constitutional democracy and held celebrations in its honor.

Even "the Balkans" – that region of endless conflict – went democratic. Croatia, Serbia, Slovenia, Bosnia-Herzegovina, and Montenegro, though beginning by slaughtering each other, ended by establishing independent democratic nation-states.

And, of course, Greece, after a tense population exchange with Turkey, a terrible civil war, and a military junta, finally established a democratic government – nepotistic and corrupt but definitely democratic. Thus, the birthplace of democracy had become democratic again.

Even Russia seemed to be moving in a democratic direction, with Gorbachev and then under Yeltsin. There were elections, and it seemed as if a free market economy would be established.

Fukuyama's projection that the nations of the world were moving in a capitalist-democratic direction seemed correct.

Then, however, the global demiurge toward democracy began to implode. The "Third Wave," as Samuel Huntington called it, was over.

Russia did not establish a high-tech capitalist economy. Instead, the former Communist Party officials and KGB operatives created a "mafia"-style economy. The corporations and even the banks became dominated by former Communist Party officials, who knew only how to rule by force, violence, and intimidation.

---

[1] Francis Fukuyama, *The End of History and the Last Man*, Free Press NY 1992.

A very democratic Russian Constitution was written, but Putin and his clique of KGB friends override the democratic institutions and rule through fraud and violence.

And then there is China, under Xi Jinping.

The capitalist economy is booming, and the middle class is growing, well-educated, and prosperous. But China still has, among its billion people, a huge class of workers and peasants, who outnumber the middle class enormously.

The Chinese regime has recruited the poor for the army and the police. They are relatively well-paid and well-treated – they are loyal to the regime.

Any push for increasing electoral participation, free speech, free press, or any other democratic phenomenon is greeted with swift repression in today's China.

And then there is Venezuela. Aristotle not only told us that a society with a majority middle class is "blessed," because its democracy will be stable and lawful, he also told us that where the poor are in the majority and organized by a demagogue so that they gain control of the assembly, "democracy is speedily ruined."[2]

For the poor, warned Aristotle, have none of the moral restraint of the middle class, and following the lead of demagogues, will legislate to take the state's wealth to themselves. But they will squander the wealth that they take.[3]

Hugo Chavez – a good man – organized Venezuela's poor into a voting majority. But unfortunately, diverting the money to the poor and away from infrastructure and economic development shattered the Venezuelan economy.

Aristotle's program for the poor was focused on giving them careers in craft workshops or cash crop farming and, thus, absorbing them into the middle class. Just giving them money was like "pouring water in a leaky jar."[4] Hugo Chavez poured the money into the poor without integrating them into the economy. Hence, not only has Venezuela's economy collapsed, but its democracy has become de-stabilized with the middle class taking to the streets and the poor counter-demonstrating.

The last region we wish to look at, in terms of the failure of democracy, is the Middle East.

Democracy, of course, did not exist in the Middle East – except in Lebanon and Israel. So it is the attempt to establish democracy in the Middle East that we should discuss.

Dictatorships existed in Iraq, Syria, and Egypt, while monarchies existed in Saudi Arabia and Jordan (and Morocco, North Africa). Iran – Persia – will be discussed separately.

The USA took over the rule, established by England and France, of developing the oil resources in the Middle East. The oil is still flowing, but the USA has been much less successful in stabilizing the political condition of the Middle Eastern nations. The USA supported the dictatorships and the monarchies by supplying

---

[2] Samuel P. Huntington, *Political Order in Changing Societies*, New Haven, Yale University Press, 1968; see also Huntington, *The Third Wave*, Norman Oklahoma, Univ. of Oklahoma Press, 1991.

[3] Aristotle, *Politics*. Barker Translation, Oxford University Press, 1963

[4] Ibid.

them with enormous amounts of military equipment. The dictators and kings used this military power to repress new populations.

But when Saddam Hussein in Iraq invaded Kuwait, the USA found itself in the peculiar situation of having to fight our own surrogate.

President George H.W. Bush was prudent in that he defeated Saddam Hussein but did not invade Iraq.

Enter "W."

The USA invasion of Iraq overthrew the dictatorship but fractionated the country into Sunni, Shia, and Kurdish divisions. None of these fractions would cooperate. Hence, George W. Bush's attempt to establish democracy in Iraq broke down; hence, a violent civil war broke out. ISIS – the most anti-democratic, anti-Western, and violent "terrorist" organizations – emerged as the leader of the Sunni faction. Their goal was to establish a new theocratic-Islamic Caliphate and to drive the "crusaders" out of the Middle East, as Saladin had driven out Richard the Lionheart, back during the Arabic "Golden Age."

Enter Barack Obama.

Barack Obama gave a speech in Cairo, encouraging an "Arab Spring," in which democracy would bloom in the desert. Unfortunately, democracy did not take root in the desert – not even on the banks of the Nile. Instead, Egypt, Syria, and Iraq exploded into violent civil wars.

In Egypt, the USA was forced to back a new military dictatorship in order to prevent the Muslim Brotherhood from establishing an Islamic theocracy in Egypt. And Russia intervened in Syria, reinforcing the rule of the dictator Assad. Iraq is still in anarchy.

Finally, even in Turkey, which since the days of Kemal Ataturk had sought to develop economically and politically like Europe, the political situation has deteriorated.

Erdogan, coming to power with a Muslim majority party – made up of poorly educated working-class voters – began to blur the lines between church and state which had been lawfully observed since the days of Ataturk.

With a failed coup against him, Erdogan cracked down on journalists, teachers, intellectuals, and anybody else who opposed his authority. In a very close vote, he won the right to extend his power in a dictatorial direction.

Given these anti-democratic events, Fukuyama's optimistic prediction began to fade.

So what is the future of democracy? And why should we maintain any hope of a world trending toward democracy?

Contents

Part I
Democracy as a Uniquely Human Political Process

Chapter 1
Humans in the Scientific State of Nature

1.1 Humans in the Scientific State of Nature

Why should we maintain any hope of a world trending towards democracy?

To answer this question, let us look at humans in the scientific state of nature."

Modern political theorists have superseded Hobbes' philosophical "state of nature"[1] with a scientific state of nature.

Theorists such as Azar Gat[2] have utilized the scientific state of nature to analyze the human proclivity for war. Conrad Lorenz[3] has emphasized human aggression and the dominance structure within human groups.

Humans *are* group animals. As Aristotle put it, "only Gods and beasts lived alone; humans are a political animal, everywhere and always found in groups."[4]

Given the fact that we live in groups, the dominance, submission, and "pecking order" of human groups have been emphasized by modern "state of nature" theorists. Books like, *The Naked Ape*,[5] *The Human Zoo*,[6] and *African Genesis*[7] describe human politics as similar to the group dynamics of chimpanzee bands – the chimps being our closes relatives, sharing much of our DNA. Jane Goodall's *In the Shadow of Man*,[8] beautifully describes chimpanzee life and emphasizes the dominance—submission and pecking order "politics" of chimpanzee bands.

However, we are not chimpanzees. We are a different species. We are homo sapiens—the hominid that "knows."

---

[1] Thomas Hobbes, *Leviathan*, Penguin, London, 1951.

[2] Azar Gat, *War in Civilization* Oxford, Oxford University Press, 2004.

[3] Konrad Lorenz *On Aggression*, N.Y., Harcourt 1963.

[4] Aristotle, *Politics*.

[5] Desmond Morris, *The Naked Ape*, NY, Amazon paperback, 2015.

[6] Desmond Morris, *The Human Zoo*, N.Y. Google paperback, 2014.

[7] Richard Audrey, African Genesis, NY Amazon paperback, 2011.

[8] Jane Goodall, *In the Shadow of Man*, Boston Houghton Mifflin, 1971.

© Springer Nature Switzerland AG 2019

R. M. Glassman, *The Future of Democracy*,

https://doi.org/10.1007/978-3-030-16111-8_1

Our key species characteristic—the characteristic that facilitated our move from an insignificant hominid to world domination—is our increased intelligence and our conscious awareness of ourselves, others, other animals, nature, and the universe.

"Eve ate of the fruit of the tree of knowledge of good and evil, and she gave some to Adam, and he ate, and their eyes were opened..."[9]

Our brain increased in size and our intelligence and awareness of the world increased dramatically. With this greater, awareness of the world and other humans, and with the consequent development of our "voice box," humans created language. And, with language, our "inter-subjective" interaction increased in depth.

Our conscious awareness of each other and our increasingly sophisticated language skills allowed humans to discuss everything and anything. Men discussed hunting strategies, women gathering destinations. Informal discussion groups emerged—sometimes gendered, sometimes not. And, the older members of the group, who had experienced more, were looked to for advice. Collective wisdom would be passed down to the next generation.

From these informal discussion groups, more formal discussion groups eventually emerged. A new form of political institutions – the "campfire" discussion council – emerged. Sometimes it was dominated by the men, when they discussed hunting and war. Sometimes it included the entire group, especially when a move to a new territory was undertaken. Often, the elders—both men and women, led the discussions.

This new, specifically human, political institution – *the democratic discussion council* —— typified most hunting – gathering societies.[10]

Dominance, submission, and pecking order status continued to exist amongst humans. There were headmen, who lead in the discussion counsel; headmen who lead in war; leading women who organized the gathering activities and helped the young women in childbirth. Men attempted to dominate through strength and weapons skills; cliques of men dominated others.

But, we are not chimpanzees. Excessive assertions of power or violence were sometimes actively inhibited within hunting—gathering bands. They would say "this headman has gotten too big," and they would slip, away in the night, leaving him alone and vulnerable.[11]

Further, old chimpanzees are not valued. Whereas the wisdom of the experienced aged was venerated amongst humans, motivating the band to keep the elders alive— if they could.[12]

Another factor that differentiates humans from chimps is this: though conscious awareness of the world, and our language skills give us our greatest species advantage, this same heightened awareness engendered "existential anxiety." That is, because we became aware of our own impending death, and, because we do not

---

[9] *Bible*, Adam & Eve Oxford Study Bible, Oxford University Press, 1991.

[10] Ronald M. Glassman, The Origins of Democracy in Tribes, City-States, and Nation-States, Dordrecht, The Netherlands, Springer International Publishers, 2017.

[11] Lorna Marshall, *Kung! Bushmen*, N.H., Yale University Press, 1958.

[12] Ronald M. Glassman, The Origins of Democracy in Tribes, City-States and Nation-States.

understand why we were born, why we are here, how we should behave, and what the vast seemingly infinite universe means, we humans become frightened.

"And – Eve and Adam ate of the tree of knowledge, and they became ashamed of their nakedness and frightened…"[13]

Emile Durkheim[14] has shown us that every human group has some sort of religious belief system: myths of creation, myths of destruction, belief in magic, spirits, and taboos, and ritual activities in which the entire group participated. Those individuals who seem to have a connection to the world of "spirits" gained high status, and sometimes power.

Chimpanzees do not bow down to a weak, old member of the band who can interpret their dreams and explain "omens". But, humans do—look at the millions who come out to touch the hand of the Pope, in this modern world, where the rational-scientific world-view is supposed to predominate!

So, what is the point here? The point is that humans—homosapiens sapiens— even conceived of in the scientific state of nature—exhibit political institutions which are more complex than, and different from, other animals.

Yes, we can succumb to power and violence, but we also have the potential to follow *spiritual leaders*, and, most importantly for this thesis, in the *human* state of nature, *democracy emerged* as a unique political institution, based on our key species characteristic—heightened intelligence and awareness and inter-subjective language skills.

Even Hobbes, in his philosophical state of nature, has humans—who had been killing each other and stealing from each other, such that "life was solitary, nasty, brutish and short"[15] — come together, and through discussion, create a "social contract" by which they give up their individual power to a "strong sovereign state", which could create order and peace.[16]

Thus, the discussion council – though gendered and age-graded – became a human political institution, and, once bands expanded and became "tribes", the tribes continued to exhibit democratic political processes—along with attempts at domination.

Let us look at both the democratic and despotic institutions of tribes.

---

[13] *Bible*, Adam & Eve, Oxford Study Bible, university of Oxford Press, 1991.

[14] Emile Durkheim, *The Elementary Forms of Religious Life*, N.Y. Free Press, 1952.

[15] Thomas Hobbes, *Leviathan*, London, Penguin, 1951.

[16] Thomas Hobbes, *Leviathan.*

Chapter 2
Democracy and Despotism in Tribal Society

2.1 Democracy in Tribal Societies

When the human group expanded beyond the hunting-gathering band level, democracy continued to be exhibited. With the larger population, the democratic discussion groups became more structured. Clan councils and representative tribal councils emerged.[1]

When homosapiens added horticulture or animal herding to their hunting-gathering activities, the population size of the human group increased. The pairing family was superseded by the extended family, or clan, and the clans of a given designated area exhibited a shared identity, language, and culture—they make up the "tribe."

In most hunting-horticultural tribes, the clans were matrilineal, organized around women's gardening role. While in herding societies, the clans were usually patrilineal, organized around men's herding role.[2]

It was typical in tribal societies that the clans elected a headman. The headman had to be a mature man because wisdom was gained through experience. The headman had to be a man, because only men could negotiate with other tribes and declare war, if negotiations failed.[3]

However, in tribes with matrilineal clans, the women had the vote – both women and men voted for the headman and, could vote to remove the headman if he was deemed incompetent.[4]

(In "suffragette" America, Susan B. Anthony announced the beginning of the movement in Seneca Falls, NY, because the Seneca women of the matrilineal clans of the Iroquois League told her that they had always had the vote).

---

[1] Glassman, Origins of Democracy in Tribes, City-States, and Nation-States.

[2] Ibid (Horticulture and Matriclans).

[3] Ibid (Herding and patriclans).

[4] Ibid (women vote in matriclans).

© Springer Nature Switzerland AG 2019
R. M. Glassman, *The Future of Democracy*,
https://doi.org/10.1007/978-3-030-16111-8_2

Still, though they could vote, a woman could not become a headperson, because only the male elders were the warrior-protectors of the tribe.

In tribes with patriclans, women could not vote or attend the tribal council.[5]

Each clan, then, chose a headman and these headmen came together in a tribal council—the council of elders. The elders – wise with experience and less "passionate" than the younger men—formed a tribal democratic discussion group, with carefully delineated rules and regulations. After debate amongst themselves, in many tribes, the elders would then sit, surrounded by an assembly of warriors, including all the younger men, and the war-chief or chiefs., In large tribal gatherings, the women and children would sit outside the circle of warriors, but close enough to hear what was going on. In some tribes, a woman could choose a man to speak for her at the tribal assembly. The Iroquois tribes exhibited this.[6]

Finally, most tribes had a "law speaker," who would open the tribal assembly with a recitation of the tribal customary laws and punishments and, the founding myths. The law speakers often sung this litany, as with the "bards" of the Celtic and Norse tribes.[7]

The tribal democracy of the Iroquois League was so well-structured that the British and Dutch colonists fashioned their "Articles of Confederations," in part, on the representative democratic structure of the Iroquois League.

Lastly, it must be emphasized that the tribal democratic assembly and council of elders, functioned as both a legislature and a judicial body. Policy was debated, and individual court cases were tried. The council of elders had the final say on court cases, while the warrior's assembly had sway on policy issues.

Often, "unanimity" in decision-making was demanded; without unanimity a policy might not get implemented. This "unanimity principle"[8] characterized most tribes, until the Greeks of the Golden Age institutionalized majority voting.

Now let us look at herding tribes.

Where animal herding was combined with some hunting and some horticulture, patriclans usually were typical. As mentioned, these clans were more male dominant. Women were excluded from voting for the clan headman. Furthermore, certain clans became designated as warrior-clans, "descended from the Gods," and gaining *aristocratic status*.[9]

Nonetheless, tribal democracy was exhibited amongst these tribes. In the Scandinavian, Dutch and German tribes, all the men and many of the women, came together for a formal meetings at designated times of year. The meetings were called "the thing" by the northern tribes.[10]

---

[5] Ibid (Norse Tribes; women could *not* vote).

[6] Ibid; see also, Morgan, *Ancient Society.*

[7] Glassman, *Origins of Democracy in Tribes, City-States, and Nation-States* (Norse Tribes, the Law Speaker) see also, *the Icelandic Sagas.*

[8] Glassman, *Origins of Democracy in Tribes, City-States and Nation-States* (The "unanimity principle" of Tribes).

[9] Glassman, *Origins of Democracy in Tribes, City-States and Nation-States.*

[10] *The Icelandic Sagas*, edited by Orlinorfur Thornsen, London, Penguin, Deluxe edition, 1997.

At the "thing" the assembly of all warriors would meet, lead by a council of aristocrats. A law-speaker would recite the rules and punishments and founding myths. Then discussion would begin. The "thing" was both a legislative and judicial body, with the aristocrats having the final say on legal decisions, with the law-speaker acting in an advisory capacity.[11]

As with the Iroquois Confederation of Tribes, the Norse tribes also held confederated gatherings. These they called the "Althing." At the Althing, all the tribes of a given region gathered on a regular basis and just as the elders dominated the "Iroquois, the Aristocrats dominated the "Viking" tribes.

The thing and Althing are well documented in *the Icelandic Sagas.*[12]

Also, in the Icelandic Sagas is the remarkable detailed description of the emergence of a unified military kingship – overriding the Althing – in Norway and Denmark.[13]

This brings us to our next point. *The Paradox of Tribes* – or should we say the paradox of human beings?!

That is, from the tribal confederations, we can already see how despotic military kingship and even theocratic despotisms, could emerge. Let us look at the office of war – chief first.

2.2 Despotism in Tribal Confederations: Kings and Priests

Once horticulture and animal herding were invented, human tribal societies expanded in population size. This lead to more encroachment on neighboring lands. And, in turn, this lead to the intensification of warfare.

Warfare had always been part of the human condition. Azar Gat in *War in Civilization,*[14] describes the violent raids and counter-raids that occurred even amongst band societies, such as the Australian Aborigines.

As warfare intensified, the status and power of the war chiefs rose. These chiefs developed loyal retinnes of young warriors, who would follow their lead in war – and even in peacetime. The authority of the clan elders was supreme in the tribal assemblies. But, the war chiefs began to hold equal status with the elders and, as warfare intensified and preparation for war became more continuous, the war chiefs began to assert their authority within the tribe and the tribal confederation. Some attempted to extend their power over the clan elders.

Fearing that the war chiefs might become despots, ruling through the force and violence of their loyal retinnes, some tribal societies created a dual office, such that two war chiefs would be elected and balance each other's power.

---

[11] Ibid.

[12] Ibid.

[13] Ibid (Kingship in Norway: Harold).

[14] Azar Gat, *War in Civilization.*

The Iroquois League exhibited this dual war chief system. And in colonial times, this dual system seems to have prevented the emergence of a despotic chieftainship.

The Spartans – famous amongst the Greeks for their warrior prowess – also exhibited a dual war chief system. The Spartans had two kings – they acted as generals in time of war and they did balance each other out in peacetime. They sat on the council of elders and spoke at the warriors' assembly – but they sometimes disagreed, and they never became despots.[15]

The Romans seem to have copied the Spartan war organization, learned, in part, from the Spartan colonies in Southern Italy. They began to fight, in phalanx formation, and they elected two war chiefs: the "consuls". Later on in history, when the Spartans created the peculiar democratic offices of the "ephors" – whose job it was to reign in the power of the Kings and the aristocratic elders – the Romans copied the ephorate by appointing the "tribunes" of the people, to reign in the power of the aristocratic senate and it's two consuls.[16]

However, in most post-tribal societies, where horticulture and animal herding replaced hunting – gathering, the war chief and his loyal retinnes claimed increasing power over and above the clan elders and the tribal assembly.

As mentioned, *The Icelandic Sagas*[17] give us the most wonderful and detailed description of this process amongst the Norwegian tribes.

According to the Sagas, King Harold gathered around him a loyal retinne of aristocratic Viking warriors. He then systematically forced the loyalty of all the other aristocrats and commoners. Those who agreed to follow his lead were rewarded with land and gifts and wealth. Those who apposed him were murdered, and their land and wealth confiscated, their families pushed off their land or killed, their women given as slaves to loyal retinne members.

In a 20 year period of consolidation, Harold annihilated all opposition ruthlessly and gathered around him an invincible regiment of paladins.

The fascinating part about this historical process is that a small group of Norwegian tribe-people refused to give in and fled to Iceland. Iceland was far enough away that Harold did not pursue these colonists – he was more interested in raiding to the South and Southwest where post-Roman treasurers awaited his raiders.

In Iceland, the runaways re-established the tribal democracy – the "thing" and the "Althing" were regularly convened, and still acted as the legislative and judicial institution of the Icelanders.

---

[15] Glassman, *Origins of Democracy in Tribes, City-States and Nation-States* (Spartans) two kinds.

[16] Glassman, *Origins of Democracy in Tribes, City-States and Nation-States* (Spartans' Ephron's) see also, Glassman, Rome's' Tribunes (in Sparta Section); see also, Polybius, *Early Roman History*, and Bk VI; London Penguin 2000; see also Titus Livins, *Early Roman History*, London, Penguin paperback 2002.

[17] Icelandic Sagas (King Harold).

The thing and the Althing were still dominated by the warrior aristocrats, but the commoners had their say and these tribal assemblies. The Icelandic tribal democracy was maintained into the Christian period (1100 A.D.) and beyond.

But, the Norwegian military chieftainship – Kingship – became the typical mode of political organization all across Europe, as the Norse tribes conquered France, Italy, Spain and Britain.

Fascinatingly, where the military Kings failed to conquer, the tribal democracy was maintained. Hence, in the high mountains of Switzerland, and the low salt marshes of the Netherlands, Norse tribal democracy continued into the era of the Enlightenment.[18]

So, the paradox of the human species continued: tribal democracy being overridden in most areas of the world yet surviving in some.

We shall describe the survival of tribal democracy in the city – states of the Middle East and Greece shortly. First, we must add one more factor to the rapidly spreading political institution of the military kingship. For, Kings are just war chiefs, unless they become conceived of as gods. Once the war chief is viewed as godly, then he becomes a "King." To be viewed as a God, the war chiefs needed the support of the priests.

2.2.1   The Power of the Priests: Theocracy and the Divine Kingship

I have described how human beings, because of our bigger brain, developed not only intelligence and speech, but a heightened awareness of ourselves in the universe. This conscious awareness is our key species characteristic – we are homosapiens, the species that "knows."

I also described the fact that this heightened awareness is a double-edged sword, at once allowing us to dominate the earth, and yet causing us "existential anxiety." The existential anxiety devolves from the knowledge that our own death is imminent, and the death of our loved ones is also inevitable. Death can occur from natural or human causes – diseases, earthquakes, murder or war. Both the natural and the social world inculcate anxieties.

As Durkheim has emphasized, most human societies have religious beliefs: myths of creation, rituals to alleviate anxiety, taboos and totems with magical powers, and a belief in the world of spirits" – harmful spirits and protective spirits.

In most human societies, shaman—male and female – arose as healers of the sick, interpreters of dreams and omens, and leaders of the religious rituals of the group.

As with the war chief, the Shaman, or priests, came to hold high status, and to gain power.[19]

---

[18] Glassman, *Origins of Democracy in Tribes, City-States and Nation-States* (Swiss and Dutch).

[19] Glassman, *Origins of Democracy in Tribes, City-States and Nation-States* (tribal shaman).

The power of the war chief is straightforward: military might, an unorganized retineue of young men who will kill anyone who does not obey the chief.

But, the priests had power as well! They could heal, using herbs and hypnotic trances, and they could kill, using poison, and hypnotic trances. They could put the fear of the spirit-world into the people—spirits could be evil and kill, or spirits could be good and heal. The priests and the priestesses knew how to invoke the spirits.

In this way, the priests developed power.

Some societies, such as those of West Africa with the Poro Cults, developed frightening theocracies – "voodoo" still scares the descendants of these West African societies in the Caribbean and Brazil.[20] And, the ancient Jews held the "prophets" in such high esteem, that they could and did, challenge the authority of the war kings.[21] In fact, after the Babylonian exile, when Cyrus the Great of Persia allowed the Jews to repatriate Israel, Ezra, "the second Moses" created a theocracy – a society ruled by a council of priests – with no war king.[22]

The Kingship was revived by the Maccabees in the Hellenistic period, but, as Josephus tells us, the council of priests – the Sanhedrin—had authority beyond the Kings.[23] The Kings were not accepted as legitimate. The Herods, the last Kings, were appointed by the Romans and never accepted by the Jews.

The theocratic Sanhedrin, as the New Testament of the Christians tells us four times over, was the ruling institution of the Jews in the Roman era.[24]

Theocracies, however, were *not typical*. Increasingly, devastating warfare made the war chieftainship more typical for post-tribal societies.

The war chiefs, however, were not accepted as fully legitimate in their domination of the tribes. Just look at the Icelanders who ran away, or, Confucius' rejection of the warring Dukes, who were causing hideous violence in their uncontrolled warfare, and violating the clan rituals that helped produce order amongst the Chinese.[25]

And, there is Aristotle's dictum that kingly domination turns their subjects into slaves[26] or Samuel's warning in the Bible that if the Jews chose a war King, he will have their sons killed in endless wars and their daughters turned to slavery,[27] and Locke, that Kings inevitably become tyrants and brutalize their subjects.[28]

---

[20] G.M. Harley, *Poro Cults of West Africa*, and, *Masks as Agents of Social Control*, N.C., Duke University Press, 1968.

[21] *Bible*, Prophets, Oxford Study Bible.

[22] *Bible*, Book of Ezra and Nehemiah, Oxford Study Bible.

[23] Josephus, *Roman-Jewish War; Jewish Antiquities*; London, Penguin paperback 1953.

[24] *The Christian Gospels'* of Mark, Matthew, Luke and John, Oxford Study Bible.

[25] Confucius, The Analects, N.Y. Amazon paperback, 2005.

[26] Aristotle, *Politics* (on Kingship).

[27] *Bible*, Book of Samuel, Oxford Study Bible.

[28] John Locke, *First Treatise on Civil Government*, Oxford, Oxford University, Press, 1952.

So, how did the war chiefs gain legitimacy? How did military chieftainship become "kingships?" How did the kingly state become what Max Weber called *"traditional authority?"*

It was the merger of military power with religious belief that created the legitimate domination we call "kingship". If the war chief becomes conceived of as "divine" – descended from the gods and, embodying god, then the people will bow down, crawl on their knees, "cow tow," and act slave-like.

Once the people believe the King is divine, then they believe he has the right to rule – they give their "consent" to be dominated. This consent is genuine where the people believe the Kind and the "Royal Family" are godlike.[29]

Of course, this legitimation is *not rational.* It is based on fear of the gods, and, fear of the King.

This *irrational legitimacy* is bolstered by the organized priesthoods that usually accompany such monarchies. Egypt is the most extreme example. There, the priests not only purveyed the belief that the Pharaohs were godly, but also administered the kingdom. They were the bureaucratic officials making sure that the economy ran well – they supervised the Nile flood-control agriculture—and that the kings were made to seem divine.[30]

The pyramids are the visible symbols of the King's godliness – even after death – their soul's being protected along with their mummified bodies.

China was similar to Egypt even though the Mandarin officials were technically secular. That is, following Confucius' ideas, a stratum of very well-educated officials, was institutionalized to administer China under the authority of the Emperor.[31]

The Emperor ruled "with the mandate from Heaven" – he was godly – no one could look into his eyes – all who approached him had to crawl on their bellies and cower before him. The Emperor could have anyone struck dead on the spot who dared to violate these rules.

And Confucius insisted that all rituals be carefully and precisely carried out – ritualized behavior characterized all formal and political interactions. And, rituals of extreme submission were enacted in relation to the Emperor.[32]

Furthermore, even though Confucius would not discuss God or the soul or the afterlife, he insisted that ancestor worship be carefully maintained.

There is no doubt that within this cultural context, the Emperor of China was conceived of as just as godly as the Pharaoh's of Egypt. And, the Mandarin officials played a similar role as the Egyptian priests in administering the empire, and, in legitimating the King.[33]

Just one more point. In order to ensure that the people really believed in their divinity, the Kings and their "royal" families developed all kinds of "manufactured

---

[29] Aristotle, *Politics* (on Kingship).

[30] Henri Frankfort, *Kingship and the Gods*, Chicago, Univ. of Chicago Press 1948.

[31] Confucius, *The Analects.*

[32] Ibid.

[33] Max Weber, *The Religion of China*, N.Y. Free Press, 1953.

charismatic" effects to enhance their divinity.[34] They dressed in magnificent clothing, wore golden crowns, held golden scepters, sat on jeweled thrones and lived in magnificent palaces. On their deaths the priests and officials made sure that their tombs were as magnificent as their palaces – for a God was being buried there, not a man.

These manufactured effects did enhance the charisma of the King, his family and his officials. The people saw someone so magnificent, that in truth, they seemed to be seeing a God.

2.2.2 Human History Becomes the History of Kings and Conquests

The divine Kingship and the Kingly-bureaucratic state spread through military conquest in most areas of the world. So common did the Kingly-bureaucratic state become that weber could call it "traditional authority,"[35] and, where it did not occur, as in ancient Greece, this was considered an anomaly—a strange atypical case. And, it did seem that way, for, once divine Kingly conquests expanded, human history became the history of Kings and battles.

In areas where the divine Kingly state became institutionalized *democracy became inconceivable*—the people were "commoners," the rulers "Gods". The King and his officials had the right to rule because it was conferred on them by the Gods. This was legitimate authority, as mentioned, because the people did consent to be ruled by the divine King. However – as we have stressed – this is *irrational* legitimacy because the King and the rulers were, of course, *not Gods.*

And, any person or group who dared oppose the rulers was killed – with great public display in order to terrorize the population into submission.

In societies like Egypt and China, the vast majority of the people did believe that the King and his officials ruled with the mandate of the Gods and were therefore godly. Hence, they did consent to such rule.

But – and we wish to emphasize this – Kings and battles do not make up all of human history. And, in fact, tribal democracy did not disappear from every area on earth. For the city-states of the Middle East and the Aegean regions continued to exhibit vestiges of tribal democracy, but now in a new form.

---

[34] Ronald M. Glassman and William Swatos, Jr., *Charisma, History and Social Structure* ("Manufactured Charisma'), N.Y. Praeger, 1981.

[35] Max Weber, *Economy and Society* "Legitimate Domination," Translated by Claus Wittich and Guenther Roth, N.Y. Bedminster Press, 1971.

Chapter 3
City-State Democracy in Sumer, Syria and Canaan-Phoenicia

3.1 City-State Democracy is Carried Over from Tribal Democracy

Long before the Greek polis emerged, there were independent city-states in the Middle East. They arose first in Sumer, then in other parts of Mesopotamia, and in Syria and Canaan-Phoenicia (Canaanite being the name conferred by the people on themselves, Phoenician the name given them by the Greeks).

In these independent city-states, tribal democracy survived and took on a new form. The council of tribal elders became the council of city fathers—an oligarchic council, based on the wealth acquired from trade: caravan trade, river trade, and sea trade. Along with the oligarchic council of city fathers, an assembly of all the citizens emerged, as an extension of the warriors' assembly that characterized most tribes.[1]

The warriors' assembly of the tribes became the citizens assembly of the city-states, and, often, these citizens continued to make up the militia of the city-states. However, in city-states of great wealth, the citizens militia was often supplemented with paid mercenaries – this latter occurring in the Phoenician city-states, but not in the Sumerian or Syrian cities. Thus, just as the council of elders and warriors' assembly characterized many tribes, the council of rich city elders and citizens assemblies characterized the city-states of the Middle East. These city-states were basically oligarchic, in that they were dominated by the rich city fathers. However, the citizens assembly did meet and did vote on important matters. Still, most of the political decision-making was done by the city fathers.

In cities where craft production became central to the trade economy, the citizens, as craftsmen, often gained increased powers, tilting the oligarchy in a more democratic direction.

---

[1] Glassman, *Origins of Democracy in Tribes, City-States and Nation-States* (city-states of the Middle East).

© Springer Nature Switzerland AG 2019
R. M. Glassman, *The Future of Democracy*,
https://doi.org/10.1007/978-3-030-16111-8_3

3.2   The City King

Further, these pre-Greek city-states had retained the office of war chief from tribal times. Each city had a war-king, who led the militia and the mercenaries during war. And, in peacetime, the city King developed much of the "manufactured charismatic" effects[2] that typified divine kingship. That is, the Kings dressed splendidly; they sat on thrones; they lived in palaces; they had crowns and scepters; their wives and mothers were magnificently attired. They, thus, exuded the manufactured effects that enhanced their charisma. Therefore, they were greatly venerated. However, in these "trade-capitalist" city-states, the rich, oligarchic, city fathers made most of the political decisions, the King's prevailing only on matters of war, and even then, often over-ruled. So, this was *not* divine kindship in the same sense as Egypt or China or the Babylonian -Assyrian-Persian Empires that came to dominate the Middle East.

In the *Epic of Gilgamesh* originally written in Sumerian, Gilgamesh, though he is a great warrior and leader of the army, must go to the council of city fathers and plead with them to go to war. When the city fathers refuse his request, he then calls the citizens assembly together and pleads his case with them. They say yes, and so Gilgamesh declares war. But the supreme authority was clearly with the council and assembly, not with the King.

3.3   The High Priest & Priestess

The city-states of the Middle East also had an institutionalized priesthood. These priests and priestesses were greatly venerated, just as they were in Egypt. The priests and priestesses did *not*, however, administer the trade-capitalist economy. They were not in charge of trade or craft production —these were administered by the merchant-rich city fathers, and the craft guilds, respectively.[3]

The priests and priestesses did, however, supervise irrigation projects where they were necessary. But, in most cases the economy was run by the merchants, bankers, craftsmen and cash-crop farmers, on their own. Whereas, the Egyptian economy was totally under the control of the priests (in *The Story of Wen Amun*, Wen Amun, a priest of the God Amun, leads the trade mission to Phoenicia)[4], the Mesopotamian economy — even under the control of the Babylonian Kingly-state – was mixed, exhibiting free trade and craft production as independent from the Kings and the

---

[2] Glassman and Swatos, *Charisma, History and Social Structure* ("Manufactured Charisma"), N.Y. Praeger.

[3] *Epic of Gilgamesh*, in Samuel Noah Kramer, *History Begins at Sumer*, Philadelphia, Univ. of Pennsylvania Press, 1950.

[4] *The Story of Wen Aun*, in *Archeology of Ancient Egypt*, East Lansing Michigan, Michigan State University, 1963.

priests. Karl Polanyi, describes this trade-capitalist independent economic sphere, though he was not yet willing to call it a true "market economy."[5]

To return to our discussion of the priests and priestesses, they held high status for they forcefully maintained the traditional religious beliefs, rituals and ceremonies of the region. The ritual sacrifices of animals and grain to the Gods and goddesses was supervised by the priesthood. And, in the face of all the rational, secular learning that emerged in these city-states (in terms of writing, weights and measures, and money and banking and contract law) the priesthood continued to insist on *human sacrifices* to placate the gods.

The sacrifice of babies to "the flames of Moloch", as the Bible tells us[6] and as Greek and Roman travelers affirmed, characterized the religious practices of the Syrian and Canaanite-Phoenician city-states.

The sacrifice of young men to the goddess of fertility was also maintained in some of these city-states. Herodotus tells us that the rivers of Lebanon would run red with the memory of the blood sacrifice of an earlier time.[7] Adonis, the young, handsome lord, would be sacrificed to the goddess of fertility, who was pictured as naked, vulva and breasts pushed forward, with snakes on her arms and lions by her side.

The priests and priestesses maintained their high status and power through the terrorization of the population with human sacrifices.[8]

So, the city-states of Mesopotamia, Syria and Phoenicia exhibited elements of oligarchy, democracy and monarchy, while retaining the traditional religion of the region. In this religion, the war god and the fertility goddess were the central figures of veneration. Frazier, in *The Golden Bow*,[9] describes "the sacred marriage rite" in which the King impersonates the war god and the high priestess, the fertility goddess. They ritually marry in a grand celebration, and then they have sex with each other to insure the fertility of the crops and the people. Sometimes a drunken sexual orgy of all the citizens followed, according to Herodotus and the Biblical prophets.

The key fact for us in this treatise is that the maintenance of the fertility religion, inhibited the emergence of the rational-scientific world-view. This religion and its priesthood also reinforced the legitimacy of the kingship — allowing the king a godly role in the sacred marriage rite ceremony. Hence, veneration of the Kings continued, even though their power was generally overridden by the oligarchic city fathers.

It was only in ancient Greece (and Rome) that the Kingship was abolished, and, traditional religion weakened. In the Greek city-states from the sixth to the fourth century BCE, with no King and no organized priesthood, oligarchy and democracy

---

[5] Karl Polanyi, *Trade and Markets in the Early Empires*, Google Paperback originally published, 1957.

[6] Bible, Leviticus (do not sacrifice babies to the flames of Moloch), Oxford Study Bible.

[7] Herodotus, *Histories* (Tyre and the Levant), London, Penguin, 1951.

[8] Glassman, *Origins of Democracy in Tribes, City-States and Nation-States* (Phoenician city-states).

[9] James, George, Frazer, *The Golden Bungh*, Amazon Books 2008.

emerged more independently and, lacking an organized priesthood, an existential quest into "the laws of nature" eventuated in both the rational-scientific world-view, and new religious cults. These new cults included, not only the "mystery cults" concerned with the soul and the afterlife, but also philosophical atheism and theism—Epicureanism insisting that there was no afterlife because the soul died with the body and that the gods did not care about humans; stoicism instating on the opposite – there is an afterlife, the soul lives on, and we must act morally and ascetically to purify ourselves for the moral god of the universe.

Let us look at the Greek city-states, for full-fledged democracy with majority voting would emerge there. And, the rational-scientific world-view and secular orientation of society would lead to what Weber called, "legal-rational authority"[10] *Democracy with constitutional guidelines* would be the new form of human political process.

---

[10] Max Weber, *Economy & Society*, Wittich & Roth, (Legitimate Domination; legal-rational authority).

Chapter 4
The City-States of Ancient Greece: Democracy, Science, and Legal-Rational Authority Emerge

4.1 The City-States of Ancient Greece

Everyone knows that Democracy came to fruition in the Greek city-states. The warriors' assembly became the citizens assembly. The council of elders became, first, a council of military aristocrats drawn exclusively from certain honored clans, but, then this council became open to all citizens. Further, the law courts, originally dominated by the elders, then the aristocrats, became open to all citizens, who sat as jurors and tried cases.

In the citizens assemblies of the ancient Greek city-states, *majority rule*[1] was introduced, replacing the "unanimity principle" which had guided tribal democracy, and, which continued in the Middle Eastern city-states until the Hellenistic era.

As the Greek city-states emerged, two processes altered the political structure: one, the rise of the overseas trade and craft economy which generated wide distinctions in wealth, producing a new class structure (delineated by Solon as chronicled by Aristotle in his Constitution of Athens)[2] and two, the institutionalization of a new military formation: the hoplite phalanx. This latter empowered the middle and working classes who made up the bulk of the heavy armored phalanx and disempowered the Aristocrats, whose horse prowess was no longer needed. (This is documented in Josiah Ober's anthology, *Demakratia.*[3]

The decline of the military aristocrats was accompanied by the rise of the capitalist rich – merchant traders, bankers, and craft-workshop owners. Many aristocratic families joined in the trading activities and became rich, but other aristocrats disdained and denigrated the new rich. In any case, the rich gained prestige through education and oratorical skills, such that they attempted to dominate the city-states

---

[1] Aristotle, *The Constitution of Athens*, London, Penguin Classics, 1968.

[2] Ibid.

[3] Josiah Ober, *Demokratia* (Hoplite Phalanx), Princeton, Princeton University Press, 1997.

© Springer Nature Switzerland AG 2019
R. M. Glassman, *The Future of Democracy*,
https://doi.org/10.1007/978-3-030-16111-8_4

as oligarchs. In many city-states they controlled the council of state by setting a wealth and property requirement on office-holding—the hallmark of oligarchy.[4]

However, in the Greek city-states – unlike the Phoenician and Syrian – the middle and working classes used their growing military power – derived from anchoring the hoplite-phalanx – to demand participation in all offices of state, as well as the assembly. Full-fledged democracy, with no oligarchic restrictions was demanded by the small farmers producing cash crops, the craftsmen in the workshops, the middlemen who moved goods to the ships and manned the ships and other middling strata.

Further the middle classes had enough money to gain some education from the many "sophists" who taught in the market places. Given their education, their moderate wealth, and their place in the phalanx, the middle classes demanded democratic governance and an end to oligarchic exclusion.[5]

Violent civil wars broke out in many Greek city-states: oligarchy of the rich vs. democracy of all the people. Sometimes the disorder became so volatile that a dictator (tyrant) temporarily took power, ruling through the force of a personal regiment and bodyguards.[6]

The civil wars between the rich and the people were further complicated by the rivalry between Sparta and Athens.[7]

Sparta supported the oligarchies – though Sparta itself was not an oligarchy but rather a unique case of tribal democracy grafted into a hoplite – phalanx militarized society, with a democratic warriors' assembly and the new institutions of the "ephors", elected to inhibit the influence of the aristocracy on the still existing council of elders. As Xenophon[8] tells us, Sparta was an antique, which all the Greek intellectuals loved to praise, but in which none of these intellectuals would really want to live.

So, Sparta supported the oligarchies simply because Athens was a democracy and the other democracies supported Athens.

Because of the internal civil wars and the external Sparta-Athens war, democratic governance in the Greek city-states did not seem stable. Thucydides describes all of this.[9]

---

[4] Aristotle *Politics*.

[5] Josiah Ober, *Demokratia*, (the middling condition); see also Aristotle, Politics (the middle class).

[6] Aristotle, *Politics*, (Tyranny); see also Plato, *The Republic* (critique of Tyranny), London, Penguin Classics, 1960.

[7] Thucydides, The *Peloponnesian War*, London, Penguin Classics 1952.

[8] Xenophon, *The Spartan Constitution*, Michel Lipka, Berlin, Walter DeGruyter, 2002.

[9] Thucydides, *Peloponnesian War*.

4.2   The Volatility of Democracy and the Necessity of Constitutional Law

The council of elders was always considered as wise and measured in its decisions. For, age not only improved wisdom but also lessened the animal passions that make men volatile.

In tribes, the elders often inhibited the young men from going to war, or, arranged for settlements between fending clans.[10] So, too, the city fathers, as elders of the city, moderated the politics of the Middle Eastern city-states.

In archaic Greek city-states, the council of aristocrats—dominated by the elder members of the aristocratic clans—did rule moderately often enough.

However, with the transition to democracy, the citizens assembly was empowered to vote on policy questions. But, these assembles often numbered in the thousands in the larger city-states. And since majority rule was institutionalized, the moderating influence of the "unanimity principle" no longer slowed own the decision-making process.

Freed from the unanimity principle and freed from the moderating control of the city elders, democracy became very volatile.[11]

The process was, thus, sped up, and could become subject to very volatile activity—so volatile that aristocratic critics likened it to the crowd psychology of a mob. Intellectual critics of democracy, such as Polybius, called it "ochlocracy," or mob-rule.[12] (This is why modern referenda also became volatile and are a bad idea – look at Brexit").

Even lovers of democracy, such as Herodotus, in the first "dialogue on the forms of government" ever written down (in *The Histories*, the section on the Persian succession to the throne), describes the flaw in democracy as its volatility—the assembly being easily swayed by demagogues to commit to dangerous or unwise policies.[13]

Plato, the most famous critic of Greek democracy, also criticizes democracy as too volatile, the people being not well-educated enough to make wise decisions— and easily swayed by demagogues for this reason.[14]

Since Plato's alternative – rule by the best – the best educated and smartest – as "Guardians" of the State – was rejected by Aristotle as ultimately leading to oligarchy, he – Aristotle – suggested a series of practical processes that could help stabilize democracy.

The keys to the stabilization of democracy for Aristotle were: one, a class structure exhibiting a *majority middle class*.[15] This middle class being made up of

---

[10] Glassman, *Origins of Democracy in Tribes, City-States and Nation-States* (Tribes).

[11] Thucydides, *Peloponnesian Luan* (volatile debates in the Athenian Assembly).

[12] Polybius, *Histories*, Bk VI (mob rule), London, Penguin, 1953.

[13] Herodotus, *Histories* (Dialogue on the Forms of Government).

[14] Plato, *The Republic* (critique of Democracy).

[15] Aristotle, *Politics* (the middle class).

prosperous small cash-crop farmers, craftsmen producing for overseas trade, middlemen in the trading economy and architects and artists involved in the building projects.

The middle class was a product of the trade-capitalist money economy that the Phoenicians had expanded out of the Middle East and into the Aegean and Mediterranean seas. This trade-capitalized economy coming to fruition with the coined money invented by the Lydians and institutionalized by the Greeks.

And two: a set of written laws—secular, rational, amendable laws—which set limits on what the democratic assembly could and could not do. The written laws limited, at least, the extreme acts of passion that often engulfed the democratic debates at the assemblies.

As Aristotle put it, "When the law rules, God and reason rule; when a man rules, we add the character of the beast."[16]

I will come back to Aristotle's theory of the middle-class majority and why the middle class stabilizes democracy—while the rich and the poor destabilize it.

First, however, I would like to discuss "law" – constitutional law. Where did it come from? Why did it emerge in *secular* form in ancient Greece? After all, there had been famous religious law codes since the days of Sumer & Babylon & Israel. From Urukagina to Hammurabi, to Moses, these law codes had all been religiously based. How did the Greek law codes become secular constitutional documents?

4.3   Trade-Capitalism and Contract Law

Money and contract law were invented by the independent merchants of Mesopotamia. By money, I do not mean coined money—that, as mentioned, would be invented by the Lydians and then perfected by the Greeks.

Money was, at first, regular measure of commodities, such as bushels of grain (or in China, strings of shells). However, the grain was too cumbersome (and the shells often broke). Eventually, bars of metal were used—copper, silver, gold, bronze.

The bars were given a designated value, depending on size, weight, and purity. Even though metal bars were heavy, they could be transported, and they did not break or spoil. Relatively sophisticated metallurgy standardized these bars into units of exchange—"money."

Money became more than just a medium of exchange. Money became "capital" because it was used to make more money. That is, money itself could be lent to a merchant so that he could go on a trading mission. It would be lent at a carefully designated interest rate. Since the money had to be returned with interest, the money had been used to make more money. Hence, money could become "capital".[17]

---

[16] Aristotle, *Politics* (on law).

[17] Karl Polanyi, *Trade & Markets*.

Specialized merchants who lent money became bankers, rather than overseas traders.

Once money and banking were introduced into trading, simple barter arrangements gave way to more complex business transactions. These "capitalist" transactions had to be carefully calculated and written down, with all the specifics made clear.

Writing had already been invented in Mesopotamia—the cuneiform of the Sumerians & Babylonians predominating over the Egyptian hieroglyphics. (Both forms of writing were invested by the priests who ran the temple economies of Egypt & Mesopotamia. Then the writing was borrowed by the independent merchant traders for business purposes, with the help of secular scribes).

Hence, with writing and money – as – capital, business transactions could be carefully written down in advance of a deal: business *contracts* became the institutionalized form for guaranteeing the sanctity and veracity of a business transaction.

These business contracts eventually gained the status of "law". There were already law courts dominated by the priests and elders of the city-states. And, these business contracts became recognized as legal documents by the already existing courts. They were allowable as evidence of the specifics of any given business transaction. Disputes over the fulfillment or lack of fulfillment of business transactions were commonplace in the Mesopotamian courts.

But, these business contracts were secular. That is, they were not religious documents, even though they were accompanied by religious curses from this god or that goddess and, they were not under the auspices of the King, though they might be accompanied by the official seal of a king.

However, in the Middle East, the courts were presided over by the priests and the elders of a given city-state. And, within the larger region, where there was kingly conquest, there emerged the grand religious law codes with which we are familiar, which delineated the punishments for designated transgressions of the religious norms and celebrated the social justice of the Kings and priests.

Amongst the Sumerians numerous grand law codes were written down, enumerating punishments and celebrating the protection of the innocent, the weak, the orphan and the widow from injustice.[18]

After the Amorite conquest of Babylon, King Hammurabi had his famous code written in stone.[19] And the laws of Moses were written down by the compilers of the Bible – the Jewish prophet taking on the rule of asserting that the laws provided social justice for the poor and the weak.[20]

As mentioned, the business contracts were often stamped with the symbols of both the religious and the kingly authority. Yet, these business contracts were rational, mathematical in their details, and secular in their intent. So, if there was a dispute, it was judged rationally according to the terms of the contract.

---

[18] Samuel Noah Kramer, *History Begins at Sumer.*

[19] *Hammurabi's' Code*, Yale University Edition, N.H. 1962.

[20] *Bible*, Ten Commandments; Leviticus; Prophets.

Therefore, contract law could become one of the bases for secular law in general, where the religious authorities were weak and where the authority of the kings was absent.

Such a situation emerged in ancient Greece, from the Archaic to the Golden Age—600–300 BCE.[21]

4.4   The Decline of Greek Olympian Religion and the Rise of the Rational-Scientific World-View

The Greek city-states of the Asia Minor coast—led by Miletus—began trading extensively with the great civilizations of the Middle East and North Africa.

Following the Phoenicians, they traded with Egypt, Syria, Babylon, Persia and Lydia. They brought back both goods and ideas. The more sophisticated religious ideas of Egypt, Mesopotamia and Persia eventuated in a questioning of the primitive conception embodied in their own tribal religion.

Xenophanes[22] questioned the conception of the gods presented in *The Iliad* and *The Odyssey*[23] by Homer, as well as the murderous and patricidal conflicts in Hesiod's *Theogeny*.[24] Xenophanes pointed out that the gods and goddesses committed every horrendous act that would render them immoral and therefore, hardly worth venerating.[25]

Heraclitus continued the critique exposing the primitive nature of the gods and their lack of acceptable morality.[26]

Eventually the more sophisticated ideas of the Babylonians, Persians, Jews and Egyptians overwhelmed the tribal Olympian religion. But, all the ideas of the great civilizations were different, so what should the Greeks believe?

The common people—those with little or no education—continued to worship the Olympian gods in the traditional way. Zeus, Hera, Athena, Aphrodite, Apollo, Artemis, Hermes and others were still worshipped, and grand temples were built to honor them. However, the better educated Greeks began the search for existential answers elsewhere. Two trends emerged: one, secular and rationally oriented; and the other mystical and spiritual.

The second trend eventuated in conceptions of the soul and an afterlife, plus conceptions of a single moral god. This line of existential questioning began by Xenophanes, led during the Golden age, to "The Mystery Cults,"[27] along with the

---

[21] Glassman, *Origins of Democracy in Tribes, City-States and Nation-States* (Greece).

[22] John Burnet, *Early Greek Philosophy*, Kessinger Publishing, 2012.

[23] Homer, *The Iliad & Odyssey*, Penguin Classics, 1952, 1953.

[24] Hesiod, *Theogony*, London, Penguin classics, 1952.

[25] John Burnet, Early Greek Philosophy (Xenophanes).

[26] John Burnet, Early Greek Philosophy (Heraclitus).

[27] The Greek Mystery Cults, see Britannica, com-topic-mystery religion.

platonic nation of "god" as the perfect "form" – the "good,"[28] and finally to the stoic theology of a moral god and a soul, purified by asceticism, which would live on.[29]

These mystical, spiritual and moral trends were significant in themselves, but the first trend changed the world. For this first trend led towards an attempt to understand the nature of the universe, life, and human society.

The first trend led to the empirical, mathematical and theoretical conception of the world we call *science*.[30]

4.5   The Rational-Scientific World-View

With the religious conception of the world declining, a group of intellectuals living along the Asia Minor coast, in various Greek city-states, began to search for more rational answers concerning the nature of the universe.

Thales[31] of Miletus is credited as being the first of the scientific thinkers. He made popular the inquiry into the "primary substance" from which all other substances were made. According to ancient Greek traditions, Thales followed the Phoenician traders to Egypt and then Babylon and the Middle East. From Egypt he learned that water—the "primeval ooze" – might be the primary substance from which all other substances emerged. But, the primeval ooze also consisted of muddy earth, so, perhaps earth was the primary substance.

Further, Egyptian and Babylonian myths also described "the breath of life" that the gods blew into living things, including humans. So, perhaps air was the primary substance.

Finally, from Persia and into Babylon, the idea that fire was the primary substance also emerged (from the pre-Zoroastrian Persian fire religion).

The wonderful thing about Thales was that he encouraged his students to *observe the world* on their own and to *theorize* about what the primary substance might be. He was not rigid, claiming that he favored water as the primary substance because it existed as a liquid, a solid (ice) and a gas (vapor). However, air, earth, fire—or some other unknown substance might be the primary substance. Thales encouraged his students to observe the world and to back up their theoretical speculations with empirical evidence to support it.[32]

His students did observe the world, and they also expanded the discussion about the primary substance to include ideas such as, "the infinite" span of the universe and, empty "space" in which material substances moved.

Thales seems to have been a great lecturer and teacher, for young men came from all over Asia Minor to listen to him.

---

[28] Plato, *Dialogue on "The Forms" in Plato's' Republic.*

[29] Zenos' Stoicism, see Britannica, com-topic Stoicism.

[30] Burnet, Early Greek Philosophy.

[31] Ibid (Thales).

[32] Ibid (Thales).

Pythagoras[33] of Samos may have heard Thales, or one of his students. For he became interested in the quest to understand the universe. Fleeing a democratic revolution in Samos (he was an aristocrat who favored oligarchy), he traveled to Miletus and then to Egypt. In Egypt, he became fascinated with mathematics.

The Egyptians were famous for their geometric measurements that allowed them to build the great pyramids and magnificent palaces and temples, with perfect precision. Geometry in its purely practical form was well-developed in Egypt.

Pythagoras, after absorbing Egyptian geometry finally settled in the city of Kroton in the Italian coast, just across from the Peloponnese. There, he founded a school of his own, wherein the search for the key to the understanding of the universe focused on measurement. Geometric measurement and, the mathematical calculations connected with it, became central for Pythagoras.

He believed that numbers and mathematical calculations, and careful measurements, were the keys to unlock the mysteries of the universe. These measurements and numerical calculations would show us the "harmonies" that underlie all activities in the universe.

When Pythagoras figured out the harmonies of the chords of stringed instruments, and therefore had a mathematical formula that could explain music, he knew he had truly found the key to understanding the universe. He looked up to the heavens and believed he could calculate "the music of the spheres," and, of course, the sun and the moon and the planets and the stars all looked like spheres. And, they all moved in a regular and mathematically predictable patterns.

The "mathematization of nature" had now joined the empirical observational quest for the primary substance.

Heraclitus[34] also may have heard Thales or one of his students. For, he too became involved in the quest for the primary substance.

Heraclitus may have traveled east from his home city of *Ephesus* towards Persia. For, he became convinced that fire was the primary substance and fire was sacred and at the core of the early Zoroastrian beliefs.

Fire fascinated Heraclitus because fire was not a stable substance. In fact, it was always changing and "change" was the key for Heraclitus in understanding the universe.

Heraclitus taught that "all things are in flux" "the same man cannot step into the same river twice for it is neither the same man nor the same river." The man is aging, and the river is flowing. The constant movement and change of all things in the universe is what Heraclitus found fascinating. And, Pythagoras was busy calculating these changes—measuring them and creating formulas for predicting them.

Did things change or was there no movement at all? Was space infinite or limited? And, what was the primary substance?

The quest for the primary substance begun by the Thales in Miletus, culminated in the work of Leukippus—also from Miletus—and his start student, Democritus. Together, they taught that the primary substance was tiny uncuttable

---

[33] Ibid (Pythagoras).
[34] Ibid (Heraclitus).

particles—atoms—moving in space—combining uncoupling and then recombining to form all the material things we can observe.

These atoms are not observable because they are so small, but they exist and are in constant motion in space. There are an infinite number of them and they can combine in infinitely different ways.[35]

Democritus came and taught in Athens at the time of Socrates, and from Athens his work and the work of all the other scientific thinkers, spread to all the Greek city-states, after the Persian Wars ended in Greece's favor.

The *rational-scientific world-view* was formulated: Empirical observation of the world; mathematical calculation to enhance our understanding; and theoretical hypothesis, which are open to debate, amendation, and alteration. Experimentation was also added to aid in calculations and to verify observations. Theories were altered if experimental findings disapproved their validity. Later scientists, such as Archimedes (of Syracuse, in the Roman era) used experiments famously.

Finally, during the Hellenistic era, Alexandria—the new Greek capital city in Egypt—became the center for scientific studies. Fascinating in this modern era of women's liberation, the last of the Alexandrian scientists was a woman—Hypatia—and horrifyingly she was brutally murdered by a Christian mob, led by a young man who had been in love with her and whom she had rejected.[36]

The rational-scientific world-view did not die with Hypatia. It continued into the Roman era. As mentioned, Archimedes of Syracuse famously continued the traditions of observation, experimentation and mathematization, along with the theorizing that characterized the scientific endeavor.

This "Greek science" was revived during the "Arabic Golden age," and enhanced by Ibn Sina's (Avicenna's) importation of Indian numerals by way of his Persian upbringing.[37] And, Ibn Rushdie's' (Averroes')[38] commentaries on the works of Aristotle stimulated the Catholic Church to revive the works of the Greeks. With Albert the Great and Thomas Aquinas affirming the importance of Aristotle's works, the Renaissance was underway. In Italy and then in Northern Europe, Greek science and the scientific endeavor spread and deepened.

Here in this treatise, we wish to emphasize that this *rational view of the world* helped to reinforce the conception of *legal authority*.[39] That is, that "the law" is rational, while humans are often irrational and emotional. As Aristotle put it: "When the law rules, god and reason rule; when a man rules we add the character of the beast.[40]

---

[35] Ibid (Leucippus and Democritus).

[36] Chilean Movie (in English), *Agora* (about Hypatia of Alexandria).

[37] Ibn Sina (Avicenna) – introduced mathematics, medicine and Greek philosophy to the Arabic Golden Age).

[38] Ibn Rushd (Averroes), (explained Aristotle's Philosophy for the Arabic-speaking world, and Thomas Aquinas, studied Ibn Rushd's commentaries translated into Latin).

[39] Max Weber, *Economy & Society*, Wittich & Roth, (Legitimate Dominations; legal-rational authority).

[40] Aristotle, *Politics*, (on law, p 145–148, Barker Trans).

So, in ancient Greece we have coming together, *contract law*—which was purely secular and involved with business transactions, and, *the rational-scientific world-view*—rather than a religious world-view.

In such a social situation it became possible to conceive of a code of rational, secular law as guiding political activity. Hence, *constitutional law*, as a limit and a guide to political actions, emerged.[41]

This constitutional law, being secular and political is by definition, different from the religious law codes which pre-existed it for centuries. And, whereas the religious law codes were guides for moral action and punishments for immoral actions, these religious law codes were *not* guides for political action. They presupposed the acceptance of kingship as the traditional form of authority.

The only limitations on the King's power was that they had to abide by the moral code. But, since the Kings ruled as military leaders and constantly engaged in violent military activity, their *use of violence to maintain order* was accepted. (This is the flaw in the Confucius system in China because even where the educated officials administered the society well, the Emperors could and did, override these officials with acts of horrendous violence, whenever they deemed it necessary).[42]

So, *traditional authority* did engender ethical law codes, but the Kings and other officials often acted violently against their subjects. The bulk of the people were *subjects*, not citizens. They had no role in their own governance, but rather were passive and "slave-like", to use Aristotle's term.

Legal-rational authority is different. It accompanies Democracy—wherein all the people participate in the political process, but it sets rational guidelines and, limits the passionate, irrational potential in the people's participatory process.

We shall now discuss Aristotle's second stabilization program for democracy—that is, the majority middle class—now that we have discussed legal-rational authority.

4.6   The Middle-Class Majority and the Stabilization of Democracy

Along with "law", Aristotle theorized that the presence of a well-educated, prosperous middle class would also help to stabilize democracy.[43]

For the middle class, he believed were moderate in tehri views and willing to compromise. They also followed the law closely. The rich thought themselves above the law, while the poor acted below it.

---

[41] Glassman, *Origins of Democracy in Tribes, City-States and Nation-States* (Constitutional law in ancient Greece).

[42] Confucius, the *Analects*.

[43] Aristotle, *Politics* (the middle class).

After establishing that the rule of law is essential for a stable government,[44] Aristotle describes why states with a majority middle class will be the most stable. Here is how Aristotle describes it:

> *"We are here concerned with the best constitution for the majority of states. Goodness itself consists of a mean; and in any state the middle class is a mean between the rich and the poor. The middle class is free from the ambition of the rich and the pettiness of the poor; it is a natural link which helps to insure political cohesion. We may thus conclude that a constitution based on this class is most likely to be generally beneficial. It will be free from faction and will be likely to be stable."*[45]

Aristotle goes on to say:

> *"Men who are in this condition are the most ready to listen to* **reason**. *Those who belong to either extreme—the over handsome, the over strong, the over noble, the over wealthy, or at the opposite extreme, the over poor, the over weak—find it hard to follow the lead of reason. Men in the first class tend more to violence and serious crime, men in the second tend too much to roguery and petty offenses.*
>
> *A state aims at being as far as it can be, a society composed of equals...and the middle class, more than any other, has this sort of composition.*
>
> *It is clear from our argument, first that the best form of political society is one where power is vested in the middle class, and second, that good government is attainable in those states where there is a large middle class—large though, if possible, to be stronger than each of the other classes, but at any rate, large enough to be stronger than either of them singly; for in that case, it's addition to either will suffice to turn the scale and will prevent either of the extremes from becoming predominant.*
>
> *It is therefore the greatest of blessings for a state that its members should possess a moderate and adequate property...when democracies have no middle class, and the poor are greatly superior in number, trouble ensues, and they are speedily ruined." (where the rich are too powerful, oligarchy replaces democracy)."*[46]

And, finally, Aristotle warns that where there are extremes of wealth and poverty, "as a reaction against both of these extremes, a tyranny (dictatorship) may emerge.

The reason I have quoted Aristotle directly here is that the theory of the middle-class majority is very relevant in the modern world of the twenty-first century, in that nations that are "developing" may not have a middle-class majority, and, even in developed nations, where the middle class is weakened by economic depression or unwise policies, democracy may become unstable.

We shall discuss this further in later chapters. Here we wish to emphasize two Aristotelian hypotheses: one, that secular rational, constitutional law helps stabilize democracy; and two, that the development and maintenance of a well-educated prosperous middle class is essential to the stability of democracy.

---

[44] Aristotle, *Politics*, Barker Trans. Oxford Press (on law, p 145–148).

[45] Aristotle, *Politics*, Barker Trans. Oxford Press, (middle class p. 178–182).

[46] Ibid p 182.

4.6.1   Trade-Capitalism as Undergirding Democratic Government

One more factor needs to be described in terms of the emergence of democracy in Greek city-state and in the Phoenician and Mesopotamia city-states as well. That is, all these city-states exhibited the *separation of economic activity from state control*. Unlike the divine kingly states wherein the priests or the kingly-bureaucratic officials controlled the economy—and these economies were very productive—in the independent city-states, the trade-capitalist economy was run by independent merchants, bankers, craftsmen, and middle men acting on their own initiative. Of course, there were state initiated projects, like temple building and road building and mining operations—but, even these were organized privately by merchants and bankers who paid and directed the work teams necessary for these large-scale projects.

I mention this because the separation of economic power from state control limits the power of the stat and encourages the kind of individual initiative that is necessary in a democratic citizenry.

This is not meant as a rebuke to modern democratic-socialism, as exhibited in the Scandinavian countries and Germany. For in these states, a capitalist economy undergirds the social-welfare state. No, it is modern communism and fascism that demanded state control of the economy.[47]

Returning to the ancient world, it was the *trade-capitalist* economy that underpinned the politics of all the independent city-state. And, this trade-capitalist economy was most highly developed by the Greeks, once they institutionalized coined money. But, before the Greeks, the Mesopotamian merchants and bankers had already instituted regulated interest charges on loans, market pricing on commodities, metal-purity standards on money, in terms of weight and percentage of coper, silver, gold, or bronze, and business contracts, as secular documents used as evidence in courts of law.[48]

In the modern world, industrial high-tech capitalism undergirds modern democracy—though the form of this economy can vary from the Japanese-Korean style on one extreme, to the American style on the other with the EU in between.

Here we wish to emphasize that the emergence of the Greek trade – capitalist economy is documented in Hesiod's *Works and Days*[49] – in which Hesiod encourages the individual initiative to grow cash-crops and arrange to bring them to the overseas trading market and, in Aristotle's commentary on the evolution of the Greek economy from family farms (Oikos, pronounced ēkos) to the trade, banking and money-market economy of his day, Aristotle discusses "just" prices and "fair" interest rates in the dynamically expanding trade-capitalist economy of his day.

---

[47] Karl Polanyi, "Aristotle Discovers the Economy," in *Trade & Markets*. Henry Regnery, 1971.
[48] Karl Polanyi, *Trade & Markets*.
[49] Hesiod, *Works and Days*, London Penguin Classics, 1954.

Karl Polanyi, in his essay, "Aristotle Discovers the Economy,"[50] describes this brilliantly. He did not believe this was a true "market economy" as yet—but if it wasn't, it certainly was close to it.

4.7   Women & Slaves Excluded from the Democracy

One last fact is necessary in terms of our discussion of democracy in the ancient city-states: women and slaves were excluded. The citizens assembly had evolved from the warriors' assemblies of the tribes. Since women were not allowed to be warriors in most tribes, they were excluded from the citizen's assemblies.

In Golden Age Greece, there was the beginning of a woman's liberation movement. Aristophanes, in his play, *The Assembly Women*,[51] has the women of Athens dress as men and attend the assembly. Once there, they outvote the men and institute laws that benefit them. The play is a farce, but it tells us that at least the discussion of women gaining the right to attend the assembly was happening.

Furthermore, women like Aspasia, Pericles' consort, were famous as intellectuals in their own right. Aspasia advocated equal education for women and partnership marriage. She also taught rhetoric and may have written Pericles's famous "Funeral Orations," in which Pericles lauds democracy. There were also women mathematicians in the Pythagorean "cult" organizations and their writings were influential as documented in the wonderful book, *Daughters of Gaia*.[52] We have already mentioned that Hypatia was the last of the astronomers at Alexandria before the Christians burned the library. And, of course, Sappho was the first of the women intellectuals to become famous—in her case for her poetry.[53]

However, with all this gender uprising, women never gained the right to attend the assembly.[54]

As for slaves, warfare was continuous in the ancient world, and prisoners of war were forced to become slaves. If Greeks were taken prisoner, they were enslaved by the city-state that won. So, there was *no ethnic* or *racial* character to the slavery. And slaves had rights: they could demand court trials and hearings, as documented by Josiah Ober, in his, *Speeches of Demosthenes*.[55]

Still, slaves were forced to work in mines and they were often mistreated—slaves could be flogged by their masters and tortured at court trials to force them to speak the truth.

So, no, the democracy was not pure, as both slaves and women were excluded.

---

[50] Karl Polanyi, "Aristotle Discovers Economy," in *Trade & Markets* also Aristotle, Politics, (on private property and the family farm (Oikos, pronounced ēkos)).

[51] Aristophanes, *The Assemblywomen*, Ann Arbor Mich. Univ. of Michigan Press 1992.

[52] Bella Vivante, *Daughters of Gaia*, Google Books, 1994.

[53] Julia Dubruff, *Sappho*, Houston, University of Houston Press 2002.

[54] Xenophon, *The Spartan Constitution*.

[55] Josiah Ober *Speeches of Demosthenes*; *Demokratia* (the trial of a slave), Princeton, University Princeton Press 1990.

Chapter 5
The Kingly-Bureaucratic State:
The Integration of Larger Political Areas

The direct democracy of the city-state was excellent for small state units. However, for larger geographic areas with much larger populations, it was unworkable.

Since continuing expansionary military conquest was an ongoing historical trend once the civilizational level was reached, the direct democracy of the city-state could not be extended in its established form.

Representative democracy, linking a league of allied city-stats, could have achieved the goal of uniting larger demographic and geographic areas.

However, in Greece, and even in Phoenicia, each city-state coveted its independence and accentuated its competition with the other city-states. Cooperation in this situation was difficult to attain, and most of these city-states refused to give up their autonomy to a central territorial unit of government.

In Greece, once the Macedonians began threatening to unite Greece through military force, a number of allied leagues of city-states did form and they developed a representative organ of state to set policy for the entire league. But, even though they were threatened militarily, they bickered and squabbled and failed to unite. The representative body never gained any real political autonomy.

In fact, the only time the Greek city-states united was earlier, during the second Persian invasion by King Xerxes. And even then, the instant the Persians were defeated, the Spartans and Athenians resumed their rivalry and split Greece with a horrendous civil war, described with great precision—and tears on the pages—by Thucydides.

Given the failure of the attempted unification it became inevitable that some sort of Kingly-bureaucratic state would unite the Greeks through force. This was, at least, partially accomplished by Philip of Macedonia. Having defeated Thebes and Athens and leaving Sparta to its isolations, Philip united Greece under his military rule. After his treacherous murder, engineered by his wife, Alexander, his son, took over the Kingship.

Alexander then led a coalition of Greek city-states out of Greece to conquer the Persian Empire. So, even in Greece, where direct city-state democracy came to perfection, Kingship had to be resorted to when the unification of larger units was necessitated.

© Springer Nature Switzerland AG 2019
R. M. Glassman, *The Future of Democracy*,
https://doi.org/10.1007/978-3-030-16111-8_5

Now, it must be remembered that tribal confederations, like the Iroquois League, successfully institutionalized representative democracy. Representatives from the clans convened in a tribal council, while representatives from each tribe sat on a confederated tribal council, at set times of the year, or when there was a crisis.[1]

However, each tribe maintained the right to abstain from the decisions reached by the confederated council, if they disagreed with it. The "unanimity principle" still prevailed.

Given this, the autonomy of each tribe superseded the authority of the representative council of the trial confederacy. So, the political integration of the larger demographic unit was not complete, not mandatory. (This reminds one of the E.U. parliament in Brussels today, where the autonomy of each European nation-state is still closely guarded).

Thus, even though representative democracy was known and was implemented by leagues of confederated city-states, it was—at this moment of developmental history—not fully successful as a unifying political institution.

Rather, military Kingship through violent conquest came to unify most civilizational areas of the world. And, once united by military force, it was held together by the institutionalization of the bureaucratic state. This bureaucratic state, made up of officials loyal to the King and under Kingly authority, began with the use of priests—who were the best educated in these societies—as Kingly-officials. Over the centuries, as education and literacy spread to secular scribes, merchants, and craftsmen, secular officials slowly replaced the priesthood.

In Egypt, the priesthood retained its ancient rule as Kingly-officials up through Roman times. In Mesopotamia the official dome was mixed—both priests and secular bureaucrats came to administer the empire through to Persian times, and even after the Greek conquest.

In China, the priesthood remained primitive—omen readers and curers of the sick—while the Kingly-officials took on the now famous Confucian style education and administered in a secular fashion. However, even in China, because Confucius emphasized the meticulous keeping of rituals and ancestor worship, the officials took on a hallowed character.

When Rome conquered the world that the Greeks had already conquered, they began their epic empire-building without a king.

The Romans even more than the Greeks, despised Kingship – with its despotic power and slave-like hold on its subjects. They had abolished Kingship early on in their history, after they threw off the Etruscan domination.[2]

Yet, once world empire demanded tight control and demographic unification, the Romans, too, reverted to Kingship. Where Caesar failed "Augustus" succeeded, even in the face of senatorial opposition.[3]

---

[1] Lewis Henry Morgan, *The Iroquois League*, and, *Ancient Society*, Charles Kerr & Co. 1909, Chicago.

[2] Polybius, *Early Rome*, see also *Livy*, Early Rome.

[3] William Shakespeare, *Julius Caesar*, Oxford, Oxford Press, 1956.

The Roman emperors, *though never gaining full legitimacy* in Rome itself, nonetheless were utilized to gain consent from the conquered populations.

The Roman emperorship—like the co-extensive Chinese emperorship—was utilized to unify a vast region of warring peoples. And though the Roman emperor was never looked upon as a god, and never ruled with "the mandate from heaven", emperor worship did succeed to some extent in creating the "Pax Romana" – a peaceful interlude of Roman unification.

Just to show that historical cases can differ very greatly, it should be mentioned that the Roman officials were not really bureaucrats. They were actually secular governors, and often entrepreneurs, whose job it was to gauge as much wealth, craft-goods and grain as they could out of the conquered peoples. They were backed-up by the power of the Roman Legions, but they never were venerated by the conquered peoples.

In fact, they were resented and rebellions against them were not uncommon.[4] No, it was not admiration (as the Koreans had for the Chinese mandarin officials), but Roman military power that kept the empire together. Nonetheless, this military power was at least partially legitimated by the institution of the Roman Emperorship.

Thus, military Kingship and the Kingly-bureaucratic state became the typical mode of unification for large-scale political units, even though they varied in their details. So much of the world became dominated by these Kingly-bureaucratic states, that even the ideas of representative government, democracy of the people and legal-rational authority disappeared. And, further after centuries of Kingly-bureaucratic rule, these democratic ideas became culturally *inconceivable.*

During the Arabic Golden Age, for instance, the works of Aristotle were translated, discussed and debated—but *not his Politics!* The caliphate was the only conceivable form of government for the Muslims of this era, and much later in history, when Sun Yat-sen—educated in Hawaii—tried to explain democracy to the Chinese people, the Chinese people could not grasp his strange "western" ideas.

The institutionalization of the Kingly-bureaucratic system of government did not change, as the Roman Empire gave way to the Arabic Empire and then to the Turkish Empire. And, in China, Korea and South East Asia, Chinese style Confucian Kingly-bureaucratic states predominated. Fancis Fukuyama in his *The Origins of Political Order*,[5] documents this.

Nothing changed until the Italian Renaissance. For, as mentioned, even though Ibn Sina and Ibn Rushd turned the attention of the intellectual world of the Middle East and Spain, toward Aristotle and other Greek philosophers, they did not recommend the Greeks' study of "the forms of government." None of them fully understood the Greek debates over oligarchy, democracy and monarchy. And, none of the Muslim intellectuals recommended dismantling the Caliphate or ruling through a democratic assembly.

In Italy, everything changed. There, independent trading cities emerged once again.

---

[4] Josephus, *Roman-Jewish War*, Amazon books, 2002.

[5] Francis Fukuyama, *The Origins of Political Order*, N.Y. Farrar, Straus, Giroux, 2011.

Chapter 6
The Renaissance City-States of Italy

Trade-capitalist city-states emerged in Northern Italy. The crusades had been launched from the new port cities of Venice and Genoa and this set off a flurry of trade with the civilizations of the Middle East.

The city-states of Italy emerged independently of each other, competing in craft production and trade. Like the Greek city-states, they saw themselves in competition with each other, often actually going to war with each other.

Unlike the Greek city-states, the Italian Renaissance cities, did not feature a powerful citizens phalanx or cavalry. Rather, the Italian cities focused on craft and trade, becoming wealthy enough to pay professional soldiers for their defense. But these professional soldiers were unreliable, often switching sides in the middle of a war, because the other side offered more money.

Machiavelli,[1] as foreign minister of Florence, attempted to copy the Athenian example by creating a citizens' militia in Florence. However, the population of Florence—and most of the Italian cities—was relatively small and the citizens preferred to concentrate on business, rather than war. So, Machiavelli's experiment ultimately failed.

If they failed at warfare, the Italian cities succeeded greatly at craft production, overseas trading, and banking. They became quite wealthy and the artistic quality of their productions was magnificent.

Because they became rich and their wares were coveted, they became targets for foreign powers. Machiavelli, as foreign minister, saw this and implored Florence and the other city-states to *unite* militarily, or risk defeat from the powerful kingdoms of France, Spain, Austria, and Germany.[2]

The city-states were so competitive with each other that they refused to heed Machiavelli's warning and they suffered the consequences: France, Spain and Austria-Germany did invade and did extort monetary payments from Florence, Venice, Genoa and many other independent city-states.

---

[1] Niccolo Machiavelli, *The Prince*, London, Penguin Classics, 1963.
[2] Ibid.

© Springer Nature Switzerland AG 2019
R. M. Glassman, *The Future of Democracy*,
https://doi.org/10.1007/978-3-030-16111-8_6

So, as in ancient Greece, no overarching political institution emerged that could unite these independent, competitive city-states in Italy.

In fact, the only unifying mechanism that existed in Italy was the Roman Catholic Church. The Church did provide a theological integration of the Italian city-states—the college of cardinals was an institution in which elected representatives from the Italian cities, and from France, Spain, Austria, Germany and England—and all the other monarchial states of Europe—did meet together.

However, it was ecclesiastical, rather than political, matters that were debated, and, even though Florence, Venice and Genoa dominated the college of cardinals and chose the Popes, the political integration of Italy never occurred.

The Italian city-states cleverly utilized the Roman Church to tax the monarchies, thus, offsetting the ransom they had to pay. But, this increasing taxation and domination of the monarchies through the Church eventually led to the Reformation wherein the Northern European monarchies broke with the Roman Catholic Church.

In any case, no unifying political institution emerged in Italy, and the Italian city-states never succeeded in establishing the kind of full-fledged democracy that Athens, Croton, Miletus, and many other Greek city-states did achieve.

The great wealth that the Italian merchants and bankers amassed, allowed them to pay professional soldiers to do their bidding. The citizens failed to organize militias powerful enough to fight these oligarchs and their mercenaries.

Florence went democratic for a short moment in history—Severino acting as the Florentine Pericles—but the Medici family was so rich that they paid mercenaries they controlled to overthrow the democracy. The Medici ruled as oligarchs for generations (while Machiavelli was forcibly retired and wrote *The Discourses*,[3] a wonderfully democratic thesis on power-limitation and the rule of law, and, *The Prince*,[4] a hideous handbook for dictators wishing to use force, violence, and terrorization to come to power and maintain their power.)

In Venice, the very rich oligarchs repressed the democratic movement emerging from the craftsmen, before democracy was even established.

The majority of Italian city-states remained oligarchic throughout their histories, and the Italian political theorists—most famously Machiavelli—became known for their analysis of power politics rather than for democratic theory.

However, Machiavelli, himself, having visited France, became enamored with the idea of a national representative parliament, with the King as the chief executive, and the rule of law superseding all personal power. Thus, Machiavelli's *Discourses on the Work of Titus Livius*[5] did advance political theory in a democratic and lawful direction. But this work of his did not become influential until the "enlightenment" of the Eighteenth century.

Let us look at this, while remembering that all the European countries were being unified by military kings. Hence, "traditional authority," that is, a military Kingship and a kingly-bureaucratic state, was emerging in all the European states.

---

[3] Niccolo Machiavelli, *The Discourses on the Work of Titus Livins* (Livy), London, Penguin, 1954.

[4] Machiavelli, *The Prince*.

[5] Machiavelli, *The Discourses on the Work of Titus Livins*.

Since there is no democracy in a Kingly-bureaucratic state, how did democracy eventually emerge in Northern Europe?

The answer is to be found in the newly arising trading cities of Northern Europe. And these trading cities grew in areas where the tribal-democratic past had not yet been fully eradicated, and, in fact, still existed in Iceland, the mountains of Switzerland and the marshes of the low countries.

Chapter 7
The Northern European City-States Unite in Leagues with Elected Representatives

The Italian city-states, as described, never allied with each other. They emerged independently and did not really face a military threat for a number off centuries. The Roman catholic church's existence as the unifier of all Christendom inhibited aggression against Italy for a substantial period of time.

In the North, things were different. Powerful military Kingships had violently unified the various territories into separate states. France, Spain, Austria and the Kingdoms of Germany could field large, well-trained armies. These armies were loyal to the King and dominated by a class of military aristocrats whose control became hereditary within certain clans.

Each European state had its King—whose succession was hereditary—and its royal aristocrats—whose succession was also hereditary. The peasants, who made up the bulk of the foot soldiers were well-trained and loyal to their local aristocratic lord who with his fellow aristocrats, made up the heavy armored cavalry that lead the lightly armored foot soldiers. The aristocratic cavalry – the "knights in shining armor" – trained for war continuously and were ruthless in war and peace, successfully repressing any rebellion from the peasants.

So, as trade and craft production seeped northward, the trade-capitalist cities that emerged found themselves surrounded by the Kingly-aristocratic military organization, which they did not have the numbers to resist.

These Northern European city-states had to make bargains with the local Kings and aristocrats in order to maintain even a semblance of independence.[1] The bargains were made, however, because the Kings and aristocrats desired the wonderful new craft goods and luxury goods which the city-states made and traded for.

As long as the city-states gave over a portion of their luxury wealth to the aristocrats and the Kings, their political and economic independence was maintained.[2]

As the cities got richer, they got bolder, desiring more independence and less taxation-in-kind. The only way they could attain more power was by allying with

---

[1] *Hanseatic League.*

[2] Max Weber, *The City.*

© Springer Nature Switzerland AG 2019
R. M. Glassman, *The Future of Democracy*,
https://doi.org/10.1007/978-3-030-16111-8_7

each other. But, why would the Northern European city-states ally with each other when the Italian (and ancient Greek) city-states would not?

One answer could be found in the still existent institutional memory of the confederated tribal councils of the Norse Tribes. "The Althing" in Scandinavia, Germany, the Netherlands, and Switzerland, and, the "Folk Moot" in Anglo-Saxon England, still existed to some extent.[3] So, the process of electing representatives to a confederated council was an institutional political process that seemed culturally consistent in Northern Europe.

The Hanseatic League was the first league of cities to emerge. And, facing the power of the Prussian kingly-state, they began electing representatives, who met in Lubeck on the Baltic Sea; for, at that time, Lubeck was the richest of the Hansa city-states.[4]

Following the lead of the Hanseatic League cities, the smaller river-cities of Germany formed a tentative league—much weaker in terms of wealth and population—but allied nonetheless, up against the monarchies of central Germany.

In Switzerland, when the Swiss mountain tribes were threatened by the Austrian Kings, a tribal confederation was founded. This federation defeated an army of heavily armored mounted knights—who could not deploy properly on the narrow mountain trails and passes. The Swiss confederation of tribes was so successful that the budding trading cities of Switzerland—Zurich, Bern, Basil, Geneva, and numerous others—joined the tribal confederation and created a representative political organization that met to face military crises and economic problems.[5]

This Swiss Confederation, consisting of elected representatives from the mountain tribes and those from the city-states, designated *no capital* – because the cities were competitive, and the tribes were quite dispersed.

Yet, eventually an institutionalized Swiss Confederation was established, exhibiting both democratic representation and constitutional legal authority.

Down in the marshy, salty, lowlands—the Netherlands—a similar process arose. The Kings, as heavily armored cavalry, avoided these vast marshy lands, for horses could get, literally, bogged down, and, the land was too filled with salt water to be productive.

However, the Dutch tribes people realized that they could live free of aristocratic and Kingly domination if they could find a way to drain the marshes. Over the centuries, the lowlanders developed the system of dykes and watermills that would characterize the Netherlands and much of present day Belgium.

The Dutch tribes—relatively free of feudal domination-reorganized their tribal-democratic system into a system of elected "water boards."[6] The waterboards oversaw the whole process of drainage of salt water and irrigation with fresh water. It was a monumental task, but they succeeded. And with this success, retained many

---

[3] Wilbert Van Vree, *Meetings, Manners, and Civilization*, London, Leicester Univ. Press, 1996.

[4] The *Hanseatic League*, Encyclopedia.com-Germany History.

[5] Glassman, *Origins of Democracy in Tribes, City-States and Nation-States* (Switzerland).

[6] Wilbert Van Vree, *Meetings, Manners and Civilization*, London, Leicester Univ. Press, 1996.

of their tribal-democratic traditions—even the "unanimity principle", and, the tradition of eating and drinking before a big meeting of all the representatives.

As in Switzerland, when the Dutch city-states arose as independent trade-capitalist city-states, these city-states—fearing invasion from the French and German Kings with their vast armies—joined the tribal waterboard confederacy, so that together they could ward off the Kingly invasions.

These Dutch city-states were jealous and competitive like the Italian city-states and often undermined each other in their struggles with France and Germany. But eventually, they became united enough to form a confederated representative institution of state. This governmental institution included representatives from each of the *many* Dutch cities, along with representatives from the waterboards of the peasant areas. It also included a representative from the one aristocratic clan of the low countries, the House of Orange.[7]

Before discussing this parliamentary democracy, with its Duke of Orange as the leader of the army, let us point out that the Dutch lowlanders, like the Swiss highlanders, were well-trained in warfare. Unlike the Italian artisans and farmers, who preferred economic activities, the Dutch and the Swiss loved heroic warfare and were able to fight the knightly aristocrats as equals. So, as with the Swiss—and because of the peculiar terrain—warfare was successfully waged against Kingly-aristocratic heavily armored cavalry incursions.

I shall not discuss the effect of the Protestant reformation on the Northern European cities as yet. But, it is significant that William of Orange, having converted to Calvinism, joined with the city-dwellers and peasants of the lowlands against his Catholic cousins in France and Spain.

The leadership of the Duke of Orange in the Dutch wars against France and Spain led the Dutch to create a new political institution: *the limited monarchy*. This is a contradiction in terms, because by definition, Kingship is absolute in power. However, the way the Dutch constitution was written, the representative parliament had all the power in economic matters and in political policy—making as well. The constitution only allowed the King to lead in war.

Thus, representative democracy with a limited monarchy— "constitutional monarchy"—became a reality, and, significantly, when England, later on, copied the Dutch model—literally crowning a younger member of the House of Orange as the new King of England in 1689—constitutional monarchy, a "mixed polity" in Aristotelian terms, became a new political reality.

What is critical for us here, is that a *new way to unify* a large region was *invented*. No longer was the Kingly-bureaucratic state the only way that a large region could be held together successfully.

The national, representative parliament—with a King or without a King—could successfully administer a large area with huge populations, keep internal order, through policing and courts, and field a well-trained army to defend its territory.

The Dutch Republic was politically and economically successful *without a King* for decades, for, sadly, the Duke of Orange was assassinated by a Catholic fanatic.

---

[7] Joop Godsblum *the Dutch Republic*.

Eventually, the Dutch re-institutionalized the monarchy—in limited fashion of course—with an heir from the House of Orange. So, both England and the Netherlands exhibited representative democracy with constitutional law, and a Kingship which would become largely ceremonial. And while the Netherlands was truly democratic, Great Britain did not remove its oligarchic voting qualifications until the 1880s! And, modern Britain is still clinging to the fantasy of a "royal" monarchy, although Britain's royals today have been reduced to common "celebrity" status (but still have a huge economic allowance).

Did the large scale representative democracies need a King? The United States of America, because of its vast continental size and its diverse populations makes the case par excellence of the success of a parliamentary representative government without any King at all. The elected presidency, of course, replaced the hereditary Kingship.

With the success of the United States, politically, economically, and militarily, *Kingship, as a unifying political institution, was no longer necessary.*

This is very revolutionary. For, remember that even the Greeks and Romans, who disliked and criticized monarchy forcefully, ended up by emulating the Kingships they were deriding. Alexander's generals divided up the vast territory of conquest into regional Kingships, and, Rome, when it acquired its empire, also institutionalized a Kingship, which overrode the oligarchic senate and the authority of the democratic tribunes of the people.

So, the American experiment of ruling a vast territory without a King was bold indeed, but it worked. So, what we have, as we move into the twenty-first century, is a model of government which is democratic—in the sense of electing representatives to a national legislature—and, legal-rational in authority structure—in that constitutional law and the court system have set the guidelines and the limits beyond which the elected representatives and the elected president, cannot go.

With the United States of America and the Dutch Republic as models, the *"nation-state"* replaced the Kingly-bureaucratic state as the model for large scale territorial integration. And, whether the nation-state in question was democratic, oligarchic or even dictatorial (France under Napoleon) none were divine-kingly anymore.

For, as Aristotle put it, *"Kingship has now gone out of fashion and any government of that type which emerges today is a personal government, or a tyranny. Kingship is a government by consent...and such a government is now an anachronism. Equality is generally diffused and there is nobody outstanding enough for the grandeur and dignity of the office of King. There is, thus, no basis of consent for such a form of government and when it is imposed by force or by fraud, it is instantly recognized as a form of tyranny...*

'Kings cease to be Kings when their subjects cease to be willing subjects, though tyrants can continue to be tyrants whether their subjects are willing or not.'"[8]

---

[8] Aristotle, Politics, Barker Trans, p. 241

This statement by Aristotle brings us to a discussion of the rise of the rational-scientific world-view in Northern Europe and the U.S.A. For, as Aristotle put it, "there was no basis for consent" for Kingship, once the people became rational-minded enough to reject that Kings were "divine." How did the people become rational-minded?

Chapter 8
The Rational-Scientific World-View after the Protestant Reformation

The rational-scientific world-view was encouraged in the Northern European city-states and emerging nation-states after the Protestant reformation

The Catholic Church, from the time of Thomas Aquinas and Albert the Great, had encouraged the study of Greek philosophy and science. However, at the time of Galileo—when Italian science was leading the world and exciting the imagination of all of Europe, the Catholic Church turned against science.

Copernicus, Galileo and others had seemed to describe a universe that was different from the Biblical description. Therefore, various fanatical Popes had condemned Copernicus posthumously and Galileo while he was still alive. Galileo—and this is critical for the history of humankind—smuggled his notebooks north to Paris.

Paris became the new center for scientific inquiry, the French Kings, defying the Popes and encouraging scientific inquiry. From Paris, science spread to the Netherlands cities, to the German cities, and to England and Scandinavia.

Science and mathematics were heralded in Northern Europe and liberated from Catholic censorship by the Protestant Reformation. Science, mathematics and medicine expanded in scope and depth beyond anything that had come before – beyond Greece, beyond Rome, beyond the Muslim Golden Age and beyond the Italian Renaissance—science now became a new international enterprise guiding all of humankind towards a rational world orientation.

Of course, religious fanaticism and mysticism and moral-spiritual trends continued in the world. Protestantism itself produced radical Calvinist sects like the Quakers and Shakers and Anabaptists and Mennonites and others, whose view of the world was anything but rational.

However, science, as a new rational world-view was carefully institutionalized in Northern Europe and the USA. The French and British established science societies that helped organize international science conferences. The Dutch and Germans established their own science councils, which met with their French and British counterparts.

© Springer Nature Switzerland AG 2019
R. M. Glassman, *The Future of Democracy*,
https://doi.org/10.1007/978-3-030-16111-8_8

New discoveries in astronomy, biology and medicine astounded the European world and firmly legitimated the scientific enterprises for all but the most fanatic religionists.

In this treatise, we wish to emphasize that the spread of, and legitimation of, the rational-scientific world-view, increased the legitimation of rational-legal authority. For, the rational study of the "laws of nature" encouraged the acceptance of constitutional laws as guiding human social and political action. Hence, legal-rational authority was replacing divine-Kingly, or, traditional, authority.[1]

Democratic nation-states were emerging, while monarchies were disappearing from the world. Of course, and Aristotle said it best again, *"Kings cease to be Kings when their subjects cease to be willing subjects, but tyrants remain tyrants whether their subjects are willing or not."*[2]

So, tyranny—dictatorship—will continue to exist. Dictatorship will haunt the modern world, and the new technology makes the spectrum of totalitarian dictatorship even more frightening.

However, before we give in to dystopian hysteria, let us look at some of the institutional factors that undergird and engender democracy.

Having discussed the rise of the democratic nation-state and legal-rational authority, one further factor must be described. That is, the industrial-capitalist economy that emerged out of the trade-capitalist economy, after the Protestant reformation, and the scientific revolution, exploded across Northern Europe.

---

[1] Max Weber, *Economy & Society*, Roth & Wittich, (Legitimate Domination).

[2] Aristotle, Politics, Barker trans (Kingship & Tyranny, p 241).

Part II
Democracy in the Modern World

Chapter 9
Free Market Capitalism Undergirds City-State and Nation-State Democracy

Tribal democracy was supported by a hunting-gathering economy. Eventually horticulture and herding supplemented hunting-gathering and allowed for a larger population to emerge in tribes. The larger population, however, lead to the intensification of warfare, which, in turn, lead to military conquests and the eventual rise of military kingship and the Kingly-bureaucratic state. These divine-Kingly-bureaucratic states completely overrode tribal democracy and pushed it into near oblivion.

As we have made central, in the Middle East and the Aegean, independent city-states emerged, always in the shadow of some Kingly-state or another, but independent enough to manage their own economy and polity.

For us, in this treatise, one key factor in understanding city-state and nation-state democracy is that some form of *capitalism undergirds the democratic (or oligarchic)* political system.

Fukuyama recognized this in his 'end of history' by-play with the ghost of Marx, when he puts forth the model for the near future as: parliamentary democracy with a capitalist economy.[1]

In the ancient world, where tribes transitioned to Kingly-bureaucratic states, and where military Kingly states conquered and absorbed all the surrounding tribes, the economy was state-run—either directed by priests, as in Egypt and early Mesopotamia, or by secular bureaucrats as in China and Persia.

However, in Mesopotamia, Syria, Phoenicia and Greece, independent trading cities emerged. And within these trading cities, the institutions of tribal democracy were carried over: the council of elders became the council of wealthy city-fathers—rich merchants and bankers; while the warriors assembly became the citizens assembly—craftsmen, cash-crop farmers, middle men and shopkeepers.

These city-states were oligarchic, rather than democratic, in their early phase. They were oligarchic because trade-capitalism was their economic basis. For, since much of the trade was controlled by the merchants and since these trade-merchants developed a money economy, they also controlled the banks.

---

[1] Francis Fukuyama, *The End of History.*

© Springer Nature Switzerland AG 2019
R. M. Glassman, *The Future of Democracy*,
https://doi.org/10.1007/978-3-030-16111-8_9

As we have described, as bankers, the merchants lent money at interest: hence, making money with money produces "capital"—money used, not just as a medium of exchange, but as an instrument to make more money.

Controlling the banks and the trade, the merchant class became wealthy, and used their wealth to gain political domination.

But, these trade economies became more and more dependent upon craft production and cash crop increases. These latter served to expand trade dramatically. In doing so, this gave the *craftsmen and free famers* enough wealth to demand higher social status and, *increased political participation*.

Thus, in most trade—capitalist city-states—whether Mesopotamian, Phoenician or Greek—the middle classes of craftsmen and farmers eventually gained enough wealth, status and education (they could read, write and do simple business calculations) to increase their power and influence at the citizens assembly—over against the power of the council of city fathers.

In this way, city-state democracy began to replace city-state oligarchy in *some* of the ancient city-states.

We have already described the rise of democracy in the Greek city-states through the combination of trade-capitalist expansion and the Hoplite phalanx military innovations. And, we have already described how the Italian city-states remained largely oligarchic.

In Northern Europe, in the Dutch and Hanseatic League German city-states, the dramatic expansion of trade and craft and cash crop production (one of the "cash crops" in Northern Europe being salted fish preserved in barrels) began to push these city-states from years of oligarchic control to a more democratic representation system.

In many of the Dutch and German city-states, the expansionary success of the trade-capitalist economy eventuated in something like the tribal democracy that had existed before the rise of the military Kings in Northern Europe.

In these city-states, the citizens assembly gained the right to vote on the final form of the policy decisions made by the city council of wealthy merchants. These city fathers maintained great influence, but the middling citizens definitely gained the right to participate.[2]

And, it should be emphasized, that like the ancient Greeks, the citizens of the Northern Europe cities made up the bulk of the militias that defended the city-states. These militias, like their ancient Greek counterparts, were well-trained, armed, and disciplined. (This did not occur in Italy, as described).

Further, because of the spread of literary and mathematical skills, the level of democracy was enhanced. Written constitutions of secular law typified these city-states and the majority vote eventually replaced the unanimity principle.[3] And with the Protestant encouragement of science and education, the emergence of legal-rational authority raised the level of democracy beyond its tribal roots.

---

[2] Max Weber, *The City* (The Plebian City), NY Free Press, 1952.

[3] Wilbert Van Vree, *Meetings, Manners & Civilization*.

Education, science and mathematical calculation typified the Northern European city-states, as trade-capitalism expanded, and the democratic processes became institutionalized.

It was in this atmosphere, in the Netherlands, Belgium, West Germany, England and Scotland that trade-capitalism—with its trade, banking and craft-cash-crop production, morphed into *industrial-capitalism*—with its machine-factory production and the application of science and technology continuously into the production process—replacing craft-production — and, its money and banking sector expanding into the stock market and other financial innovations. Remember that *industrial-capitalism was, and is, both industrial and capitalist.*[4]

Weber, of course, famously and controversially theorized that it was the Protestant Reformation—and specifically the Calvinist "puritans" religious trend—that engendered the industrial revolution.[5] Capitalism entering a new phase, industrial-capitalism replacing trade-capitalism.

Now, Marx had already emphasized the distinction between trade-capitalism and industrial-capitalism. Marx described in detail, the new form of capitalism—industrial-capitalism with giant corporations — in his posthumous work, *Das Capital*, compiled by Engels.[6]

Now, whether this new form of capitalism was brought about through material causes, as Marx theorized, or by spiritual courses, as Weber theorized, is open to debate—will it ever be resolved? — but what is *not* debated is the fact that industrial-capitalism did emerge in England, Scotland, Flanders, the Netherlands, and then, the United States of America.

Industrial-capitalism, characterized by machine-factory production and the application of science and technology to the productive process—*is capitalism.* That is, the use of money as capital in order to make more money is institutionalized in the banking and financial system.

The new Dutch innovation of selling shares to individual investors on a stock exchange, created a capitalism that was *even more capitalistic* than trade-capitalism. New financial institutions emerged and were encouraged to expand their range of involvement beyond the banking system. Nothing like this occurred, even in ancient Greece![7]

And free market forces were allowed to guide economic transactions, even though they engendered great instability in the system. Adam Smith praised "the invisible hand of the market,"[8] and Jeremy Bentham[9] believed it would create a Utopian economy, but Karl Marx warned of the *business cycle* of boom and bust that typified free market dynamics.

---

[4] Karl Marx, *Das Capital*, N.Y. International Publishers, 1948.

[5] Max Weber, *The Protestant Ethnic and the Spirit of Capitalism*, Free Press, 1951.

[6] Marx, *Das Capital*.

[7] Karl Polanyi, *The Great Transformation*, Google Books. 2006.

[8] Adam Smith, *The Wealth of Nations*, London, Penguin Classics, 1951.

[9] Jeremy Betham, *Collected Works*, John Bowring, Edinburgh, William Tait, Google Books, 2009.

Like it or hate it, market dynamics have become part of industrial-capitalism. Such market dynamics had characterized trade-capitalism, but not in such an all-encompassing way—if we can believe Karl Polanyi in his *Trade and Markets* anthology.[10]

So, industrial-capitalism is capitalist—it was *not* just an industrial revolution. An industrial-capitalist revolution is what it was.

But, again, let us emphasize that with the industrial sector—the machine-factory sector—there was *the encouragement of the application* of rational science to create the practical technology necessary to improve the machine-production process, and, the products themselves.

Industrial-capitalism—as both Weber and Marx asserted vividly—is the most productive and innovative economic system that human beings have ever created.

State run monopolies tend to be inefficient and wasteful, bogged down in government bureaucracy and political interferences. Therefore, the industrial capitalists—businessmen, factory owners, bankers, and stock market managers—wanted no government control over the economy.

The free market does produce the most efficient, innovative and productive economy. That is exemplified by the changeover to the "capitalist road" in China from the state run communist party-controlled economy. When this occurred, China's economy took off.[11]

However, as Marx warned—with the passion and eloquence of a Biblical prophet—capitalism, in its new iteration of industrial-capitalism, engenders such wide wealth distinctions that oligarchic dominance stifles democracy.

Marx's solution, that the means of production should be taken away from the rich capitalists and placed in the control of a "temporary dictatorship" of the communist party intellectuals, was no solution at all.[12] For once you have a government run economy and an all-powerful communist party elite, what you get is: an inefficient, poorly run economy and an authoritarian dictatorial polity. The state *does not* "wither away" and the workers cannot manage the high technology factory economy.

Weber agreed that industrial-capitalism did produce huge inequalities in wealth and power. But, since industrial-capitalism is the most productive and innovative economy he believed it should be retained *but balanced* by *the Socialist-Democratic parties.* For these parties through electoral majorities, could insure that the working class and the middle class could gain their fair share of the industrial wealth, through good wages, high salaries and social safety-net programs. Also, a free educational system for all citizens was championed by the Social-Democrats.

So, let us agree with Weber that the industrial-capitalist system should be institutionalized because of its efficiency and technological innovation. And, let us agree that the middle and working classes must be empowered, educated, and financially

---

[10] Karl Polanyi, *Trade & Markets.*

[11] Ronald M. Glassman, *China in Transition: Communism, Capitalism, Democracy,* N.Y. Greenwood-Praeger, 1991.

[12] Karl Marx and Fredrich Engels, *The Communist Manifesto,* N.Y. International Publishers, 1948.

secure. These latter factors are, of course, part of an ongoing political struggle even in the most advanced industrial-capitalist nations.

The tendency towards oligarchic accumulations of wealth and the squeezing down of workers' wages and middle-class salaries is intrinsic to capitalism—in all of its forms. And, it must be guarded against in all of the modern countries wherein the representative democracy is undergirded by industrial-capitalism.

Now, before we look at the modern world, we wish to emphasize a number of key factors which characterize industrial-capitalism, and, which help to stabilize modern democracy. These factors account for the fact that modern democracies are accompanied by a capitalist form of economy.

Chapter 10
Four Ways Free Market Capitalism Reinforces Legal-Rational Democracy

10.1 One: The Separation of the Economy from the Polity

When one thinks of the separation of powers, one thinks of Montesquieu and *The Federalist Papers* of the USA founding fathers. Montesquieu in his *Spirit of the Laws,*[1] and Hamilton, Madison and Jay[2] describe the separating of the legislative, judiciary, and executive branches of government, as enunciated in the American Constitution and as the hallmark of democratic governance.

However, it is also the case that with a capitalist economy, the control and direction of the economy is separated from government control.

This is critically important, in that it limits the power of the state—beyond the constitutional limitations.

And, in another vein, where a vibrant capitalist economy is institutionalized, it encourages men who are power seekers to turn their energies towards wealth accumulation. Thus, men of power become tycoons instead of dictators. To paraphrase John Maynard Keynes, *"I would rather have someone tyrannize over my bank account than over my life."*[3]

In legal-rational representative democratic nation-states, there is a balance between the power of the business upper class and the elected representatives of the people. The rich financiers and corporate executives pay well-trained lobbyists to gain influence over the party-political process. While, the elected representatives hold businesses and banks in check through taxation and regulatory agencies.

In a perfect situation, the rich capitalists and the elected representatives of the middle and working classes balance each other. But, of course, there are no perfect situations. Therefore, the prospect of oligarchic overinfluence of the democratic government is often a reality—as it is in the USA in 2019. There is rarely a perfect

---

[1] Montesquieu, *The Spirit of the Laws*, London, Penguin, 1956.

[2] Hamilton, Madison, Jay, *The Federalist Papers*, Random House, 1956.

[3] John Maynard Keynes, Biography, by *Robert Skidelsky*, N.Y. Public Affairs, 2009.

© Springer Nature Switzerland AG 2019
R. M. Glassman, *The Future of Democracy*,
https://doi.org/10.1007/978-3-030-16111-8_10

balance, although Germany comes close and the problems of both oligarchic over-influence, and, too much government interference are both real.

In this treatise, we wish to emphasize that the separation of power between the market economy and the elected government is a good thing for democracy because it creates a secondary limitation of the power of the state, beyond the constitutional separation of powers.

10.2   Two: Contract Law and Patent Law

From the trade-capitalism of the ancient city-states to the high-technology industrial capitalism of the twenty-first century, all business transactions are grounded in contract law. Without a legally binding, detailed contract, no business transactions would be possible.

In the ancient world, beginning in Sumer, where writing first emerged, contract law emerged with it. At first used to document the goods stored in the temples and accounted by the priests, writing was then applied to the trading process which was expanding up and down the Tigris and Euphrates rivers (and with the caravans that crossed the desert).

The earliest contracts were made binding by affixing the seal of the regional war-king, and by attaching curses of the local gods. Breaking a contract in any way would bring down the wrath of the Kingly courts upon the transgressor with harsh punishments and, the transgressor would suffer the curses of the gods on himself and his family.

Thus, contract law was backed up by political and religious power. This power was necessary in order to sanctify and fortify the veracity of the legal contracts. But, the contracts were honored even more so by the fact that they benefitted both parties entering into them.

That is, trade was lucrative, and the merchants and the craftsmen who produced the trade-goods benefitted financially from these business transactions. One could lose at trade if ships were sunk or caravans attacked by thieves but gaining wealth from trade was more common. Therefore, with wealth to gain, and punishments for breaking contracts harsh, contracts were usually honored.

Contract law, then, became an integral part of trade-capitalism as it emerged in Mesopotamia and spread to the sea trade of the Mediterranean.

For instance, the Bible tells us that Abraham was a caravan merchant, organizing donkey caravans, first in and around Harran near the Euphrates river and then in Canaan, when he and his tribes migrated there. This merchant orientation was so ingrained, that Abraham enters into a "covenant" with God. The concept of a covenant—though used for religious purposes—comes right out of the contract law that bound merchants to legally defined activities.

Centuries later, during the British enlightenment, in the era of expanding capitalism and banking in Northern Europe, Scotland and England, Thomas Hobbes would write of the people entering into a "social contract" in order to set up a government and raise people out of "the state of nature" – in which there was no law and no government and in which life was "solitary, nasty, brutish and short."[4]

Long before the Enlightenment, contract law was raised to a new level in the ancient Greek city-states. Contract law, regulating secular business transactions, had become so deeply ingrained in the Greek trading cities, that when they wrote their law codes, they evolved away from the religiously based law codes of the great civilizations, and towards secular "constitutional" law codes, regarding political processes, rather than moral norms.[5] The moral law codes existed as well,[6] but constitutional law, like contract law, was secular in its orientation.

Why am I discussing contract law? Because, where free market capitalism is institutionalized as the basic economy of a nation, contract law must be carefully institutionalized as well. And once contract law is fully institutionalized and honored, then constitutional law becomes a possibility as well.

The case of contemporary China can illustrate what I mean. In a book that I wrote on China, entitled, *China in Transition: Communism, Capitalism, Democracy,*[7] I describe how the Chinese Communist party, once it embarked on "the capitalist road," was suddenly confronted with the system of contract law and patent law that circumscribe the modern high tech industrial-capitalist economies of the USA, the E.U. and the U.K.

Once China entered into this globally expanding economic network, its businesses were bound by contract law. No company would do business with a Chinese company without legal guarantees. Therefore, reluctantly, and sometimes not fully complying, the Chinese businesses began to uphold the legal contracts that all businesses must adhere to.

This process has been difficult for the Chinese regime to accept, because they are used to political control of all activities—including economic activities—in China. However, the remarkable success of the Chinese businesses has overridden the authoritarian regimes' proclivity for control.

Now, I am fully aware that the Chinese businessmen have cheated whenever they can, and often do not fully comply with the contract. I am also aware that the Communist party dictatorial government still controls large state industries and directs large scale infrastructure projects.

Still, as the capitalist sector of the economy grows, and the businessmen, bankers, stock brokers and others see their profits soar, there has been more of an effort to comply with contract law. And, again, even though the Chinese have continued to violate patent law and literary rights, enormous pressure has been put on the Chinese by the Europeans and Americans and Japanese corporations to comply with these business laws.

---

[4] Thomas Hobbes, *Leviathan.*

[5] Aristotle, *The Constitution of Athens.*

[6] Glassman, *Origins of Democracy in Tribes, City-States and Nation-States* (The Gorton Law Code of Crete-section on constitutional law in ancient Greece).

[7] Glassman, *China in Transition: Communism, Capitalism, Democracy.*

The more successful Chinese capitalism becomes, the more likely will the Chinese capitalists comply with contract law. And, as we have emphasized, once contract law becomes fully accepted, it can lead to the legitimation of constitutional law, covering the protection of the rights of all the people, not just businesses.

Demands for constitutional guidelines, limiting and directing political activities, often follow the institutionalization of contract law—which limits and guides economic activities.

We cannot be naïve. We know that authoritarian—nearly totalitarian—regimes like that of contemporary China do not disappear of their own accord. Marx's notion of "the withering away of the state" was Utopian at best, and at its worst it encouraged "the temporary dictatorship of the proletariat." For once dictators take power, they do not give it up peacefully.

Xi in China has become more authoritarian than his predecessor, repressing any real attempts at freedom of speech, press, and religion.

However, the spectacular growth of the capitalist economy with its expanding contract law and patent law has set the stage for a general acceptance of the rule of law over the rule of men. And, further, the modern high tech industrial-capitalist economy is dependent on science and the application of science to technology.

Once science is established, the rational-scientific world-view spreads in the educated portion of the population, and, with the need for excellent science and engineering, the educated portion of the population grows dramatically.

These latter phenomena are happening in China (& India). So, let us look at the impact of the rational-scientific world-view on the populations. And, on the growth of a well-educated, prosperous middle class that accompanies it. For, the rational-scientific world-view and a well-educated prosperous middle class bode well for the future *possibility* of democracy.

10.3   Three: The Rational-Scientific World-View

We are fully aware that science can be, and has been, used by authoritarian and totalitarian regimes. Nazi Germany, Stalinist Russia and now Kim Jong Un's North Korea, have effectively organized, supported, and utilized scientists to develop military power and computer technology to support authoritarian political processes.

In no way is science linked only with democracy or capitalism. Even in ancient Greece, scientists such as Archimedes of Syracuse—along with their scientific discoveries—invented military weaponry, rather than consumer products. And, of course, Nobel, in the modern world, after inventing dynamite, tried to atone by leaving his fortune for the Nobel Peace Prizes.

So, why am I highlighting the rational-scientific world-view and linking it with legal-rational democracy? It is the legal-rational segment of modern democracy that we wish to focus on.

That is, legal authority is based on secular law. Secular law is rational and amendable—like scientific theory. What distinguishes scientific theory from religious

doctrine is the fact that scientific theories are open to rational debate, empirical veri-
fication and alteration. The whole process of scientific theorizing, hypothesizing,
experimentation and mathematization is *rational*.

Now, as Kuhn[8] has pointed out, even the best scientists can become irrational
when evidence shows that the abandonment of a long-held theory becomes necessary. But Kuhn also shows that in the long run, rationality wins out and revolutionary scientific theories, like Einstein's Relativity Theory, do become accepted.

The rational norms of science eventually override the irrational attachments to
certain established theories.

Also, and this is critical, the mathematical character of scientific thinking rein-
forces the rationality of the theorizing. Since mathematics is based on logic, it is the
ultimate rational process of human thinking. No one is quite sure why the "mathematization of nature" works. But, it does, insofar as it gives us defined measurements of the laws of motion, and the laws governing the processes of the universe in
general.

Mathematical equations and formulas help scientists predict the events in the
universe and explain them. However—and the scientists have warned about this—
these mathematical formulas can *not* be used to predict the fluctuations in the stock
market—as became evident in 2008, when the Black-Scholes[9] and other MIT generated formulas, failed to predict the mortgage-based crash. In fact, the mathematical
formulas do poorly in predicting most *human social phenomena*, such as the effect
of the birth control pill on human sexual interaction, or women's liberation on the
divorce rate, or the demand for gay marriage, once gays "came out."

Humans do not always act logically. Sometimes they act irrationally, emotionally, or willfully. Also, new technological inventions, like the birth control pill or the
smart phone, add new elements to society that were "not in the equation"
previously.

Social science generalizations can be made, as both Weber[10] and Durkheim[11]
have shown, but the element of continuing global change makes the generalizations
more difficult—but not impossible. Cross-cultural and trans-historical generalizations have been, and will continue to be, helpful in analyzing human societies.

However, mathematics has been remarkable in its application to the physical
sciences.

The combination of mathematical logic and calculation, with rational theorizing
and empirical observation and experimentation—the "scientific method" – does
engender a rational world-view amongst populations educated to its principles.
And, even though such educated populations can become irrationally patriotic,

---

[8] Thomas Kuhn, *The Structure of Scientific Revolutions*, Chicago, Univ. of Chicago Press, 1962.

[9] Black-Scholes algorithms for predicting stock market fluctuations—failed; see Wikipedia.com-
Black Scholes Algorithms.

[10] Max Weber, *The Methodology of the Social Sciences,* N.Y. Free Press, 1949 (Shils & Finch,
editors).

[11] Emile Durkheim, *The Rules of Sociological Method*, N.Y. Free Press, 1956.

"tribal", and, or, spiritually religious (both Newton and Einstein retained strong religious beliefs), their basic orientation to the world may still be rational.

With this rational-scientific world-view, modern populations, which are well educated begin to believe that they should be included in the political decision-making process. They begin to feel themselves competent enough to want to participate in the electoral process, or to run for office themselves, or, at least to be able to express themselves freely in literature, journalism, and the arts.

One can see this already in the educated middle classes of China, India, and other rapidly developing nations. One can see this in Russia as well, even though they may back Putin for patriotic reasons. They may vote for Putin, reveling in his annexation of Crimea and reassertion of Russian world power, but they know that Putin is overriding the constitutional law of Russia, and that he is murdering his opposition. The Russian middle class—well-educated and especially well-trained in the sciences—do not like the authoritarian encroachments on what was supposed to be a democratic process of government. And, they do not like the "kleptocracy" of the "oligarchs" surrounding Putin, with their perversion of the capitalist economy from market forces to pure force.

Now, both China and Russia have had long histories and ingrained cultures of Kingly-bureaucratic authoritarian government. And, both China and Russia have had communist authoritarian rule. However, both nations are also still in transition to capitalist economic development and legal-rational authority. The may never become legal-rational and democratic, but it is too soon to tell. Certainly, the rational-scientific world-view is spreading as the population becomes more educated. And— this will be our next highlighted focus—in Russia, China, India, Latin America, and other areas of the developing world, there is a growing, well-educated middle class emerging. And, these middle classes, like those of Aristotle's Athens, tend to be reasonable, lawful, and willing to compromise.

As Aristotle put it, "Blessed is the state with a majority middle class, for democracy is most stable when the middle class is in the majority and can outvote the poor and the rich."[12,13]

10.4   Four: The Majority Middle Class and Democracy

I have written many books on the middle class and its link with stable democracy. They include: *The Middle Class and Democracy in Historical Perspective* (E.J. Brill); *For Democracy: The Noble Character and Tragic Flaws of the Middle Class (Praeger)*[14]; *The New Middle Class and Democracy in Global Perspective*

---

[12] Aristotle, *Politics* (middle class).

[13] Ronald M. Glassman, *The Middle class and Democracy in Historical Perspective*, E.J. Brill, Leiden, The Netherlands, 2002.

[14] Ronald M. Glassman and William Swatos, Jr. and Peter Kivisto *For Democracy: The Noble Character and Tragic Flaws of the Middle Class*, N.Y. Praeger, 1993.

(MacMillan)[15]; *Caring Capitalism* (MacMillan).[16] So, what is the link between an educated prosperous middle class and the stability of democracy?

Aristotle theorized that a majority middle class would stabilize democracy, because the middle class is reasonable and lawful. They are less likely to become extreme and fall under the sway of demagogues. The poor tend to be angry and uneducated and feel neglected by the law—below the law. Thus, they commit petty crimes and acts of violence. And, the rich tend to be arrogant and believe themselves to be above the law. They use their wealth to subvert the law, and sometimes commit big crimes.[17]

The middle class, Aristotle observed, tends to follow the law and honor the law and opt for the policy positions in a reasonable manner that allows for compromise. Having enough wealth to be comfortable, but not so much to corrupt them, and, being educated enough to understand policy implications, the middle class is ideal for the stabilization of democracy.

Aristotle further observed, that where the poor are in the majority and can out-vote the middle class, "democracy is speedily ruined."[18] Why? Because the poor tend to be angry and uneducated, and they fall under the sway of charismatic dema-gogues, who promise them that they will confiscate the wealth of the rich and dis-tribute it to the poor.

Contemporary Venezuela exemplifies this. There, Hugo Chavez organized the poor, gained their vote, and distributed the wealth of the oil economy to the poor—not in terms of education and career training, but in terms of giveaways that had to be repeated, once the first grants ran out. The economy collapsed, and, as Aristotle warned, the democracy was "speedily ruined."

Aristotle also warned that the rich, if they control the vote, buying off the vote with their enormous wealth, also subvert democracy. If democracy is moved in an oligarchic direction, the rich will rule in their own interest, and not in the interest of all the people.

In the modern world that has been a growing trend wherein the super-rich avoid paying taxes through bogus banking systems, such as those of Cyprus, the Cayman Islands, and Switzerland. And, with their accumulating wealth, the rich over-influence the representative democratic process through the use of well-trained lob-byists and lawyers who attempt to control both the electoral process and the legislative process.

Where the rich, and, or, the poor have too much influence, extremes of political positions, and the lack of compromise, can lead to increasing violence and political instability.

However, where the middle class can outvote the rich and the poor, and retain control over the political process, the extremes of politics generated by the rich and

---

[15] Ronald M. Glassman, *The New Middle Class and Democracy and Global Perspective*, N.Y. MacMillan, 2003.

[16] Ronald M. Glassman, *Caring Capitalism*, N.Y. MacMillan, 2008.

[17] Aristotle, *Politics* (rich, poor, and middle class).

[18] Aristotle, *Politics* (poor).

the poor can be contained. Therefore, it is of the essence that if a stable democracy is the goal, then the establishment of a well-educated, prosperous, majority middle class becomes absolutely necessary.

Aristotle offered *practical programs* for absorbing the poor and containing the power of the rich.

For the poor, he suggested training them in craft workshops, so that they could have a lifetime career. Or, attaching them to cash-crop producing farms, again, so that they could gain a career. Just giving the poor money would be like "pouring water into a leaky jar."[19]

The E.U. follows this advice—especially in Germany, Scandinavia, and the Netherlands. There, immigrants get training and are placed in factories and other industrial jobs. In France, where there are more immigrants—especially North African Muslims—this has been done, but less successfully.

As for the rich, Aristotle believed that the middle class—having the voting majority—would introduce "wise legislation"[20] that would tax the rich enough to fund civic projects that would benefit all of the people. He also believed that the rich could be socialized to have a civic conscience, such that they would give voluntarily to civic projects and to religious festivals.

And, it should be noted that the rich of the ancient Greek city-states were often generous in their support of civic and religious projects. Still, the middle-class majority had to insure this latter with their "wise legislation."

Obviously, the increasing trend, in the twenty-first century, of the rich in the industrial-capitalist societies to avoid paying taxes and to ignore the civic needs of the societies they live in, is very worrisome. In the USA, a wealthy candidate for the presidency, Mitt Romney, admitted that he had his money in the Cayman Islands. And, most blatantly, Donald Trump would not release his tax returns at all—because he rarely paid taxes, and, because much of his money was linked to Russian-oligarchs' money laundering.

Finally, the decline of the middle class in any democratic nation bodes ill. Because where the middle-class declines, extremes of politics emerge, and unlawful activities increase. All of this destabilizes democracy.

In the USA in the twenty-first century, the decline of the middle class has led to the emergence of extremes in politics. The "Tea Party" fundamentalist conservatives, the Bernie Sanders socialists, right wing Neo-Nazi racists, P.C. extremists who do not recognize the right to free speech, and more.

The American middle class needs help with college tuition costs—which escalated wildly from nearly free from 1945–1970, to $20,000–$60,000 dollars a year. This has been ruinous for the middle class and their children who are now saddled with enormous student loans.

Mortgage prices and rentals have gone through the roof—pardon the pun—and are bankrupting the middle class and forcing their children to live at home.

---

[19] Aristotle, *Politics* (poor-"leaky jar").

[20] Aristotle, *Politics* (wise legislation by the middle class).

Healthcare costs and the cost of prescription drugs have also gone way up and weakened the American middle class economically.

With the middle class declining economically, American democracy has become unstable. The compromises that characterized American democracy since WW II, have now become impossible and obstructionary gridlock politics is now the norm.

Hopefully, policies helpful to the middle class will emerge in the near future. There are glimmers of hope in this regard: Governor Cuomo of NY has legislated that college tuition is *free* at all State universities. New Jersey has made 2 year colleges tuition free and Georgia has had a program of free tuition at its state universities for a number of years.

In the E.U. a Financial Transaction Tax—FTT—has been implemented in all stock transactions. Because of computerized trading, there are literally millions of stock transactions occurring every day. Therefore, a tiny tax on each transaction can bring in billions of dollars of tax revenue. Thus, FTT revenue can be earmarked to pay for health insurance, college tuition, childcare, and other increasingly expensive necessities of modern living.

The USA could enact an FTT and if they did, the tax revenue would be enormous, as there is more stock trading in the USA than anywhere else in the world. Of course, the "catch 22" is that the financial rich have enough lobbyists to prevent this in the USA. The idea for the FTT originally came from John Maynard Keynes,[21] and it will be instituted in the U.K.—unless Brexit stalls it. As for the USA, eventually the FTT will catch on as our deficit continues to balloon.

With or without the FTT, the financial condition of the American middle class must be bolstered if democratic stability is to return.

10.5 Is there a Numerical Formula Relating to a Middle-Class Majority?

When Seymour Martin Lipset popularized Aristotle's "Middle Class thesis," in his book *Political Man,*[22] his students—trained in American "Functionalist" sociology—wanted a numerical attribution to the "middle class thesis." What constitutes a majority? How large does the middle class have to be?

There is no absolute numerical formula for determining when and if a middle class is in the majority. And, the middle class can be split between two or more parties in modern nation-states—as they are in the USA with liberal-Republicans and moderate Democrats, or, in Germany, with Conservatives and Social Democrats.

The key here is that a large well-educated, prosperous, middle class can serve to stabilize democratic regimes. Whereas, extremes of wealth and poverty can destabilize democratic regimes.

---

[21] Keynes, *Biography.*

[22] Seymour Martin Lipset, *Political Man,* Random House, 1953.

Of course, massive immigration like that of the Muslims into Europe or the Mexicans (and Central Americas) into the USA, can result in extremism. However, the middle-class majority in the E.U. countries and the USA has held the extremism in check — while the right-wing parties have gained more seats in the European parliaments, and, Donald Trump was elected president in the USA, the middle-class moderates have asserted themselves, such that rational programs for assimilation of the new immigrants are beginning to prevail.

So, to reassert our main point: *the existence of a majority middle class does stabilize democracy*, even in its modern form and *the steady expansion of a well-educated, prosperous middle class, does improve the prospects for developing a democratic political process.*

Let us present a few case studies to illustrate this thesis—and to show the complexities that are involved when we are dealing with human societies, rather than electrons or bees.

The structural fact of the growth and expansion of a well-educated prosperous middle class must be placed within the specific cultural and historical realities of the given nations in question. Huntington[23] has emphasized the cultural resistance to democracy in many societies, and this is problematical. The specific history of a society can also effect the changes in the present and near future.

Nonetheless, structural changes, such as the introduction of a capitalist economy, science education, contract law, and modern technological devices of global communication capacity—along with the growth of a new middle class—can and do alter societies developing in similar economic, social, and political ways.

Let us look at specific case histories to trace both the *structural similarities*, and, the *cultural and historical peculiarities* involved.

---

[23] Samuel P. Huntington, *Political Order in Changing Societies.*

Chapter 11
Case Studies of Socio-Political Change in Some of the Developing Nations

11.1 India

In India, where there is a growing, well-educated, prosperous middle class, the democratic government—inspired by the British long-term occupation and the British-style educational system—has remained stable, even though the poor vastly outnumber the middle class. This is because in India the poor live dispersed widely in the Indian countryside. They live in villages remote from the cities. In these villages, with their families intact, they tend to vote moderately and to allow the national legislature to be guided by the emerging middle class.

Further, the Hindu caste system[1] created a theological passivity for the poor, in which they see themselves as having inherited the "degraded souls" of the individuals who had exhibited "bad karma." So, they believe they deserve their low status. Illustrating this is the social phenomenon that a poor Indian farmer will kill himself for failing to produce enough, rather than turning his anger on the rich.

The poor of the cities are wretched, but so far, they too have been politically passive. Although, recently Hindu fanatics have been able to rile them up—but against Muslims, and liberated women—not against the government.

So, in India, though the well-educated, prosperous middle class is by no means a majority, it acts to stabilize the democratic regime. Both the years of British education, emphasizing the rule of law and parliamentary procedure, and, the Hindu theology of the transmigration of the soul (with its caste system) have pacified the poor and enhanced the status of the new middle class. This new Indian middle class is rapidly expanding, and contributing to the success of the high tech industrial capitalist economy which they are actively engaged in.

The middle class in India is very entrepreneurial, and quite skilled at technology. Their influence in expanding the Indian economy and stabilizing the Indian polity has been profound.

---

[1] Max Weber, *The Religion of India*, NY Free Press, 1950.

© Springer Nature Switzerland AG 2019
R. M. Glassman, *The Future of Democracy*,
https://doi.org/10.1007/978-3-030-16111-8_11

Finally, do not discount the remarkable effect of the British educational system. For, wherever it has been successfully institutionalized, the middle class has grown and been ingrained with the spirit of legal-authority and democratic debate. India, Hong Kong, Cyprus, Kenya, Singapore, and other British colonial regions, all exhibit legal-democratic forms of government. So, along with "divide and con-quer"—the worst element of British colonialism—the British proclivity for law and reasonable debate have greatly influenced the former British colonies in a demo-cratic direction.

One last fact is also important, concerning both the politics and economics of India. Because India exhibited different languages, the establishment of the English language as the official language made sense. This allowed the Indian middle class to excel in the educational system and become open to the entire cultural tradition of British and American literature and learning.

Furthermore, it allowed the Indian middle class to easily become part of the global capitalist economy. Indians are being used by British and American compa-nies wherever English language skills are needed, and, lower salaries can produce more profit.

Members of the Indian new middle class have found it easy to move between Silicon Valley in the USA and the high-tech hubs in India.

India also has a tradition of mathematical learning. This goes back beyond the Arabic Golden Age—Arabic numerals actually being Indian numerals. This Indian proclivity for mathematics has given India boost in the capitalist high tech economy, which is developing in India. And, this rapid economic growth has expanded the middle class dramatically and enhanced India's political stability as well.

11.2   China

In China, where a rapidly expanding capitalist economy has grown beyond all expectations, a well-educated prosperous middle class is emerging. They are by no means a majority, the peasantry and the working poor making up a vast majority.

But, let us look at Hong Kong first. For, in Hong Kong—a British colony like India, — a stable democratic regime was established.

As in India, British educational systems and years of British rule, inculcated a reverence for law and parliamentary representations. Not that the British ruled Hong Kong in that way! Hardly. The British were racist and authoritarian with the Chinese—and earlier had unleashed the "opium war" to weaken China.

Nonetheless, when the British left, they helped set up a parliamentary democratic regime with a constitutional law framework.

The Hong Kong Chinese love it. And even though they have the same Confucian moral background—and some Buddhist proclivities—the democratic regime had been stable before the Beijing takeover. In fact, consistent with the Aristotelian hypothesis, the Hong Kong Chinese developed a successful system for upgrading the condition of the poor Chinese who were flooding in from the mainland.

A dramatically expanding capitalist economy was developing in "the new territories," just across from Hong Kong Island (and connected to the Kowloon mainland which was part of Hong Kong), and under Hong Kong control. The Hong Kong Chinese made sure that the poor were trained and absorbed into factory jobs, and they created new housing for these poor immigrants as well.

Further, they moved the "boat people"—wretchedly poor—into housing units, and educated their children, absorbing them into the expanding economy.

By absorbing the poor and educating the middle class well, the Hong Kong Chinese began to create the middle-class stability that Aristotle commended. The rich of Hong Kong—emerging as a banking, financial, and corporate elite—were supportive of the democratic regime, fearing the Beijing government politically and economically.

Because of this fear of Beijing, the Hong Kong rich strongly reinforced the progressive policies of the middle class. So worried were they about a Beijing takeover, that the rich bought condos in Toronto (to-run-to), Vancouver and California.

Why am I discussing Hong Kong? Because this example shows that even where a culture is antithetical to "western" democratic ideas, as Huntington asserts, democracy can emerge and even be deeply desired. Of course, Hong Kong had years of British counter-socialization to override the Kingly-bureaucratic state culture and the Confucian family deference and ritual patterns that had characterized Chinese culture.

Having described Hong Kong, now let us turn to China itself.

We should remember that when Sun Yat-sen attempted to introduce democratic ideas and institutions into China his efforts failed. The Chinese, as Huntington[2] hypothesized, simply could not grasp these strange, "western" ideas.

The Confucian-influenced political system had been stable for millennia. It consisted of: one, an emperor—with absolute power, like the father of a Chinese family—and, the emperor ruled "with the mandate from Heaven" – he was a divine King. And, two, an institutionalized, *merit-based* system for well-educated officials—the "mandarins"—guided the emperor towards "benevolent" policies—policies that would benefit the people.[3]

This system existed, and was successful, for so many centuries, that *no other political system was conceivable.*

Even though the political system bounced back and forth between emperors who were truly benevolent and emperors who were hideously violent and tyrannical, and, even though the mandarin officials rigged the systems so that their sons could pass the exams and gain official positions, enough smart peasant youths were recruited into the system, and enough emperors were benevolent, so that the people lent their consent to this system, such that *it was deeply legitimated.*

---

[2] Samuel Huntington, *Political Order.*
[3] Max Weber, *The Religion of China*, N.Y. Free Press, 1950.

Also, where an emperor was wildly incompetent or brutal, the Confucian ideology allowed for the rebellion of the people and the *revoking of the mandate from Heaven*. Thus, the people had the right to revolt.[4]

But, the revolt was only directed at installing a new emperor, who would attend the peoples' needs. No revolutionary changes in the political system were intended, nor were they conceivable, as China remained closed-off from the outside world. (The Great Wall was both real and metaphoric).

So, a new "good" emperor would be installed and the meritocratically selected, well-educated officials would help the new emperor rule benevolently.

Further, elaborate rituals were maintained for all social interactions, as Confucius had made central, with ancestor worship and family deference patterns reinforced as part of Confucian ethics.[5]

In this cultural context, western political ideas and institutions were difficult to understand or implement. But, when China was invaded and easily defeated by the Europeans—whom the Chinese thought they were superior to—something had to change.

Sun Yat-sen, and then his protégé, Chiang Kai-shek, though unsuccessful in explaining western ideas to the Chinese, used military force to attempt to somehow modernize China politically and economically. They were challenged, also by military force, by a new group of communists, influenced by and supported by, the new Russian Community party.

Ironically, the Chinese communists were thoroughly defeated by Chiang Kai-shek and his western-trained army, but the Japanese invasion of the 1930s, altered this situation. Chiang was defeated by the Japanese who began an interlude of very cruel domination.

During WWII, the USA supported Chiang Kai-shek and his Kuomintang party. But the Russians secretly supported Mao Tse-Tong and his Communist party. After WWII the USA reasserted support for the Kuomintang, thinking they would win an easy victory over the Communists. The Russians, however, had trained Mao's forces well and, Mao had created an "ideal commune" which the Chinese peasants came to believe was more "benevolent" than Chiang's people.

The Communists unexpectedly won the civil war of 1948 and Mao became the head of the new communist government.

Now, there is no doubt that Mao's communism was *consonant* with Confucian traditions—in its early years.[6] The focus was on the modernization of the economy, the creation of a modern educational system, and the improvement of the health and welfare of the people.

Mao was "the last emperor" and the communist party officials acted like mandarin officials—at least during the first 10 years of Mao's regime.

The "Great Leap Forward" and the "Cultural Revolution" changed the people's perception, however. The great leap failed, and thousands died from forced labor

---

[4] Ibid.

[5] Confucius, *The Analects.*

[6] Glassman, *China in Transition: Communism, Capitalism, Democracy*, Praeger-Greenwood.

and famine. Mao tried again, with his "cultural revolution". He set the young people loose on a mission of change—destroy Confucianism and, everything western! This attempt, not only failed, but it disrupted China completely.

Mao retired to a Buddhist monastery and soon thereafter, died. Before he died, he brought back Deng Chao Ping and told him to try the "capitalist road."

Once China embarked on the "capitalist road," the dazzling success of the new Chinese capitalist economy generated a large and growing new middle class.[7] With the need for science and technology that the modern capitalist economy demands, this new middle class is becoming increasingly well-educated, and, rationally-scientific oriented.

The Chinese university system is expanding and improving, but the need for well-trained individuals is so urgent that the Chinese government has allowed thousands of Chinese students to study abroad—in the USA, the EU and the UK. I myself, in a "Great Books" program at NYU taught hundreds of Chinese students over a 20 year period. These students did not just study science, they took a wide range of classes and learned the spectrum *of liberal arts* and sciences offered—including the study of the ancient Greek and Enlightenment political theorists, who debated the forms of government and advocated legal-authority and democracy—from Aristotle, to Locke, to Jefferson, the Chinese students were opened to "western" ideas on politics.

What will this mean for the new middle class that is rapidly emerging in China?

The middle class in China (2017–18) is expanding, becoming prosperous, and well-versed in the rational-scientific world-view. They are also learning about the American, British and European models of parliamentary democratic government.

Does this mean that democracy will miraculously arise in China? Certainly not. However, what is happening—and this is typical—is that the middle-class has begun to raise issues of freedom of speech, press, religion, and artistic expression. The middle class in China is not assertively political. Generations of communist despotism and millennia of divine-Kingly domination have made China's middle class reticent to raise political issues. They are also fearful because *the regime's police are everywhere*, and they clamp down on anyone whom the government decides is challenging them.

Also, the spectacular economic expansion and prosperity has lent a modicum of legitimation to the current regime.

Middle classes are rarely revolutionary—that is why Aristotle commends them for their moderation and lawfulness. And given the stable capitalist development and the high rate of upward mobility, the middle class in China is not likely to take any political risks.

But, the middle classes' proclivity for law and moderation does turn them against corruption and the governmental use of excessive violence. The middle class in China is becoming quite aware of corruption and violence and is critical of it.

In this sense, the Chinese middle class is becoming a *possible base* for a stable modern democracy. But, it must be understood that the poor peasants and workers—

---

[7] Ibid.

numbering in the one-half billions—not only greatly outnumber the middle class but are easily coopted into supporting the authoritarian regime in terms of recruitment for the police and the military. As long as the police and the military are well-paid and well-treated, they will back the despotism. The despotism gives them power over the middle classes, whom they resent for their prosperity and superior education.

The workers and peasants are not educated to the rational-scientific world-view, nor have they studied anything about a Bill of Rights or Constitutional Law or participatory democracy.

Still, there is hope for a future of democracy in China: first, high tech capitalism is grounded in *contract* law, science and technology; second, as the middle class becomes well-educated and learned in science, engineering, mathematics and the social sciences, a general comfort with some modicum of political freedom and political participation usually emerges. When, and if, the next generation of communist party leaders is recruited from the new middle class, these proclivities could influence these leaders.

Gorbachev and his contemporaries are examples of this. Once Gorbachev and the younger leaders of the Russian communist party saw that western Europe and the USA were outproducing them and living a much more affluent lifestyle, Gorbachev and his colleagues tried to institute a more liberal political system and economy. This did eventuate in a democratic revolution in Russia and some of the Soviet Republics.

However, the break-up of the Soviet Union was so sudden and disruptive, and, the loss of Russian power in the world so "shamefully" perceived, that the Russians allowed Putin and his clique to reestablish a despotism and override the democratic constitution that had been so clearly written.

The Chinese leadership today, is aware of the disruption that accrued when the Soviet Union broke up. So, they will not allow any liberalization of political control. They do not want to lose their outer provinces, such as Tibet or the Moslem provinces, because these areas are rich in natural resources, and connect China to the old "silk road."

However, in 20 years, where a new leadership emerges, the desire for political freedom and democratic participation may overwhelm the fear of disorder. Xi Jinping, the current leader, is not from the new middle class, his father was one of the original communist leader in the era of Mao. He is attempting to rule with a "cult of personality." However, again, in 20 years, the new leadership *may* be different, and, China will be more fully developed economically.

11.3   Russia

Russia like China, had a history and culture of Kingly-bureaucratic authoritarian rule. And, as Francis Fukuyama has suggested in his book, *The Origins of Political Order,*[8] the Russian monarchy was influenced by the Mongol Kingship of the "Golden Horde" that dominated Southern Russia for many centuries.

So, the Russian monarchy was much more despotic and violent than its Western European counterparts.

Unlike China, however, the Russian Kings, aristocrats and intellectuals were influenced by the "Enlightenment". Under Catherine the Great, French intellectuals were invited to the court, and their books and pamphlets were widely read. Voltaire[9] especially, impressed Catherine and other Russians.

When the French Revolution occurred, it scared the monarch and the barons so greatly, that the ideas of the French "Philsophe" were rejected. Still, the Enlightenment reached Russia, and the ideas of freedom of speech, press, and electoral representation in a national parliament, continued to circulate.

Criticism of the Christian religion—a la Voltaire—were absorbed by the intellectuals and debated in their works. The whole atmosphere of pre-revolutionary France was reproduced in Russia—but only amongst the intelligencia.

The peasants, who made up the vast majority of Russians, knew nothing of these ideas.

But again, the entire artistic community was influenced: art, architecture, music, dance (ballet), and literature exploded into the Russian urban world. Ballet was taken to a new level, St. Petersburg, looked like Paris, and plays and novels poured forth enriching the culture of the urban Russians.

No such western-oriented cultural exchange emerged in China.

The Russians learned how to set up a national parliament, and this "Duma" became a slowly evolving reality. The model was supposed to emulate the Netherlands and Great Britain, with a limited monarchy joined to a legislative parliament. The Russian Kings acquiesced to the establishment of a representative parliament, but, they and the aristocrats, retained absolute power. Hence, the form of democracy was instituted, but the process was overridden by the Kings and barons.

Along with these political institutions borrowed from Western Europe, the beginnings of a capitalist-industrial economy were also brought into Russia by Dutch, German, and British businessmen, bankers, and factory owners.

The new royal city of St. Petersburg was built with Russian labor but planned by European architects and engineers.

Now, as the industrial revolution emerged in England, Scotland, Flanders, and the Netherlands, it emerged, not only with machine-factory production, but also

---

[8] Francis Fukuyama, *The Origins of Political Order*, Farrar, Straus and Giroux, 2012.

[9] Voltaire, *Candide* and other writings, Google Books, 2009.

with capitalist banking and stock market financial institutions. Hence the new economic category: industrial-capitalism.[10]

Industrial-capitalism was brought into Russia, as mentioned, by Dutch, German and English entrepreneurs. The Dutch helped mechanize farming and build canals near the Baltic Sea. The English erected some cloth factories and the Germans initiated metal-working factories.

None of these industrial-capitalist institutions took hold in Russia in any significant way. But, the idea of machine-factory production became well-understood.

11.3.1   Enter, Marx, Lenin and Trotsky

The Enlightenment ideas had barely penetrated Russian political culture, when *the Communist Manifesto*[11] was written by Marx and Engels. Between 1860–1900 the idea of a communist revolution began to sweep all of Europe.

Constitutional monarchy with a capitalist-industrial economy had not really been implemented in Russia. The Russian Kings and barons used repressive force and violence to retain their absolute power. Revolutionaries, inspired by the French, demanded real parliamentary democracy. But, the monarchy resisted such democratization repressively. The industrial-capitalist economy was also making little progress in Russia.

Into this mix of reactionary monarchists and revolutionary democrats, was added the new Utopian idea of a classless society with a temporary dictatorship of the communist intellectuals, ruling in the name of the worker (until the workers would become sufficiently educated to rule for themselves).

Since Russia did not yet have an industrial-capitalist economy, the Russian, Community Party, under Lenin's leadership, added, that the temporary dictatorship would also undertake a *rapid industrialization* of Russia—without the capitalist business and banking class.[12]

This was new, for Marx had predicted that the communist revolutions would occur in Germany and England, where the industrial-capitalist economy was already institutionalized and successful. The Communists would take over this economy and run it for the workers. But, in Russia, an industrial economy had to be developed almost from scratch!

Marxism-Leninism became a new ideology beyond that of Marx and Engels. It included the notion of a rapid industrialization directed by the communist party state. It also included the establishment of a western-style educational system focused on science and technology, along with the arts and literature.

---

[10] Marx, *Das Capital.*

[11] Marx-Engels, *Communist Manifesto.*

[12] Marxism-Leninism became a new program for rapid industrialization, Britannica. com-topic-Leninism.

And, equality of all classes –including women, who would be liberated from the domination of men and the confines of the family, to enter the work force in all professions. To accomplish the liberation of women—which had been a hallmark of Marx's utopianism, borrowed from Plato (in his *Republic*,[13] women were liberated and could become "guardians", gaining the same education as men—mentally and physically)—Lenin established state nurseries (a Platonic idea) placed at all the work places and universities, where women could be with their children, and even breast feed them while on breaks).

And, of course, everyone was to make equal pay. "From each according to his abilities-to each according to his needs."[14]

This Marxist-Leninist utopian vision—with its communist dictatorship – was more *consonant* with the Russian authoritarian political culture then the democratic participation system of western democracies. And, of course, Russia needed a rapid industrialization, and this the communists promised.

Consonant or not, without the humiliating defeat of the Russian Kingly-state by the Germans, in WWI, communism might never have become institutionalized. Forced by the aristocratic officers to charge into the German gunfire, with few guns of their own, the Russian army units—famed and feared for their "Kozak" bravery and violence—were forced to retreat in humiliation. These army units were turned against the Russian King by Lenin and his communist allies. They stormed the Kingly court and overthrew the traditional monarchy.

But, was the new government to be parliamentary-democratic or a temporary dictatorship of the proletariat (run by the communist party intellectuals)? A parliament was elected, and the democratic faction—the Mensheviks'—won. The Bolshevik's who wanted a dictatorship, were in the minority, but repudiated the parliamentary government.

The history of the split between the two factions, and the civil war against the aristocrats, is well-known. First, the monarchists—the White Russians—had to be defeated. Then the victorious revolutionaries had to decide which system to adopt. Obviously, the Leninist-communists—the Red's—won. The Menshevik's and their leader, Kerensky, fled to the West. Lenin and his associate Trotsky (who had organized the Red Army) took control.

They successfully created an industrial factory system, but without capitalist profit incentive and efficiency demands, the industrial system, run by communist party officials, became bureaucratic and inefficient. Industrial production, however, did occur in Russia, and it was especially successful in the military sector (as it is today).

And, the communists did create an excellent educational system based on the German system, and oriented towards mathematics, science, and engineering. It was overlaid by censorship and communist party propaganda in history, the arts, and literature. Science and engineering, though, directed towards military technology

---

[13] Plato, *The Republic* (liberated women).

[14] Marx-Engels, *Communist Manifesto*.

was allowed more leeway. (The biology of Lamarckian principles being the big exception showing real perversion of the scientific methodology and theorizing).

Even with this heavy-handed control of the universities, communism seemed like a big success. The industrial economy was growing, Russian scientists were surprising the world, women were liberated—there were more women doctors than men by the 1930s and easy divorce in cases of abusive marriage was encouraged.

Then Lenin died, and Trotsky was outmaneuvered by Stalin. The Stalinist take-over and purges warning the Europeans that if the Enlightenment political theorists such as Locke, Montesquieu, J.S. Mill, Jefferson, Hamilton and Madison, were ignored, and a "temporary dictatorship" established, tyrannical, despotic, repressive and violent government would emerge. Stalin followed Machiavelli's program, uti-lizing murder and terror on a scale never seen before (but, unfortunately, soon sur-passed by Hitler and his Nazis).

Stalin altered communist party rule from authoritarian-utopian to totalitarian-terror. Stalin was responsible for more Russian deaths than the Germans in WWII. The hideous Stalinist atrocities, his secret police and the terrorist tactics shocked the world—but only after WWII. Before that, these events in Russia were overshadowed by the rise of the Fascist terror in Italy, Spain and Germany.

After Stalin's death, Khrushchev admitted to the world that Stalin had ruled through terror and committed acts of mass murder, including the systems of forced labor in Siberia, from which few ever returned.

From 1960–1980, under the less repressive, but still dictatorial regime, a large, well-educated, somewhat prosperous, middle class emerged in Russia.

The Russian middle class was not only well-educated in the rational-scientific world-view, but also in the entire European, American and classical Greek litera-ture, art, and social science traditions. The Russians knew Shakespeare as well as Chekov, Herodotus, as well as Tolstoy, Beethoven as well as Rimsky-Korsakov.

As an example of how well and how widely science was taught, a young woman from a small city in the North of Russia (parallel to Finland), emigrated to the USA and in my class at NYU volunteered to write the equation for "the first nanosecond" of the "big bang" on the blackboard. She dazzled the American students, who knew about the "big bang" theory and Stephen Hawking, but who certainly knew nothing of the mathematical calculations that Hawking, and his contemporaries had utilized.

Thus, the Russian middle class is well-educated and rational-scientific in their orientation to the world. There is also a major revival of the Russian Orthodox Christian Church occurring and, given the sociopathic behavior engendered by the Stalinist and post-Stalinist communist party officials, this religious revival is not surprising. Let us hope it takes a humanistic direction—though Putin is using it to reinforce Russian traditional values on families, gays, and, unfortunately, authori-tarian politics.

So, is this Russian middle class an Aristotelian base for a future stable democracy?

The Aristotelian theory states that a majority middle class will stabilize democracy, because the middle class is moderate, reasonable, and lawful in its political influence.

In Russia, first of all, the middle class is large and growing, and well-educated, but there has been an out-migration to Europe America and Israel, and the working class and the farmers still outnumber them.

Further, though the middle class is well-educated, they are not prosperous by European or American standard. This is because the Russian economy is not growing and has become dependent on the exportation of oil and natural gas. I will come back to the economy shortly.

The well-educated, scientifically oriented Russian middle class did generate a desire for more political freedom, and more consumer-oriented capitalist-industrial production.

After Brezhnev's death—and he was more "Stalinist" than Khrushchev (crushing Czechoslovakia and repressing dissent forcefully)—many of the older communist party leaders also died in rapid succession. The party then chose a younger leadership. Gorbachev and other young communist leaders took key communist party positions.

Gorbachev was, himself, a member of the new middle class emerging in Russia by the 1980s. He had visited Europe and Canada and saw that the economies and lifestyle of the Western societies were far more advanced than that of Russia. Gorbachev attempted to institute more capitalist entrepreneurialism and more political freedom: "Glasnost" and "Perestroika." But, the communist party functionaries interfered with these attempts and blocked change. In frustration, Gorbachev dismantled the communist party government and called for a new constitution, delineating a bill of rights and electoral government.

But Gorbachev was not only the leader of Russia, he was the leader of the Soviet Union. His sudden move towards democratization in Russia excited the nationalist spirit of the other Soviet Republics, which promptly declared their independence from the Russian-dominated Soviet Union.

Republics, such as Armenia and Azerbaijan declared independence, and, of course, Poland, Czechoslovakia, Romania, Hungary and the Baltic Republics finally gained their independence. Even the Ukraine, which had been historically connected to Russia, but which hated the domination by the Moscow government, broke with Russia.

Now, Russia is a massive country, but it had controlled Ukraine and the countries on its Southern border for a long time. So, it was a shock to the Russians to realize that they had lost so much political authority. Thus, there was a mixed reaction in Russia to the break-up of the Soviet Union: shock that they had lost their power on the world stage, and excitement over the possibility of gaining freedom and democracy in Russia itself.

A new parliament was elected, guided by an excellent institution. Boris Yeltsin was elected president and, a consumer-oriented capitalist economy was initiated.

Yeltsin, however, became an out-of-control alcoholic—a drunk—shaming the Russians. And, opposition leaders failed to form a majority against him. Vladimir Putin was then handpicked by Yeltsin to succeed him.

Whatever the historical details, Putin became president and promptly overrode the democratic constitution by re-empowering the KGB—the secret police—and surrounding himself with a loyal clique of KGB operatives.

So, a despotic government, engaging in the assassination of opposition leaders and journalists, but retaining the façade of democratic electoral procedure, now exists in Russia. The economy too was perverted into a violent, unlawful direction.

11.4   The Peculiar Nature of the Russian Economy: Oligarchic Kleptocracy and Mafia-Style Violence

The communist party had controlled the Russian economy since the days of Lenin. There never was a free market industrial-capitalist economy in Russia. However, under Gorbachev and Yeltsin, capitalist enterprises and banks did emerge, and, there was foreign investment coming into Russia. So, such an economy, could have served as a base for a stable democratic government.

Under Putin, all this changed. Putin gave control of all the major industries and banks to his personal friends—his loyal clique. These men were not capitalists, they were KGB men—violent, despotic, and unimpressed with the rules of contract law.

These Putin cronies became billionaire "oligarchs", controlling all the major industrial and financial firms of Russia. They did not run the economy according to contract law and business etiquette. They simply threatened anyone who got in their way. They tortured and murdered anyone who blocked their control

The economy is controlled by these violent oligarchs who use force and intimidation instead of business acumen, to get their way. This "mafia-style" capitalism is something new in the world of economics. It would probably have *failed* as an economic system if it were not for the fact that Russia has enormous reserves of oil, natural gas, and so many other minerals that are needed by other nations. Russia's productive economy is smaller than that of California!

Putin has been clever enough to use some of the ill-gotten billions to fake a fancy consumer economy. Gucci and Pucci and Chanel, and other luxury producers of upscale consumer goods, have opened stores in Moscow, Petersburg, and other cities. VW and other automakers sell their cars in Russia. Thus, the billionaires sport the high-end luxury goods, and, the middle class has just enough money to buy some of these goods and eat out in an occasional upscale restaurant. The middle class does buy cars, television sets, computers, cellphones, high fashion and anything else exhibited in the shopping area, and, online.

Hence, the middle class in Russia is emulating the lifestyle by their European counterparts, but the economy is a "substitution-capitalist" economy, like that of

Third World countries decades ago. And, worse, the representative democracy has no power and legal-rational authority does not exist.

So, why does the Russian middle class not demand political rights and economic opportunities?

First, they are afraid. Demonstrations for democracy *do* occur, but the opposition leadership is systemically murdered. Second, because Putin has successfully tapped into Russian *patriotism* — the loss of Russian territory and world prestige really bothers the Russians. Crimea and the Black Sea ports had always hosted the Russian fleet, but suddenly the Ukraine had those. The Russians have backed Putin in his takeover of Crimea and assertion of control over the Russian fleet.

Putin's reassertion of world power in the Middle East and Turkey and at the U.N. has also been strongly approved by most Russians.

So, Putin has strong backing, and as long as the consumer goods keep flowing—along with the oil—and Russia's prestige in the world keeps increasing, he will gain enough legitimacy to prevent the democratic demi-urge of the educated middle class from gaining social support.

Putin's clever revival of the Russian Orthodox Church has also gained him strong support from the working class and peasants, who are less educated and less democratically inclined.

Lacking a lawful economic system and depending on a third-world style oil export economy, the middle class of Russia exists on a shaky, shady economic base. And Putin is young – He will be around for a long time.

Still, given the democratic character of the Russian constitution, and the excellent educational system, it is possible that after Putin, with Russia's place in the world restored, a trend away from tyranny and towards electoral democracy and legal-rational authority could occur. Leaders and their followers are still risking their lives in ongoing demonstrations *for democracy* in all the large cities of Russia. So, a glimmer of hope still exists for the future of democracy in Russia.

11.5   The Middle East: Why the "Arab Spring" Turned to Winter

When Barack Obama made his speech in Cairo, encouraging an "Arab Spring" of democracy and law, many scholars and diplomats in Europe, the USA, and, Egypt, thought that he was right: it was time for a democratic movement in Egypt and the entire Muslim Middle East.

An attempt was made in Egypt to remove the military regime headed by Mubarak, and to hold elections in order to establish a democratic parliament.

Since the military regime in Egypt has been trained, armed, and supported by the USA, when we pressured the military regime, they eventually agreed to attempt to establish a parliamentary democratic government.

Of course, it took huge demonstrations in Cairo to finally force the military to allow elections to occur. Mubarak, who opposed the elections, had to be arrested to avert further disruptions. Now the demonstrations in Cairo were largely peaceful, and the desire of the Egyptian people for democracy was genuine. The demonstrations were led by the middle class—well-educated individuals and groups. But, the working class and the poor seemed also to want democratic elections.

The process unfolded so quickly that there were no organized political parties in Egypt. Parties did form, but their platforms were unclear. All they wanted was political power exerted through a democratically elected parliament.

The Egyptian economy was very weak. There was very little of an industrial-capitalist economy. Most people worked in the tourist industry, for the government, or in small shops and small farms. The economy is entrepreneurial, but at a really low level—very small businesses with low profits and lower wages.

Further, the majority of the populations is not middle class, not well-educated, not immersed in the rational-scientific world-view. The majority of the population is working class or poor.

Most importantly, the vast majority of Egyptians are very religious Muslims. The Muslims gather at their mosques and the Muslim priests (Imams) provide the poorer people with social services and a caring environment. The Koran[15] is strong on caring for the poor, the sick, the orphaned, the widowed. And the mosque communities raise money for this purpose.

11.6   Enter the Muslim Brotherhood

The Muslim Brotherhood is an intellectual-theological movement, which has spread from Egypt all across the Muslim world. Its ideology is that "Sharia Law" – the religious laws of the Koran – should become the basis for all political and moral policies. Constitutional law—secular and democratic—is rejected as a "western" system incompatible with Islam.

Given this socio-economic-theological situation, it is not surprising that when elections were held, The Muslim Brotherhood—running as a political party—gained the majority of the seats in the new parliament.

Once this occurred, the Muslim Brotherhood's leaders voted to alter the secular constitution towards Sharia Law. They wished to create a theocracy, with their leader as "Caliph" – the head of state and mosque. This had been Muslim tradition, dating back to the Golden Age of the Muslim Empire. But, of course, this new government of the Muslim Brotherhood would not be democratic anymore. Nor would human political rights be honored. Rather, a repressive Muslim, theocratic despotism would enforce Sharia Law aggressively.

---

[15] *The Koran* (Q'uran) (you *must* give to the poor, the widow, the sick) London, Penguin Classics, 1960.

Once this reality hit the American government officials—and Barack Obama himself—the USA moved quickly to nullify the election and return to a military-authoritarian rule.

The educated middle class grudgingly accepted this return to military rule, because they believe that the Muslim Brotherhood's theocracy would be worse. And also, because the Moslem Brotherhood had no plan to expand or modernize the economy—while the military regime, with American assistance—has a modest plan for economic modernization.

So, Egypt returned to military rule and democracy has been put on hold. The economy is bolstered by American aid, but it is growing very slowly. There are more and more cars in Cairo, but no traffic lights!? And to make things worse, the tourist industry is being hampered greatly by Islamist terror attacks and constant threats of attack.

It will be a very long time before a majority middle class emerges. Worse, the rational-scientific world-view is rejected by the radical Islamists—who, ironically, use every form of modern technology to violently disrupt the modernization—"westernization"—of the Muslim nations.

Even during the Arabic Golden age, when Ibn Sina,[16] Ibn Rushd,[17] and other Muslim intellectuals, learned, utilized and expanded "Greek science," the theology of Al Ghazali prevailed and Greek science—at first actively encouraged by the Caliphs—was, in the end, repressed. The Arabic Golden Age ended, as the Italian Renaissance—which it stimulated—began. Without Ibn Rushd, there would have been no Thomas Aquinas. But, the work of Ibn Rushd was banned, and the Arabic civilization sank back, into petty tribalism.

11.7   Syria and Iraq

Both Syria and Iraq have large cities: Damascus, Aleppo, Baghdad and others. Within these cities, a small, well-educated middle class emerged. The economy of both countries is based primarily on oil.

Oil fueled the modernization process—pardon the pun. Modern buildings and many cars gave the cities a veneer of modernization.

Unfortunately, the vast majority of the population is still relatively poor or working class. Whether as proprietors of city shops or as farmers, the majority of the populations of Syria and Iraq is working class. They are educated enough to be able to read, write and do simple calculations. They run businesses well, but they are small and local.[18]

---

[16] Ibn Sina (Avicenna), Britannica.com-Avicenna.

[17] Ibn Rushd (Avaroees), Britannica.com-Avaroees.

[18] Al Ghazali (against Greek philosophy) Britannica.com, Arabic Golden Age.

So, there is no well-educated, prosperous, majority middle class—though, as mentioned, this class is growing. There are excellent doctors, journalists, literary figures, and university professors.

It is not the lack of a middle class that is the main problem in these countries. The problem is that in the countryside and within the city neighborhoods, the people are divided by *tribal* and *religious* identifications, which are powerful in their hold. And worse, these tribes and religious sects hate each other with a vengeance and engage in violent actions against each other.

The Shia-Sunni split is virulent and stirred up by Iran and Saudi Arabia who arm each side against the other. Along with the Shia-Sunni, Muslim divide, there are small tribal groups that are also at each other's throats.

Add to this the Al Qaeda and ISIS movements amongst the Sunni Muslims, which is directed against the USA, the EU and the UK, but which is also directed against the Shia factions supported by Iran.

There are also Kurds, Turkmen, Christians (The Jews were forced to leave) and others—all making different demands, and all set against each other.

Radical Islam, the competition between Iran and Saudi Arabia, the Cold War between the USA and Russia, the Kurdish independence movement (opposed by the Turks)—it is all too much for a democratic parliamentary system to accommodate.

Violent, repressive, military dictatorships held Syria and Iraq together. When Saddam Hussein was ousted and killed, after the USA invasion, Iraq broke apart into three entities: Shia, Sunni, and Kurdish. The Shia now dominate Baghdad and Eastern Iraq, with Iran training and arming the Shia military quite well. The Sunnis, in frustration with their oust from Baghdad, joined with ISIS, but were defeated by the U.S.A. backed Kurds and the Iran-backed Shia. The Kurds want an independent state with their capital at Mosul, but the Shia militias and Turkmen—along with Sunni protestors—forced the Kurds to back off.

The Kurds are the most modernist faction in Iraq: they have liberated women—who fight alongside the men—they have separated their Muslim faith from their political organization, and they might be able to establish a legal-democratic state, except for the fact that the Turks won't allow it to happen.

Iraq is in anarchy. American, Turkish and Iranian involvement have not created anything like political stability. And, the educated middle class has fled.

Syria is also in a condition of complete anarchy. Syria was held together, like Iraq, by a violent, repressive, dictatorship. Assad himself, and his father who preceded him as dictator, is a member of a minority tribal and religious group. He and they are loosely connected to the Shia Moslem faction. To stay in power, he and they allied themselves with the Syrian Christians, against the Sunni majority.

Just to show that the education of the dictator alone does not create change, Assad—while his father was dictator—received an excellent British education, and married a woman who also has a British degree. But this British education did not make Assad into a British-style, lawful-democratic ruler.

Pressured by the Sunni majority to hold democratic elections, after Obama's "Arab Spring" speech, he realized that he and his minority Shia sect would be defeated by the Sunni majority, and forced out of power.

It did not help that the Sunnis were led by extremist Al-Qaeda-oriented radical Islamists, who themselves would have overthrown the democracy and moved the nations towards "Sharia Law" and Moslem caliphate.

Backed by the Russians, who have a vital naval and air base on the coast of Syria, Assad chose to repress the Sunni demand for elections and violently attack the Sunnis—first in Damascus, then all across Syria.

The country broke up into a hideous civil war, with every small faction fighting every other faction. The USA attempted to back the moderate Sunnis, but when all-out war occurred, the radical Islamists took over the leadership of the Sunni rebellion. The USA was therefore, stymied, and the Russian-backed Assad dictatorship has been propped up. Syria is still in a shamble—all the major cities have been bombed into oblivion and there is no reconciliation in sight.

In terms of the future of democracy, Syria and Iraq are certainly not models for any optimism.

11.8   What About Iran? Persia and the Possibility for Democracy in the Near Future

Iran—Persia—has a long and distinguished history. The Persians were involved with both the Jews and the Greeks, influencing the theological and political outcome of "Western Civilization". When Cyrus the Great allowed the Jews to return to Israel, they brought with them the Zoroastrianism dualism that led to the theology of God and the Devil, Heaven and Hill, the apocalypse and the Messiah-savior. The Persian invasion of Greece forced the Greeks to temporarily unite, and to analyze their unique forms of government—democracy, oligarchy and tyranny—over against the Persian form of government—traditional monarchy with a bureaucratic state.

The Persians were very much aware of their historical link with the Jews and the Greeks. And since they were defeated by the Greeks, under Alexander the Great, Persian historians obsessed over the Greeks—described their great civilization prior to the Greek conquest and then later regaining of independence with the Parthian dynasties successfully rebelling against both Greece and Rome.

During the Arabic Golden Age centuries later, the Persians were still interested in Greek culture and its mysterious strengths (the Jews had been dispersed by the Romans and displaced by the Christians by the time of the Arabic Golden Age).

When the Arabs failed to take Constantinople and the Greeks continued to seem mysteriously gifted, Arabic scholars were encouraged to study Greek philosophy to try to absorb this Greek knowledge. The Caliphs of Baghdad had Greek works of philosophy, mathematics, science, logic and medicine translated into Arabic. In Baghdad, they created a great library of Greek works in translation, called "The House of Wisdom."[19]

---

[19] In Baghdad, during the Arabic Golden Age, a caliph had a grand library built called "The house of Wisdom," Britannica.com, Arabic Golden Age.

Prominent amongst the Arabic scholars were Persians—again fascinated by the Greeks and again fueling the historical link with them. Ibn Sina (Avicenna),[20] a Persian, was the first to popularize Aristotle's logic and Galen's medical books. Ibn Sina also was a mathematical genius who took Greek mathematics and combined it with Indian numerals, thus making calculations much easier to transcribe.

Many Persians participated in the Arabic Golden Age, bringing Greek philosophy and science into the mainstream of Middle Eastern Culture, influencing Arabic speaking intellectuals from Baghdad to Spain. Before Al Ghazali's ban (and the Mongol invasion of Baghdad) ended the Arabic Golden Age, the Italian Renaissance was engendered by it—as mentioned, there could not have been a Thomas Aquinas without Ibn Rushd, and Ibn Sina—and the Persians once again felt their history as intertwined with the Greeks.

Why am I mentioning this? Because, as the Persians moved into the modern world in the twentieth century, they revived their connection to their heroic past. Unlike the Arabs, who had a tribal past of disunification and constant feuding, and unlike the Egyptians, whose past was too distant to identify with—though they are happy to take the tourists to its monuments, the Persians have been able to identify themselves with their civilizational past and move forward with great pride in terms of their future. During the 1960s and 1970s, more Persian students studied abroad than any other group. And, they went back to Iran as an educated middle class to try to modernize and democratize Iran. Of course, Iran's history took a different turn.

Let us look at this unexpected detour.

The oil discoveries in the Middle East brought the European powers into it, competing for control of the oil fields. There was oil in Persia as well as Mesopotamia and Arabia.

The British took charge of Persia after Germany's defeat in WWI. Having dismantled the Turkish Empire (the Turks sided with Germany in WWI), the British attempted to stabilize the Middle East, after the Turkish governors were pushed out.

In Persia—which was renamed Iran—the British installed an army officer, loyal to them, as King. The "Shah", or King of Iran, was a modernist, who worked with the British, allowing them to exploit the oil and using the oil money to build modern cities and roads and universities.

After WWII, the USA took over Britain's role in the Middle East. In Iran, we backed the Shah—now the son of the previous King—and continued to encourage him to modernize Iran. He did this, not only using oil money to modernize Teheran and other cities, but also refurbishing the ancient cities of the Persian Empire, thus reinforcing Iran's link with its glorious Persian past.

So many students returned, and so many others graduated from Persian universities, that this new educated middle class began to demand a transition to democracy. The problem was that the Russians began to influence the middle class and to radicalize the students against the Shah.

In a panic, the Americans armed the Shah's government, which created a police forcer and militia to stamp out communism amongst the students of the new middle

---

[20] Ibn Sina popularized Aristotle's *Logic* and Galeus book of Physiology.

class. Unfortunately, the Shah—who had had a good reputation, and might have made for a perfect limited monarch in a democratic parliamentary regime—became a violent dictator, hated by the new middle class he was arresting and repressing.

While this Cold War drama was playing out, the Ayatollah Khomeini was organizing the Shiite hierarchy of Iran in the back country. The working class of the cities and the farmers of the country side are religious Muslims. They wanted modernization, but the communist atheism scared them, and, the American liberal culture of the new middle class repelled them—there was too much freedom, and women were encouraged to be liberated.

When the new middle class demanded elections, and the Americans gave in, so as not to appear as hypocrites, Mohammed Mossadegh, a leftist, won the election, and the Americans panicked. They helped the Shah overthrow Mossadegh, disbanded the parliament, and allowed the Shah to rule as a repressive military dictator.

The Shah became too repressive, and under President Jimmy Carter an uprising against the Shah forced him out. The American diplomats at our embassy were taken hostage, and all other Americans expelled. The USA had lost its hold on Iran, but, so had the Russians! In a surprise to the world, the Ayatollah Khomeini and the Shia clerics took charge of the revolution and created a theocracy in Iran. It was anti-American—America was "the Great Satan" – but it was also anti-Russian, for they were atheist communists.

The new middle class, however, was well-educated, and quite large and influential in the cities. Under pressure from this educated class, the Ayatollah allowed for the institutionalization of a parliamentary – democratic system, with elections and a constitution of secular laws.

However, the theocratic authority of the Ayatollahs was supreme. Therefore, Sharia Law was also instituted, and it superseded secular law, where they were in conflict.

Also, the representatives who run for office—including the candidates for president—must be approved by the Ayatollahs' theocrats council. So, these are not free elections.

Yet, interestingly, over the years, the Ayatollahs have allowed a wider range of candidate to run for officer. And, as the educated middle class expands—and it is expanding dramatically—and as this middle class absorbs the national-scientific world-view—which the Ayatollah's need for their nuclear ambitions—the demand for really free elections, and legal-rational protections for individual human rights, has intensified.

The middle class is much larger and more influential in Iran than in other nations of the Middle East. And unlike Syria and Iraq, *Iran is not split up by tribal rivalries*. The Persians have seen themselves as a civilizational entity for centuries. They are proud of their unified cultural tradition. They have been linked with, and competitive with the Western civilizations since the time of the Greeks. This civilizational unity has created the possibility for a modern nationhood.

Without the violent tribal rivalries of the Arabic countries, and far more modern than Egypt in its economic and scientific development, Iran could slowly begin to exhibit more and more of a free electoral process.

Now, the Ayatollah's theocracy has the loyalty of the Iranian Guard—the well-trained, well-disciplined, well-armed army of Iran. They fought loyally for Iran against Iraq, when the USA encouraged Saddam Hussein to invade Iran. And, eventually after the USA invasion of Iraq eliminated Saddam Hussein's dictatorship, the Iranian militias took over Eastern Iraq and Baghdad. So, the Iranian army is loyal to the theocracy in Iran, and wherever they are sent to fight.

The Persian troops, linked with the Ayatollahs have prevented the middle class from establishing a true legal-democratic government. But, the successful modernization of the economy and the continued growth of the middle class—with their high level of university education—has pushed the theocracy and the army to allow for more freedom of expression and freer elections.

One last factor. The new middle class does not like it that Iran is disliked in Europe and America. They feel a bond with Western civilization and want to be part of it. Even on Israel, the Iranian intellectuals were more comfortable with the Shah's alliance with Israel, than in the Ahmadinejad's denial of the Holocaust. Ahmadinejad was so unpopular that eventually pressure from the middle class forced the Ayatollahs to run more moderate, better educated, candidates for the presidency.

So, with each uprising by the middle class, the Ayatollahs have allowed more electoral freedom and put forth more modernist, less Islamist candidates. Will the Ayatollahs be pushed out of power? Will the Persian guard join the middle class?

Not yet. But there is hope for increasing democratization in Iran. The Persians are anxious to take their place besides the advanced nations of the world. They have a sense of themselves as civilizationally superior and this could serve them well—in the near future—in terms of establishing a stable democratic government.

11.9   The Case of Spain and the Hope for the Future of Democracy

The case of Spin, from the 1920s to the present can shed some light on the hope for a legal-democratic future in the world.

Spain had been a traditional monarchy. And even this monarchy, strongly supported by the Catholic Church in the war against Islam (and Judaism), barely held the nation together—with Portugal separating early-on, and Catalan attempting to separate now, in 2017.

The Spanish monarchy had, for centuries, been propped-up economically by the treasures of the New World. The Spanish Conquistadors sent a steady stream of wealth to Spain from the colonies.

However, when the Latin American countries rebelled, and gained independence, the Spanish economy—which had not industrialized and was not capitalist—collapsed. The monarchy slowly collapsed as well.

Hence, by the beginnings of the twentieth century, Spain faced both an economic and political crisis. The Spaniards began to emulate their European neighbors by establishing the rudiments of a capitalist-industrial economy and the institutions of parliamentary democracy.

In the 1920s–1940s, when Spain began to democratize, the democracy was unstable, and Spain erupted into a violent, merciless, brutal civil war—chronicled by Hemingway, in *For Whom the Bell Tolls*.[21] Extremist factions took over—fascists and communists—with true democrats caught in the middle and eventually pushed aside.

Spanish intellectuals, like Miguel de Unamuno[22]—who was eventually murdered by the fascists—came to believe that Spanish culture was anathema to democratic norms, such that democratic government could never be institutionalized.

Bull-fighting, wherein the bull was eventually killed, and many matadors died too was loved—and it was a blood sport. Personal duals over "honor' or women, rather than rational discussion, were encouraged. Don Juanism, or the seduction and domination of women, was not only normative, but it was considered heroic.[23] The glorification of blood violence seemed to characterize Spanish culture—at the time of Columbus the converso priest, Las Casas, described the "Rape of the Indies,"[24] in which the "Conquistadors" committed the mass brutalization of the Native Americans—beyond Christian moral bounds.

Helped by the Italian fascists and German Nazis, the Spanish fascists won the civil war. They established a dictatorship, led by General Francisco Franco They repressed violently any democratic revolutionaries. Spanish culture, as Unamano warned, and as Samuel Huntington[25] theorized years later, was against democracy.

Yet, after WWII, the dictator, Franco, shaken by Germany's loss and fascism's fall in Italy, surprisingly, pushed out the Spanish fascists, and began to copy Italy, Germany and France, in their rapid economic recovery.

By the 1960s, Spain was developing a fast-growing industrial-capitalist economy similar to that of Italy and France (though not quite up to that of Germany). The Spanish corporations were productive and efficient, their unions militant, but cooperative like those of France.

The Spanish economy took off, and a large, well-educated middle class emerged. This middle class still liked bull fights, but they became more rational-scientific in their world-view.

With the help of King Juan Carlos—who had been anti-fascist all along—the monarchy was restored in limited, constitutional form, as in England, and when

---

[21] Ernest Hemingway, *For Whom the Bell Tolls*, N.Y. Random House, 1949.

[22] Miguel de Unamuno, *Blood Wedding*, *Plays of Unamuno*, Google Books 2010.

[23] The legend of Don Juan was told in many versions—some heroic, some tragic.

[24] Las Casas, *The Rape of the Indies*, Amazon Books, 2011.

[25] Samuel Huntington, *Political Order in Changing Societies*.

Franco died, a truly legal-democratic regime was firmly institutionalized. This legal-democratic regime, with the help of the restored monarchy has become strongly legitimated in Spain,

And yes, Spanish culture is changing as the moderate, lawful, middle class expands. A women's liberation movement has counter-balanced the Don Juanism, and the blood violence has been relegated to literature, and is now seen as a relic of past history. The mistreatment of the Native Americans and the Jews (during the Inquisition) has been brought into the open and the modern Spaniards are attempting humanistic reconciliation in the present to erase the violence of the past. Even the Catholic Church under the recent Popes, has encouraged humanistic reconciliation in Spain and in its former colonies.

So, Spain is now a successful member of the E.U. Its economy is relatively strong, and most importantly for this treatise, Spain's government is truly democratic and, it is functioning well. Even the terrorist attacks by Muslims in Spain—and there have been many—have not pushed Spain towards extremisms. Spain's response has been less extremist than Hungary's, or the Le Pen Party in France.

Finally, the recent attempt by Catalan to secede from Spain is a warning that "tribal", ethnic identity is still a problem for any country in which such differences exist. Just look at the former Yugoslavia or Czechoslovakia.

However, in this case—and the others mentioned—Catalan would have created its own legal-democratic government, even though it would have separated from Spain (as did the Croatians, Serbs, Slovenians, Czechs, and Slovaks).

Huntington's thesis on culture against democracy is still strong.[26] However, the case of Spain shows that even in a country with a culture negative to democracy and steeped in violence and domination, the emergence of a productive industrial-capitalist economy linked into the global capitalist economy, and, the expansion of a university educated middle class with a rational-scientific world-view, can override the original cultural complex.

The Spanish people are still Spanish, but they are also well-educated, prosperous, and scientifically oriented.

As Aristotle put it, "blessed is a country with a majority middle class," because the middle class is educated, moderate, reasonable, lawful and willing to compromise.[27]

If Spain can change so dramatically in its politics, so can other nations where the middle class expands, education tends towards the rational-scientific world-view, and an industrial-capitalist economy undergirds the whole process.

South Korea would be another example. And, horrifyingly, North Korea exemplifies the opposite process. The human paradox continues.

This is the paradox of the human species: we can act rationally and discuss policy and participate in leadership; we can also act irrationally and succumb to our animal instincts of dominance, submission and territoriality.

---

[26] Ibid.

[27] Aristotle, *Politics* (the middle class).

I shall discuss the ever-present danger of despotism, and the even worse problem of high technology totalitarianism. It is easy to re-enlist Orwell in this world of cyber surveillance and computer-generated crime—"Big Brother" is already watching us.

First, however, let us look at the hope for democracy in the near future.

Chapter 12
The Resurgence of Fascism in the Mid-Twenty First Century

12.1 Introduction

Having grown up with the newsreel images of Hitler and Mussolini in the movie theaters during the 1950's, I never thought that I would see a resurgence of fascism in my lifetime. The defeat of fascism by American democracy seemed to have put an end to this violent, despotic, militaristic, and racist ideology. But then, I also did not know that communism – that other despotic ideological movement – would collapse, also in my lifetime.

These events tell us two things: one, that human historical change is difficult to predict; and two, that despotic ideological movements will continue to arise and decline, because they are part of the human paradox, in terms of politics.

New despotic ideologies such as todays Islamism will continue to arise from sources previously unsuspected. And, the striving for a democratic alternative to these violent, despotic "isms" will also continue.

So, with neo-fascism on the rise again in Europe and in the USA, I thought it necessary to add a few sociological insights concerning it. A full discussion of this neo-fascist upsurge is not possible in this work. I refer the reader to such books as Madeline Albright's[1] recent work on the new rise of fascism, and Robert Kuttner's[2] new book on the link between "globalization" and fascism.

With great trepidation, let me add some sociological insights to the political phenomenon of despotic, militaristic, violent, racist, fascism.

---

[1] Madeline Albright, Fascism: A Warning, Google Books, 2018; see also, Steven Levitsky and Daniel Ziblatt, *How Democracies Die* , Amazon, 2018.

[2] Robert Kuttner, Can Democracy Survive Global Capitalism, Amazon Books, 2018.

© Springer Nature Switzerland AG 2019
R. M. Glassman, *The Future of Democracy*,
https://doi.org/10.1007/978-3-030-16111-8_12

12.2   The Resurgence of Fascism

There have been three trends in contemporary societies (2000–2020) which have regenerated the fascist movement that arose originally in the 1920's to 1930's. They are: one, the *outsourcing of jobs* to Asia, Latin America, and other low wage societies. This trend is part of the general *globalization* process generated by the remarkably productive high technology capitalist economies of the twenty-first century; two, the massive *immigration* from the Muslim Middle East and Africa into Europe, and the equally massive migration from Latin America into the USA; and three, *women's liberation* into the labor market.

All three of these trends negatively impact the male working class in Europe and the USA. It is this male working class that has formed the backbone of the neo-fascist voting blocks in Europe and the USA.

It was the male working class who, in the 1920's and 1930's formed the basic support of the original fascist movements in Italy, Spain, Germany, and France.

12.3   The Social Democratic Parties Cave in to the Globalization Pressure

The Social Democratic parties were phenomenally successful in Europe, gaining for their workers: pensions, vacations, good working conditions, free health care, free schools and universities, and so much more. The working class in Europe did so well in the 1960's to the 1990's that it looked like a worker's paradise had been achieved – not only in Germany, but in France, the Netherlands, Scandinavia, Italy, and even Spain.

However, the globalization of the capitalist economies led to a huge outsourcing of industrial jobs to low wage nations, such as China, India, and Mexico. Once this occurred, the Social Democratic parties were forced to make compromises in order to keep the European sector of the new global capitalist economy competitive. Since they were not willing to give up the wonderful welfare state programs, they compromised on wages.

The workers in Germany, and all the other EU countries, agreed to take wage cuts, and, some benefits were cut as well. Gerhard Schroeder of Germany led the way to such compromises – he had to do it in order to save the German industrial economy. The other European nations reluctantly followed his lead.

But, this left the Social Democrats unpopular with their own constituents – the workers. These disgruntled, disillusioned workers could have turned to extreme left parties – some did. However, the extreme left wing parties had been discredited since the fall of Communism.

Therefore, many of the workers began to turn to the right wing parties. Theses right wing parties often had demagogic leaders, who knew how to engage and agitate the angry workers. In Hungary, Poland, Italy, Greece, and even France, right wing parties and their demagogue leaders have expanded.

In the United States, the Democratic Party, during and after the Roosevelt years, played the same role for the American workers as the Social Democratic parties played in Europe. The New Deal secured for the American workers: pensions, excellent working conditions, high wages, and job security.

However, just as in Europe, from the 1980's onward, the globalization of the world's capitalist economies led to the outsourcing of jobs to Asia and Latin America. The American workers began to be laid off, the unions lost their power, and industrial jobs began to disappear.

The Democratic Party lost its labor core, and turned to liberal suburban voters as a new core constituency. But their concerns focused on racial justice, women's issues, gay liberation, and high tech careers. The concerns of the American workers were pushed aside in favor of this new liberal agenda.

Therefore, the workers came to feel that the Democratic Party no longer represented them. They stayed loyal to the Democrats – everywhere except in the South, where racism had pushed the white workers into the Republican Party since the Nixon years (and after Johnson passed the Civil Rights Act). In the Mid-West and North East, the workers continued to vote Democratic, until Trump cleverly tapped into their anger and frustration.

Trump generated the same kind of neo-fascist rhetoric as the European right wing parties. And, Trump gets his support largely from the white, male working class, who see globalization as a threat to new jobs. And, of course, the massive immigration from Latin America threatened them as well. We shall discuss the immigration issue next.

However, it is the globalization of the world capitalist economies that really threatens the workers' jobs – in both Europe and America.

Now globalization has many positive aspects – when the world's nations are linked together by trade and interlocking production, this is good for world peace. And, globalization can lead to a new global culture, through which the worlds' nations may share common values and open systems of communication. The new middle classes around the world have much in common with each other – and that is a good thing, and could lead to a world of mutual understanding – even where cultural differences remain strong.

However, here in this section we wish to emphasize that the globalization process does lead to a weakening of the position of the working class in the developed nations. Eventually, the children of this working class will get jobs in the high tech sector of the developed economies – Pittsburgh and Stuttgart are good examples. There the old steel and auto jobs have yielded to high tech jobs, and the workers in these high tech industries are doing well. Similarly in the Netherlands, Phillips-Norelco has created high tech jobs for the workers in the Netherlands. During the transition, however, the old working class will be angry, confused, and open to manipulation by demagogues, such as Trump, Le Pen, and Orban (of Hungary).

So globalization, in the short run will dislocate the workers and makes them angry and irrational.

Various books, such as Robert Kuttner's[3] have blamed this swing to the right on globalization and the outsourcing of jobs. There is no doubt that this is the core of the problem.

However, there is more.

12.4   The Immigration Problem: Job Competition and Xenophobic "Tribalism"

Just as the workers of Europe and the USA were being compromised by the outsourcing of jobs, the immigration crisis occurred.

In the USA, the immigration from Latin America had a long history, but the political and economic instability in Central America and parts of South America engendered a massive surge of immigration from these countries from the 1990's onward.

Similarly, the Syrian civil war drove millions of Syrians into Europe, and African migration followed in its wake.

These immigrants – in the USA and in Europe – posed a threat to the working class. The worker's jobs were already in jeopardy from globalization, and now these new immigrants were willing to work for less, since they were desperate.

Furthermore – and this occurred in all the European countries and even the UK – the immigrants generated a "tribal" nationalism in the indigenous populations. In the UK, the Celtic, and Anglo-Saxton Britain's voted for "Brexit" in order to stop the "open borders" immigration policy in the EU. In Hungary, the Magyar citizens voted to fence out all immigrants and refuse them even safe passage to Germany. In Greece, where the immigrants have been treated very well and cared for humanely, and, where the majority of the immigrants have been sent north to Germany or south back to Turkey, a Neo-Nazi party, called the Golden Dawn, has won many votes and engaged in acts of violence – all generated against the immigration policy.

Recently – and this brings neo-fascism full circle with the original fascist movement – in Italy, a coalition of right wing parties has won on a platform of anti-immigration, pro-nationalist, and economic development.

Racism, anti-Islam and tribal-nationalism have been revived all across Europe. The immigration crisis has definitely inflamed this movement.

In the USA, the same kind of anti-immigrant nationalism led to Trump's demagogic electoral victory. His opening remarks were (paraphrase) "Some of the immigrants are rapists, some murderers, and some......very nice people...."

---

[3] Ibid.

The Syrian Civil War is winding down, and African immigrants have been forcibly slowed down – through Libya. Given this slowing of immigration, the neo-fascist parties may lose some of their edge.

In the USA, the Trump administrations' tough border policy may also slow immigration. The USA has always been a nation of immigrants, and the USA has always been good at assimilating the immigrants to the "American Dream" of upward economic mobility and democratic politics of freedom.

The Europeans are not good at such assimilation. And the "European Dream" is less clearly articulated. But, Europe has a low birth rate and really needs immigration to fill the labor force. Therefore, a policy of economic stimulation in Germany and France and economic development in Southern Italy would help the situation.

The UK is moderately good in assimilating immigrants, and, hopefully, will slowly return to, at least, economic integration with the EU. And, the case of the Netherlands is interesting in this regard: The Dutch assimilated their Indonesian colonists well (1960–1980), but have had difficulty with the Muslim immigrants, because the Muslim religious culture conflicts with the liberal sexual and gender liberation of the Dutch culture.

I mention this, because it is also true in Scandinavia, Germany, and France. So, Muslim assimilation has been slow, and conflict-ridden, leading to incidents of violence – exacerbated by the radical Islamic movement.

One more issue – less obvious – has fueled the neo-fascist movements in Europe and the USA. That is, women's liberation.

12.5   Women's Liberation as a Threat to Macho Masculinity

The liberation of women, into the job market created even more competition for jobs – and the male workers felt especially threatened by the women's movement. For, women are often better than their brothers at school. And, women often have more marketable skills than their working class brothers – being absorbed as nurses, teachers, social workers, and lower level office workers.

Further, and this has created a revolutionary change in modern society, the women do not want to stay home and take care of the children and the household anymore. This is exciting for women, who have expanded their career horizons and limited the birth rate dramatically. But this is depressing for men – especially working class men – who have lost their household partners. The men would work hard in factory jobs, while the women maintained the household and family. This traditional male-female gender role integration is gone now.

In Italy, young men go home to their mothers for food and laundry, while their girlfriends have their own apartments and their own careers. There is sexual activity, but no child-rearing or household work done by the girlfriends. In Italy, these men have been called, "mammone," because they go home to mama. But, it is the women who have made the change – they do not want children – the birth rate is dangerously low in Europe – and they certainly do not want to do extensive household work.

Men, in order to assert their declining power, go to gyms to work out and look like Arnold Schwarzenegger, join the military as volunteer soldiers, and, join the militaristic, nationalistic, male macho neo-fascist movement. Some women join too, on nationalistic grounds, but, these movements have been largely dominated by men. (Even Marina Le Pen was a follower of her father, who first established the right wing neo-fascist nationalist party in France).

In the USA, working class men form the core of Donald Trump's supporters, and not only did they hate Hillary Clinton but they also hate Nancy Pelosi – it is an irrational, anti-women hatred; in my view this hatred is generated by the jealousy and loss of power that the working class men feel, as women get ahead in the world, outperform them in school, getting better jobs then men in the new high tech economy.

So there are at least three causes for the neo-fascist revival; globalization and outsourcing; immigration; and the women's movement,

There is also a fourth factor which is also generating right wing politics. That is, traditional religious values vs. the new "politically correct" values.

12.6   Traditional Religious Values on Family, Gender, Sex, Gays and more, vs the New P.C. Values

Another factor I wish to emphasize which has generated right wing political actions is the problem of traditional religious values, relating to family, gender, child-rearing, gays, lesbians, abortion, and more.

These traditional religious values have been challenged by the women's movement, the LGBT movement, and the "youth" movements, which involve rock music, drugs, and liberal sexuality.

In Europe, it is the Catholic Church which has been challenged – the Protestant Churches in Northern Europe have accepted the newer values, while the Catholic Church has been slow to change.

In the USA, it is both the Protestant fundamentalists and the Catholic Church which feel under attack from the women, the gays, and the youth.

Being "politically correct" – P.C. – means being for women's liberation, gay liberation, abortion (as a choice), and for racial equality. Tribal-nationalism is rejected in favor of internationalism, multi-culturalism, and global inclusiveness.

These PC principles clash with traditional religious family values, abortion as a choice, women's work role, and the Biblical prohibition against homosexuality.

Therefore, the right wing parties – in Europe and the USA – tend to emphasize the traditional religious values – Vladimir Putin has cleverly utilized the Russian Orthodox Church to bolster his political position by openly opposing the PC values – especially on gay liberation and macho masculinity. It has worked for Putin and it is working for Trump. It also works for the Italian, Hungarian, and Polish right wing leaders as well.

In the USA, the Protestant fundamentalists have supported Trump – and Vice-President Pence – and have gotten in return the appointment of right wing judges – on the Supreme Court and the local courts nationwide – who support traditional religious values.

One must understand that the liberation of women and gays and sexuality is new. And, the rejection of traditional religious values is a by-product of these remarkable social changes. Social change always creates crises in societies. And such crises are often used by charismatic leaders to gain power.[4] Sometimes charismatic leaders have a positive effect on societies going through drastic social changes – Martin Luther King Jr., Ghandi, and Franklin Roosevelt come to mind.

However, sometimes the charismatic leaders have a terrible effect on societies undergoing change: Mussolini, Hitler, and now Erdogan in Turkey, Orban in Hungary, Putin in Russia – and, yes, Trump in the USA.

None of these new leaders may become totalitarian dictators because of both our historical memory, and, the democratic safeguards put in place after WWII in Europe and by the founding fathers in the USA.

Let us hope the new fascist movements are contained before they can become totalitarian.

12.7   Some Practical Programs to Combat Neo-Fascism

It is very difficult to stop the momentum of any ideological movement which sweeps a region. But, here are a few programs that could help reduce the influences of the new-fascist ideology in the mid-twenty first century.

12.8   Programs to Ease the Impact of Globalization

The outsourcing of jobs to low wage areas of the world will continue. It is part of the process of world capitalism. And, this process leaves the workers in the developed countries with, either reduced wages and benefits, or no jobs at all.

Therefore, in the developed nations, programs for the retraining of blue collar workers – and the training of young workers – should focus on the new kinds of jobs that are available in the developed nations.

That is, jobs connected to the high technology systems and products that are available. Jobs such as installing cable television and WI-FI connections, installing and maintaining the new electrical grid and the windmills and solar panels linked with it. IT workers – the "techies", who seem to work miracles on our computers when we can't get them to work.

---

[4] Ronald M. Glassman and William Swatos Jr.,Charisma, History, and Social Structure, N.Y. Prager-Greenword, 1990.

Also, given the effects of climate change, where storms and floods and fires seem to be increasing in numbers and intensity, modern developed societies need more workers trained to combat these disasters and rebuild what has been destroyed.

Technical jobs connected to the medical, dental and hospital professions have also expanded dramatically in all of the developed nations. These jobs provide men and women of the old working class with new kinds of working class jobs.

All these new jobs are connected to the high tech economy. Such jobs can be generated so as to absorb the younger blue collar workers, and absorb at least some of the older blue collar workers.

In the USA, the city of Pittsburgh provided a perfect example of what I am discussing. The steel and coal jobs are gone, but Pittsburgh – with the help of Carnegie-Mellon University – has become a high tech city employing thousands of new tech-connected workers. Not just college graduates with engineering and technical skills, but blue collar workers who have been trained for the lower level tech jobs. These lower level tech jobs pay well, because they are usually connected to the big tech companies such as Comcast, Apple, Amazon, and others.

So, to sum up, lower level technical jobs are becoming more available in the developed nations, as the blue collar factory jobs are being outsourced to Asia and Latin America. Training programs and career-line jobs can eventually ease the impact of the globalization processes outsourcing. This could reduce the anger of the displaced workers, and therefore reduce the political support of the neo-fascist parties.

These kinds of jobs are now becoming available, not only in the USA and Germany, but also in Spain, Italy, France, the Netherlands, Sweden, and the UK. Spain, Northern Italy and Ireland are dynamically developing their high technology sectors of their economies. Southern Italy and Greece have fallen behind, and neo-fascist parties have been doing well there, unfortunately.

12.9   The Immigration Crisis

The massive immigration from Syria into Europe, and the equally large immigration from Latin America into the USA definitely generated a right wing backlash and fed the neo-fascist movement in Europe and the Trump phenomenon in the USA. So, what exactly can be done to stem the tide?

In terms of Syria, the civil war is winding down. Many Syrians will eventually go back home and rebuild some of their great cities. Aleppo is now almost a ghost town – people will return if the war ends. Of course, with Assad as dictator, they may not wish to return. However, many will want to rebuild the once flourishing country.

Muslims from the Middle East may continue to flee to Europe unless Iraq is somehow reconfigured so that peace and normal economic activities can return to that fragmented country.

And North Africa needs investment and modernization as well. Morocco, Algeria, Tunisia, and Libya need major investments or immigration to Europe will continue. Morocco and Tunisia are making progress economically, but Libya is still fragmented and Algeria has seen slow modernization of the economy.

Europe, it should be mentioned, has an aging labor force, and needs immigration to keep its industries competitive.

In terms of Mexico and Central America, the Catholic Church must ease its birth control ban. These countries are over-populated and poor.

Investment in Mexico has been somewhat successful – jobs are now available in Mexico in the factory sector. However, Central America is not doing well – Guatemala, El Salvador, and Nicaragua are poor, disorganized and violent. Immigrants are fleeing the violence and coming to America.

And, even though Trump right wingers are hysterical – the USA needs these immigrants – especially in the agriculture and food industries. Still, as long as the immigration seems excessive, it will inflame right wing neo-fascist ideology.

So, there is no immediate solution to the immigration situation, except that the flow of immigrants has been reduced by the right wing reactions to it, and the reduction of immigration will reduce the hysteria of the right wing parties.

Global immigration will continue, and therefore xenophobic "tribalism" will continue to fuel neo-fascist parties.

However, when the immigration is from the new middle class, rather than the poor, it is usually received with much less agitation. In the USA, UK, and EU, when an immigrant is a doctor, scientist, an engineer, a professor, or a nurse, nobody reacts. It is when the immigrants are poor and uneducated that people become frightened and xenophobically tribal.

In the short term, poor immigrants from the Middle East, Africa, Latin America, and Asia will bolster the neo-fascist nationalist -tribalist parties. But, in the long run, as the world develops economically and educationally, the idea of the global village on "the big blue marble" moving in space, will prevail. However, that is a long time away.

12.10 Women's Liberation

Women's liberation from the family and child-rearing and into the labor force will continue. And this process does threaten male workers. Men who are left behind and who see women getting ahead, do become resentful. And such men, in order to assert their macho masculinity do find the neo-fascist parties intriguing. They join; they assert their masculinity through violence against immigrants or threats of violence.

The neo-fascist parties tend to be very masculine oriented with dominating dictatorial male leaders.

Marine LePen is the exception that proves the rule – her father was the founder of the party in France. In the USA, Trump is the embodiment of a male bully.

Threatening immigrants, calling them murderers and rapists, threatening reporters, embracing dictators like Putin, Kim, and Erdogan, and bragging about assaulting women and engaging in sexual affairs.

Of course there are women who condone such macho men. However, the core supporters of this neo-fascist movement continue to be working class men, who are not well educated, and who want violent solutions to the social and economical problems.

The only way to move these men away from the neo-fascist movement is to train them and re-train them, to fit into the new high tech job market. Women are going to continue to work, excel in education, and move up in the work force. So, working class men must be encouraged to do better in school and to go on towards a more technical career.

As for marriage and child-rearing, American men are making enough concessions towards women to sustain the new patterns of dual career couples, and nursery school child care. The American birthrate is stable.

The European men – especially the Italians – have been unwilling to do any household or child-rearing work. Therefore – since the women are working – the birthrate has fallen dangerously low.

Macho masculinity and Don Juanism continue to characterize many European men – and this was the cultural standard in the European countries. But, as long as this is the case, the birthrate will be low and the marriage rate will continue to decline.

Europe needs a men's movement to go along with the women's liberation movement. Until a new masculinity is developed, the birth rate will remain low, and, the appeal of new-fascist parties will remain high. Vladimir Putin has put himself forward as an icon of macho-masculinity, and his neo-fascist dictatorial style has become a model for such leaders as Orban in Hungary, and Erdogan in Turkey.

12.11   Rapid Social Change, Anomie, Deviance and Political Extremism

Emile Durkheim, in his seminal work, *Suicide*,[5] describes the fact that during periods of rapid social change, the traditional norms and values of a society decline, and new norms and values slowly take their place.

However, during the period of transition when the new norms and values have not yet taken hold and the old norms and values have lost their influence – a condition of "anomie" exists in society. Anomie means that all the norms and values are called into question, and there is general confusion about what is "right" and what is "wrong". This produces a loss of meaning in the society – what is the meaning of life? How should one live?

---

[5] Emile Durkheim, Suicide, N.Y., Free Press, 1952.

In this condition of anomie, rates of deviance skyrocket: suicide, murder, divorce, drug and alcohol abuse, family breakup – all of these deviances increase.

Along with deviance, political extremism also increases. Since in a period of anomie no one seems to have the answers to right and wrong issues, extremist political ideologies emerge proporting to have the answers to all of the social problems plaguing society.

Hence, right wing and left wing ideologies – like fascism and communism – arise. Also, radical religious movements emerge – like Islamism, Protestant fundamentalism, or the Zen Buddhism of the American "hippies" in the 1960's.

These religious movements all purport to have the answers to social ills – all attempt to give meaning to society in which meaning has been lost. Science, rationalism, and secular humanism give way to radical religious definitions of right and wrong, good and evil.

The world's modern societies are going through a period of rapid social change. The old religious values of the Judeo-Christian, Islamic, and Confucian traditions are giving way to new P.C. values and norms.

By P.C. – "politically correct" – we mean; women's liberation, gay liberation, racial equality, and multiculturalism. These new norms and values are spreading worldwide. But they run counter to the religious values, wherein women's place is within the family, motherhood is venerated, fathers dominate mothers, children know their place, gays are hidden "in the closet", the white race is dominant, and "God" is imminent – involved in our everyday lives.

Given the clash of norms and values that this represents, rates of deviance have skyrocketed, as Durkheim theorized they would: suicide, murder, drug and alcohol abuse, divorce, and family breakup – all these deviances have had rising rates.

So, too, political extremist movements have increased.

Now, the neo-fascist movement in Europe and the USA has been exacerbated by the immigration crisis. However, it has been reinforced by the anomic loss of norms, values, and increasingly exacerbated by the global P.C. trends. Women's liberation, gay liberation, and multiculturalism – these will not go away. So, the reactions against them will continue as well.

To sum up then:

Globalization, immigration, the women's movement, and the P.C. changes will all continue. Given these de-stabilizing – but exciting – world trends, neo-fascism and other extremist "isms" will continue to de-stabilize the politics of the modern nation-states.

Therefore, the teaching of Democracy and the programs that help stabilize Democracy must be continually reinforced.

Chapter 13
Words vs Violence: Democratic Debate and Civility in Political Discourse

13.1 Introduction

This week, in October 2018, an angry supporter of President Trump sent bombs to all the critics of Trump, whom Trump specifically mentioned in his speeches. Instead of debating with words and voting on election day, this individual turned to violence to express his political views.

In the same week, another individual acted out his political views with violence, instead of words. He burst into a synagogue on the Sabbath, and mowed down a room full of worshipers with an assault weapon. He didn't argue his point or debate his issues, he just used violence to act out his irrational feelings.

That week was a bad week for democracy. For democracy is based on the rational discussion of differing views, and the debating of the differing issues with words. Violent fighting is prohibited by rational lawful rules of procedure in all democracies.

Democracy is defined by discussion, debate, and majority voting. And the procedures for the discussion, debate, and vote are always carefully spelled out in the constitutional law codes. If violence, fighting, and killing replace rational, lawful debate, democracy disappears.

We established at the outset of this treatise, that the unique characteristic of homo sapiens, as a species, is consciousness – the intelligent awareness of ourselves, others, nature, the world, and the universe. This is the species characteristic that has allowed homo sapiens to dominate the earth. And, this "cognitive revolution," as Yuval Noah Harari[1] calls it, allowed humans to diverge from animal politics, and use their intellectual faculties to discuss difficult issues, such that the collective wisdom of the group could lead it to a thoughtful resolution of problematic situations.

---

[1] Yuval Noah Harari, Sapiens, A Brief History of Humankind, Amazon Paperback, 2017.

© Springer Nature Switzerland AG 2019
R. M. Glassman, *The Future of Democracy*,
https://doi.org/10.1007/978-3-030-16111-8_13

Whereas animal politics – such as that of chimpanzee bands – consists of direct, violent, fighting to determine leadership, and enforce order,[2] human politics can consist of discussion and debate, rather than violence. And, the smartest and wisest members of the group can take leadership roles, not just the strongest, most aggressive, and the most violent.

Of course, since homo sapiens is, at once, both human and animal, at any time humans can revert to animal politics. Discussion and debate can lead to heated exchanges, and rational debate can lead to irrational, emotional rage and violence. The purely human characteristic of consciousness and intelligent awareness can be overridden by animal violence, physical domination, and acquiescent fear and submission.

War chiefs, kings, and dictators can and do dominate human societies and engender fearful acquiescent behavior in the subject peoples. However, we humans always have the potential for the institutionalization of rational-democratic political systems.

The history of homo sapiens is not just the history of Kings and battles,[3] it is also the history of democracy and great debates. And, within the history of democracy itself, there has been an evolutionary trend – from tribal democracy to city-state democracy to nation-state democracy – toward ever-improving lawful procedures governing debating rules, voting rules, the limitation of the power of the state, and the explicit designation of individual rights.[4]

Thus, lawful rules governing the process of democratic debate had to emerge; lawful voting procedures had to be explicitly designated; the military and police power of the state had to be explicitly limited by law; individual rights, which the state cannot take away, had to be made explicit in a lawful Bill of Rights; and the use of violence by individuals against their political opponents has to be reined in by customary norms relating to proper debating procedure.

So, words must replace violence in human political interaction if democratic human politics is to be maintained against the ever-potential animal violence and domination.

All across the world, in the year 2018, journalists have been jailed or killed. Without a free press, there is no free speech, and without free speech, there are no free debates, and without debates, there are no words. When words are inhibited, violent actions take their place.

Donald Trump has called the press the "enemy of the people." He attacks the press in every speech. He encourages his crowds to beat up reporters. And, he purveys "false news" – lies – in all his speeches.

Democracy depends on debate and the rational discussion of issues. Without a free press, this cannot occur.

---

[2] Jane Goodall, *In the Shadow of Man*, Amazon Paperback, 2015.

[3] Reinhard Bendix, *Kings or People*, Amazon Paperback.

[4] Ronald M. Glassman, *The Origins of Democracy in Tribes, City-States and Nation-States*, The Netherlands, Springer International, 2017 (2 Volumes).

And, it is not just Donald Trump who has turned on the press. Look what just happened with Saudi Arabia and a journalist who was brutally murdered and his body dismembered. This took place in Turkey, at the Saudi Consulate. The killing was ordered by the new Saudi ruler, Prince "MBS."

And ironically, this horrific deed against a journalist was described – in all its gory details – by Recep Tayyip Erdoğan, the president of Turkey, who has in the past year, after an attempted coup against him, arrested and jailed *hundreds* of journalists.

Vladimir Putin, in Russia, keeps the trappings of democracy intact. Elections are held, and debates do occur. However, opposition leaders are jailed or killed, and journalists are routinely poisoned. Words are too dangerous for Putin and Erdoğan, so they resort to violence to silence them.

Similar violence against journalists and opposition groups has occurred in Hungary and the Philippines. Orbán in Hungry has, not only crackdown on journalists, but is closing an entire University in Budapest. That university, founded by George Soros, was dedicated to democratic norms and values. Soros, a Hungarian-born Jew, who fled Hungary and made his fortune on Wall Street, funded the University in Budapest because he knew that after generations of monarchy, Nazism, and communism, the Hungarians might need tutoring in how to establish and maintain a legal-democratic political system. It seems Soros was correct, and now Orbán – who went to Oxford on a Soros scholarship – is making Soros into a villain. Not only does this have anti-Semitic overtones, but it is anathema to democracy as well.

And, yes, Trump villainizes Soros as well, and one of the bombs sent this week, October 2018, was sent to George Soros.

In this emerging world of the twenty-first century, unfortunately, violence is replacing words in many nations – even nations that are still democratic.

13.2   Civility in Debate vs. Extremist Views

For democracy to function, violent fighting must give way to rational debate.

In tribal democracies, such as that of the Iroquois League,[5] weapons were not allowed at the tribal council, and the clan heads had to be chosen from amongst the elders, for it was determined that young men were often too volatile. Furthermore, the debates took place within a religious atmosphere. That is, the great spirits were invoked before and after the proceedings, and the assembly was warned that bad behavior would bring down curses from the spirit world.

Finally, when the debates were completed, and the vote taken, the unanimity principle was invoked, such that all the elders and all the warriors at the assembly had to agree on the decision.[6] If there were individuals who did not agree, the

---

[5] Lewis Henry Morgan, *Ancient Society published in 1877, Classics of Anthropology,* Amazon.

[6] Ronald M. Glassman, *The Origins of Democracy in Tribes, City-States and Nation-States,* Springer International.

discussion would go on until they gave in, and voted their agreement. And, if unanimity could not be gained, often the decision was not implemented. Sometimes the unanimity process would go on for weeks.

Once unanimity was reached, religious invocations would consecrate the decision, and it would be implemented. In this way, violent conflict was avoided in the Iroquois Leagues' democracy.[7]

Amongst the ancient Greeks, a similar situation existed during the archaic period. "Wise elders" – selected only from certain aristocrat clans – met at a council meeting and recommended policies. Then these policies were submitted to the warriors' assembly. As with the Iroquois, no weapons were allowed at the warriors' assembly. The warriors voted yes or no on the proposals submitted by the aristocratic elders. Unanimity was demanded, and the process could be slow – the warriors voting by stamping their feet or shouting, until a consensus had been reached.[8]

However, once the Greeks developed trading cities, and the city-states replaced the tribes as the political units, tribal democracy was slowly replaced with city-state democracy.

Aristotle tells us[9] in the Constitution of Athens, that after the time of Solon – the "lawgiver" – the old military aristocracy lost its power, and a class-based system emerged.[10] The council of elders was replaced with a council of wealthy individuals, who took turns by lot. These wealthy individuals had the leisure time to gain an education, and so they were still considered as "wise," and they continue to make recommendations to the warriors' assembly. This assembly – though still a warriors' assembly[11] – was now also class-based. The middle class of craftsmen and farmers – both producing for the new money, trade-capitalist economy – held the majority in prosperous cities, while the poor – day laborers and seasonal farm laborers (rowers on the ships) held the majority in the less prosperous cities.[12]

In the trade-capitalist city-states, the warriors' assembly became the *citizens assembly*, and the counsel was dominated by the well-educated rich, rather than the tribal elders. Weapons were still barred, but, the unanimity principle was dropped – decisions had to be reached more quickly in the volatile economic and political world of the competing Greek city-states.

Majority vote was institutionalized, and a decision could pass by one vote – Aristotle describes these new voting procedures in the *Constitution of Athens*.[13]

But, how were these decisions debated, and how was violence averted?

Because the citizens' assemblies could number in the thousands, tribal, ritualized debate gave way to charismatic and clever speechmaking – the kind of speechmaking

---

[7] *Ibid.*

[8] Aristotle, *Politics*, (on Sparta), Oxford, UK, Oxford University Press, 1952.

[9] Aristotle, *The Constitution of Athens*, Oxford, UK, Oxford University Press, 1954.

[10] *Ibid.* (*See Solon's Reforms*).

[11] Josiah Ober, *Demokratia*, Princeton, NJ, Princeton University Press, 1990 (See articles on Hoplites).

[12] Aristotle, *Politics*.

[13] Aristotle, *The Constitution of Athens*.

that could sway a crowd – crowd psychology comes into play here, with brilliant charismatic rhetors – men who used logical arguments and became known as great debaters – and clever demagogues – men who could manipulate the assembly through irrational and emotional appeals.

Both great orators and clever demagogues spoke at the citizens' assemblies and attempted to convince the citizens on how to vote.

After each side's advocates had spoken, a vote was taken. Since there was no unanimity principle, the losing side was often disappointed and angry. However, the issue could be brought up again, and if voted the same way, the losing side had to accept the decision.

Constitutional laws were passed regulating the rules of debate and the conditions under which the decisions could be challenged, or left standing.

Greek city-state democracy was volatile, and demagogic speakers could manipulate the crowd at the assembly – Plato criticized democracy strongly because of this latter.[14] However, Plato notwithstanding, the Greeks – in many city-states – from Croton in Italy to Miletus and Halicarnassus in Asia Minor – learned to accept majority rule and to participate actively, but nonviolently, in the discussion, debate, and voting process.

Schools of rhetoric sprang up, first in Italy, then all across Greece and Asia Minor, in which men – mostly wealthy men of leisure – could learn how to argue logically on *any* issue – even take both sides and argue them equally well, and, they learned how to play on the emotions of the crowd at the assembly and manipulate them. The schools of rhetoric produced both great debaters and manipulative demagogues.

The key for us here is that violence was not used – the citizens did not fight physically, they used words. They debated, they did not duel.

This does not mean that there were not riots or that violence never broke out. However, by and large, the citizens accepted the new rules of democratic debate and majority decision-making. Tyranny – dictatorship – was denigrated, by the great theorists such as Plato and Aristotle, and by the people at large. Where tyranny existed, those city-states, such as Syracuse in Sicily, were held in low esteem. And where non-Greeks lived under monarchy, the great kings were considered tyrants – the regimes turning citizens into slaves.[15]

Greek city-state democracy with its schools of rhetoric and great debaters lasted throughout the Hellenistic period and into the Roman Era. Romans, such as Cicero, adored rhetoric and debate, and brought Greek teachers of rhetoric to Rome.

Of course, with the collapse of the Roman Empire, the Greek city-states declined as well. And, as is so well-known, it was not until the Renaissance, centuries later, that the Greek ideas about democracy and its functioning were revived.

As we described in an earlier chapter, the Italian city-states went through a similar process of development as the Greek, when trade-capitalism and craft production were revived. And though Florence had a "moment" of democracy, most of the

---

[14] Plato, *The Republic*, London, Penguin Classics, 1950, (See Plato's Critique of Democracy).

[15] Aristotle, *Politics*. (See Aristotle on Monarchy).

Italian city-states retained oligarchic regimes which were despotic – no debate was allowed, and the citizens' assemblies were disbanded.[16]

So, let us turn to the Viking tribes of Northwest Europe and then the slow evolution of representative democracy amongst the city-states of the Netherlands, Switzerland and West Germany.

Let us begin with Viking tribal democracy.

Among the Scandinavian tribes, the tribal democracy was similar to that of the Iroquois. No weapons were allowed at the tribal assembly, and a council of aristocrats met first, and gave their decisions to the warriors' assembly.

However, the aristocrats – as amongst the archaic Greeks – were the leading warriors. Their clans were "royal" clans from which the best warriors were trained. These Viking warriors were not known as "wise elders," as they were amongst the Iroquois and the archaic Greeks. Rather, they were known for their heroism in battle and their tendency to be violent within the tribe.[17]

So, amongst the Norse Tribes, we have tribal democracy: the aristocratic leaders meet in council and make decisions; they submit these decisions to the warriors' assembly for a vote; the vote must be unanimous, or no decision is taken. And, the assembly proceedings are surrounded with religious incantations, a reciting of the customary laws, by a "law speaker," and the invocation of curses from the gods against anyone who breaks the laws or refuses to abide by the unanimous decision.

The problem, according to the *Islandic Sagas,*[18] is that the aristocratic clan leaders were so prone to violence, that once the democratic assembly was disbanded, they would, often enough, refuse to accept the decisions and engage in violence against their opponents. Either a duel to the death, or clan retributions against the opposing clan were *routinely* engaged in.

The words of the democracy were overruled by the violence of the aristocrats. Now, the Iroquois were just as warlike as the Vikings, and they tortured war prisoners mercilessly. However, they came to value and fully accept their democratic political procedures. Of course, there was clan violence and retribution, but the elders were known as "peace chiefs," and the founder of Iroquois democracy, Hiawatha,[19] was venerated as a God (as was the clan matron who facilitated his peace efforts – hence women gained the vote to choose the clan elders – according to the *founding myth*).

Amongst the Viking tribes, the "law speakers" were venerated, but aristocratic violence overrode democratic procedures quite regularly, and, Odin, the High God, was a God of Death, who brought violence wherever he went.[20]

---

[16] Venice remained staunchly oligarchic; on democratic movement was repressed violently.

[17] Islandic Sagas, edited by Oronol Fur Thorson, Penguin Paperback, 2000, London & NY. See also, Glassman, *The Origins of Democracy in Tribes, City-States and Nation-States.*

[18] *Ibid.*

[19] Henry Wadsworth Longfellow, *The sons of Hiawatha*, Amazon Paperback. (Hiawatha, a skilled orator, convinced the warring tribes of central New York State to join together in the Iroquois League).

[20] Ronald M. Glassman, *The Origins of Democracy in Tribes, City-States and Nation-States.* (See the section on Norse Tribes).

Why do I focus on this? Because, when city-states emerged in Northwest Europe, as trade-capitalist, craft-producing cities, the transition from tribal democracy to city-state, and then nation-state democracy, had to include social norms that would override and inhibit the violence inherent in Norse tribal democracy. As Thorkild Jacobsen[21] tells us, sometimes the Norse tribesmen ate and drank at huge feasts before they convened their assemblies. And in this drunken state, they were more likely to vote unanimously, and less likely to turn to violence.

This, however, was no solution. A more modern form of democratic procedure was needed.

13.3   The Emergence of Representative Parliamentary Democracy and the Need for Non-Violent Rules of Procedure

Wilbert Van Vree, in his wonderful book *Meetings, Manners, and Civilization*[22] describes in detail how the Dutch Republic slowly moved from the unanimity principle to majority rule, and from drunken assemblies to more formal, civilized assemblies.

Make no mistake about it, the problem of violence and dueling and rioting, and refusing to accept majority decisions plagued the Dutch Republic, and the German Hanseatic League cities as well. And in the Netherlands, Germany and England, the religious wars generated by the Protestant Reformation made the situation worse – the charismatic leader of the Dutch against the Spanish and French, William of Orange, was murdered by a Catholic fanatic because he, William, had converted to Protestantism. It took a century or more before the Dutch (and Swiss) could develop procedures for majority rule and inhibit the violence that close decisions generated. Dueling with swords, rather than debating with words remained culturally acceptable for a long time.

The cultural change that truly ushered in the age of democratic debate and non-violent democratic procedures, emerged from England, rather than from the Netherlands – even though the Netherlands became truly democratic before England.

---

[21] Thorkild Jacobsen, *Primitive Democracy in Ancient Mesopotamia*, 1943, Journal of Near Eastern Studies, Vol. 2 #3, July 1943 – Published by The University of Chicago Press (Paperback).

[22] Wilbert Van Vree, *Meetings, Manners and Civilizations*, Bloomsburg, UK Leicester University Press, 6/1/2001 (Paperback).

13.4   The English "Gentlemen" Create a New "Civilized" Order

The emergence of the British "Gentry," as a new commercial class in the countryside, replacing the feudal knighthood is detailed famously by Tawney.[23] Tawney describes the "Enclosure Movement," whereby the English countryside was converted to sheep farming and the woolens industry. Merchant-oriented "gentry" bought up the land, expelled the peasants and paid off the feudal knights, such that they moved nearby to the Kingly Court.

The gentry became wealthy on the woolens industry – British woolen clothing selling well in Europe.

But, why were these woolens' merchants called "gentlemen?" Why not some other term to designate a rich businessman who lived in the countryside? You could not use the term *burgher* because they did not live in a city.

The answer seems to be that these businessmen-farmers wanted to create an image for themselves that was different from the feudal military aristocrats they were replacing. The British military aristocrats, like all the Norse aristocrats, were volatile and violent – insult them and you had to fight them. But the woolens' manufacturers wanted to do business, and business transactions are governed by lawful contracts. You do not use violence, you use contract law, signed on by two parties, who peacefully engage in trade.

Hence, to reinforce their identity as businessmen – even though they did not live in a city, they needed a name that signified lawful, nonviolent transactions.

Furthermore, in order to do business, one needed a modicum of education in mathematical calculations, literacy and law. Profits, losses, and legal contracts had to be understood. So, unlike the feudal lords, who cared more for fighting than for learning, the gentry had to be educated.

As educated men, they rejected the rough language of the feudal lords, and the bastardized language of the Celtic peasants. Both the harsh Germanic guttural sounds of the Anglo-Saxon-Danish-Norwegian lords, and the brogue-laden sound of the peasants, were rejected in favor of a smooth, learned, erudite version of the emerging English language.

Up until the gentry emerged as a new class, the upper class spoke either Latin or French, while the lower classes spoke Celtic (Gaelic) when English was spoken by either the upper or lower feudal classes, it was unacceptable to the new learned gentry.

So, the gentry became learned and lawful, and spoke a sophisticated refined English – with a large vocabulary, including Latin and French words that were "Anglicized."

But still, why "gentlemen" – "gentle," after all, means non-violent, peaceful, composed.

---

[23] R.H. Tawney, *Religion and the Rise of Capitalism*, Amazon Paperback.

The answer comes from Calvinist Puritanism. Puritanism is all about controlling one's *passions*. Our animal passions – sex, violence, the desire for food, urination, defecation – all of these animal passions had to be controlled. Sex was considered sinful, and violence morally wrong. All the passions were animalistic, and humans had to be spiritual and learn to contain these animal instincts.

Though the Church of England, the Anglican Church, never became fully Puritan – persecuting the Puritans, and driving many of them to leave and go to the New World – the Puritan ideas about controlling one's passions and acting in a well-mannered way became culturally dominant in England, even to some extent amongst the Celtic Catholics.

Thus, the gentry attained the designation "gentlemen," because they eschewed violence, followed the law, and comported themselves in such a way as to control their passions. They were truly gentle men, and because of their excellent educational level, they were "genteel" in their social relationships, and erudite in their use of language.

So, now let us return to our focus on democratic rules of procedure, especially the use of words, not violence.

13.5   The Gentry and the English Parliament

The gentry and the city merchants had money from the new trade – capitalist economy. The King and the feudal lords needed money. Therefore, a representative Parliament from the countryside woolens districts and the cities, met regularly with the King and the Lords.

I have discussed this earlier, and in detail in the *Origins of Democracy in Tribes, City-States, and Nation-States*.[24]

Here we wish to emphasize that the English Parliament adopted specific rules of order and other lawful procedures that inhibited violence and allowed for spirited debate of policies, and a majority vote.[25]

With the "gentlemen" in charge of the parliament, the passions were frowned upon, and civilized debate was encouraged.

With the gentry in the majority in parliament, rhetoric – Greek style debate – was revived. Part of the classical revival in education was, not only philosophy and science, but also debating. British debating clubs emerged at Oxford and Cambridge, and logical and clever debating skills became encouraged.

England was not yet a democracy, however, the King could disband parliament at anytime he wanted, and the Lords still held power.

I cannot go into the English "Civil War" (or Revolution or Puritan revolt) here, except to say that when Oliver Cromwell[26] and his new model army defeated the

---

[24] Ronald M. Glassman, *The Origins of Democracy in Tribes, City-States and Nation-States*.

[25] Wilbert Van Vree, *Meetings, Manners and Civilizations*.

[26] Christopher Hill, *God's Englishman: Oliver Cromwell and the English Revolution*, published 1970, now Google Books.

feudal army of the King and the Lords, a full-fledged democracy did emerge for a short time. Cromwell and the Puritan craftsmen and Yeomen farmers in his army sat in parliament with the gentry. The King was beheaded (Charles I) and the Lords were expelled.

After Cromwell's death, chaos occurred in England, with monarchists, democrats, and oligarchic parties vying for power. In 1688, with the help of the Dutch Republic, a constitutionally limited monarchy based on the Dutch model and installing a Dutch King – another William of Orange – was established. Unlike the Dutch, the English constitutionally limited monarchy was an oligarchy, not a democracy. The rich gentry and merchants dominated the new parliament in 1688–1689.

With no "unruly" craftsmen or farmers, and with a highly educated gentry in control, the very "civilized" rules of procedure that characterized Great Britain to the world were adopted. The passions were controlled with Puritan vigor, and debate and majority voting could proceed without the fear of violence disturbing the process.

Wilbert Van Vree describes how the Dutch then adapted these British procedures to their parliament – the States General – and how they did become slowly institutionalized.[27] The Dutch were Calvinists, but not Puritan – sex was considered natural, and violence was still culturally encouraged. Over time, however, as the Dutch became educated, the gentlemanly culture, encouraged by Erasmus – the most famous Dutchman of his time – and institutionalized in nearby England – took hold in the Netherlands.

As late as 1910, Max Weber,[28] in Germany, believed that the Germans – immersed in their military culture – would never be able to adapt to "Anglo-Saxon Conventions" and accept a democratic style of government.

13.6   American Democracy and Frontier Violence

After 1688 in England, a limited monarchy was established, as we have mentioned – a Dutch King was brought over, because the British heirs would not accept the constitutional limitations of power that was demanded by the parliament.

However, the parliament itself would not accept the demands of the artisans and small farmers to gain democratic representation. The gentry were firmly in control of the parliament – they were well-educated, well-mannered, law-abiding, and rich. A property qualification was established, such that only the rich could sit in parliament. But, this was oligarchy, not democracy. The gentry called it, "The Glorious Revolution" of 1688, but the middling and poorer citizens saw it as a fraudulent revolution.

---

[27] Wilbert Van Vree, *Meetings, Manners and Civilizations*.

[28] Max Weber, on "Anglo Saxon Conventions," in *Economy and Society*, Trans. Guenther Roth and Claus Wittich, NY, Bedminster Press, 1981.

Disgusted with this turn of political events, and also with the Church of England's refusal to fully evolve towards true Calvinist Puritanism, thousands of craftsmen and free farmers fled the British Isles for the New World. There they settled what became the Northern Colonies, and established both Puritan churches – the little, white, unadorned churches – and full-fledged democracy – representative government with no property qualification and no King at all – limited or unlimited.

The first warship built by the fledgling United States in their war against England was called, "The Oliver Cromwell."[29]

Not only did these northern American settlers establish local democratic representative democracies, but since they were Puritans, and believed in reigning in the passions, they established a peaceful, lawful, set of procedures for debating the issues. They also established free public schools, so that they would become educated enough to argue the issues intelligently.

So, violence was banned from the political process. But, then the wars with the Indians began. The very same Indians who had saved "the pilgrims" of The Mayflower, were turned upon and killed in "King Phillip's War" – King Philip was the name the Indian War Chief had taken.

Violence against the Indians increased as the Indians fought back to retain their lands. Disease, however, hit the Indian so hard – the Native Americans had no immunity to measles and smallpox – that the wars in the Northern Colonies ended. The Indians were pushed aside onto reservations, and the Puritan British colonists established a well-run lawful democratic political system, that would eventually spawn a remarkable industrial-capitalist economy, similar to that which would emerge in England, Scotland, and the Netherlands.

The American South was settled differently. Some of the feudal lords who were pushed off the land in Great Britain during the gentry's take over of the countryside, were encouraged to settle Virginia – where the original British colony had failed – the Carolinas, and Georgia.

Thus, British feudal lords did settle the American South. They brought with them serfs and "indentured servants," and attempted to establish a lordly lifestyle. However, the serfs and servants from Britain discovered that in this vast frontier nation, they could escape from the lords and claim their own land.

Losing their serf base, the Lords attempted to enserf the Indians. But, Indian men would not farm the land – this was women's work and taboo for men. The Indians also died off from disease.

Fortuitously – and history is full of such coincidences – the Portuguese were at that moment in history bringing thousands of Africans from West Africa to Brazil. For, whereas the Spaniards had conquered the Aztec, Mayan, and Inca empires and had millions of people to enserf, the Portuguese had taken Brazil, a land of the Amazon Jungle with "naked primitives" living deep in the rainforest.

Vasco da Gama had discovered the sea route around Africa to India and the Spice Islands. Along this route, the Portuguese had established many ports of call. In West Africa, they traded their steel goods and guns for gold. The "Gold Coast," however,

---

[29] The Warship, Oliver Cromwell, was the first warship build in America – in Essex, CT.

began to run low on gold. Therefore, the African Kingdoms which were at war with one another, began to trade their war captives – slaves – to the Portuguese. When the Portuguese discovered that these Africans could take the heat and humidity of Brazil, and that they knew how to farm – both men and women farmed in West Africa – they realized that these African slaves were more valuable than gold. Hence, the expansion of the slave trade to epic proportions.

The Portuguese stopped at Cuba and Dominica to get supplies for their further trip to Brazil. English and Dutch sea captains stopped there too.

When the British Lords of the American South were told about these slaves from Africa, they began buying them in great numbers. The South, then, became a very different country than the North. It became a slave society dominated by feudal lords. Violence against the African slaves became endemic, as slaves began to out-number the British settlers. This violence came to characterize the South, and, the violence was turned against the Native Americans by Southern military leaders, who wanted to exterminate them.

Racism and violence were institutionalized in the American South.

So, how is it that the most famous democratic theorists came from the South? Washington, Jefferson, Madison, and many more, helped write the Declaration of Independence, the Constitution, and the Bill of Rights.

History plays tricks and humans are complex and difficult to predict. Many of the Southern aristocrats sent their sons abroad – especially to Paris, which was the center of learning from 1750 to 1800 – and these young men were exposed to the ideas of Voltaire, Condoset, Montesquieu, and the other "philosophe," espousing radical, democratic ideas: freedom of speech and religion, the limitation of the power of the state, checks and balances on state power, and lawful procedures of parliamentary representative government – without a king or a pope.

So imbued with the radical democratic ideas of France, the young Southern aristocrats helped establish the democracy of the USA. Once elected to the presidency or the Congress, these Southerners acted in a genteel way – words and laws, not violence, characterized the American democratic procedure.

But, but, but, these Southern aristocrats reneged on their promise to free their slaves. Instead, the South became more violent, against the Africans and the Native Americans.

So, we have a paradox in American history and culture: the North was truly democratic and lawful, while the South degenerated into ever-increasing violence and race hatred.

The Civil War did not end the paradox, it worsened it. Lincoln was the first president to be assassinated – Southern violence had now spread to the halls of government in Washington DC.

Reconstruction was halted with Lincoln's death, and for the next hundred years – 1864 to 1964 – violence and lawlessness in the American South continued. The Ku Klux Klan, a white supremacist organization, attacked, lynched, murdered and denied African-Americans their constitutional rights.

13.7   The Frontier and Gun Violence

The Northerners spread West into Ohio, Indiana, Michigan, Wisconsin, Minnesota, Kansas, Nebraska, and more. In settling the land for farming, they confronted the Indians. Violence between the Indians and the settlers exploded. The USA government sent troops, but confrontations with the Indians could occur at any moment. So, the settlers armed themselves. Guns were manufactured in great numbers, and all the frontier farmers – the men and the women – learned to shoot, and shoot well.

The Indians lacked guns, or had far fewer guns, and eventually they were defeated and pushed onto reservations – I need not go into the well-known history of General Custer and his genocidal war against the Indians of the West, for though Custer was killed, the Indians eventually lost and were pushed aside. The tradition of being armed with guns, however, did not disappear.

From the South, settlers moved into Texas and the Great Plains – this was good cattle country. The Plains' Indians lived off the buffalo herds and rode on horseback. The Buffalo were systematically killed off, so that the Indians would starve – men like "Buffalo Bill" became famous for killing off the Buffalo. Since the Plains' Indians had horses, they could appear out of nowhere and raid and kill. So, both the farming settlers and the cowboys and ranchers who were running huge herds of cattle where the buffalo once roamed, armed themselves.

Ranchers, cowboys, farmers – they all had guns. Drunken cowboys shot up frontier towns, ranchers used these cowboys as armed gangs, violating the land laws and ruling through fear and violence. Outlaws formed their own gangs – armed with guns and violence – as crime escalated in the West. Indians still rode their horses, and, they obtained guns. It was "The Wild, Wild West" – lawless – a place where guns gave power and anarchy reigned.

Slowly, slowly, between 1870 and 1900, government and law were brought to the frontier. Elected governors and senators, law courts and judges, schools, and railroads, eventually bought the western territories into the democratic and lawful nation.

The guns, however, remained. The frontier culture had created a "frontier mentality," and Westerners held onto their guns as a right – and it *was* written into the Bill of Rights. The Second Amendment protects the right to bear arms – it was included in the Bill of Rights to protect the revolutionary militias fighting the British for independence. But, it has, unfortunately, been interpreted by the Supreme Court to mean the right of every citizen to have guns.

The frontier mentality and the Second Amendment would create a situation of violent behavior in society at large, while at the same time, the USA was establishing a peaceful, lawful, democracy, in which debates on policies were voted upon by majority, and wherein such decisions were supposed to be lawfully accepted.

But the combination of frontier mentality and the ready availability of guns engendered a violent society. The USA has one of the highest rates of murder and violent assaults of any of the advanced industrial democracies. More murders occur in a day than occur in a year in Japan or France.

And, since the assassination of Lincoln, we have had other presidents assassinated – McKinley and John F. Kennedy come to mind. There was an attempt to shoot Teddy Roosevelt – he was saved by his cigar case in his jacket pocket near his heart, there was an attempt to shoot Franklin Roosevelt in Florida – the Governor of Florida, standing next to him, was killed. Ronald Reagan was shot, but survived, while Bobby Kennedy, running for the nomination, was killed – shot in the head – in California. So, too, was Martin Luther King Jr. shot and killed.

13.8   Gun Violence Continues to Plague American Democracy

Gun violence spiked after World War I, when organized crime syndicates had machine guns, and ordinary citizens bought better rifles and handguns. Then, the Great Depression and World War II engendered a decline in violence and gun ownership in America. After World War II, with so many men killed overseas, a quieter, gentler society emerged – especially in the West. Then, however, the 1960s Civil Rights movement in the South, the anti-Vietnam War movement in the North and California, and the subsequent women's and gay liberation movements, broke the fabric of American society to the core. Puritanism was rejected, patriotism was rejected, racism, sexism, and discrimination against gays were rejected – but those Americans who still held firmly to Puritan sexual norms and the older conceptions of the family, became angry and embattled.

The "moral majority" in the heartland of the Midwest, and racism in the South, let loose the *anomic* violence that still plagues this nation. The more the norms and values of the country were challenged and changing, the worse the anomic violence became.

Then something occurred that made this situation much worse. The war in the Middle East generated the need for soldiers. Because the Vietnam War draft had led to so much protesting, *a volunteer army* was created by Congress. The volunteer army caused *no protests*, because if you did not want to serve, you did not have to. And, the volunteer army is better trained and has higher morale than the drafted Army.

The wars in the Middle East and Afghanistan seemed never to end. And during these wars, the soldiers were equipped with more deadly guns. The automatic rifle – the "assault weapon" – was deployed. It shoots like a machine gun and is loaded with the deadliest bullets invented.

Unfortunately, these assault weapons – American-made, Russian-made, Israeli made – have become readily available, and, they are not expensive. Attempts by Congress to make them illegal have failed.

Enter the NRA (the National Rifle Association). Gun manufacturers, like any other capitalist – industrial corporations, want to maximize their profits. So, they advertise, sell their guns in as many outlets as they can, and they sell them on the Internet. Anybody can get a gun anywhere.

With the help of the NRA, guns flooded the market, and Congress was paid off with huge campaign funding – legal – not to stop it. Backed by the Second Amendment, Americans have become armed with assault weapons – weapons of war not used for hunting or target shooting or self-protection.

To make things worse, Middle Eastern Muslims, reacting to America's increasing involvement in their affairs, established terrorist organizations such as Al Qaeda and Isis!

These terrorists recruit young men by using the internet and set them against the USA. Some of them have succeeded in bombing and shooting up America.

The threat of terrorism engendered even more Americans to buy assault weapons. After all, if the Muslim radicals have declared war on us, then we better be armed against them.

With even more Americans buying guns and deadly ammunition, the threat of violence escalated even further.

The result has been the worst epidemic of mass shootings this nation has ever seen. The shooter in Las Vegas killed more people than had ever been killed in a mass shooting. He had no known motive, yet was armed with dozens of assault weapons. The shooting in Pittsburgh at a Jewish synagogue was the worst anti-Semitic episode in America's history. These terrible mass shootings will continue, because Americans are armed with weapons of war, and our cultural fabric has been torn apart by rapid social change. In an atmosphere of *anomie* – confusion over values and the loss of norms – violence escalates[30] both random and targeted violence. It should also be established that individuals suffering various kinds of mental illnesses will tend to *act out their violent fantasies.* Under more stable social conditions, such individuals fantasize, but do not act out violence. Since the anomic conditions caused by rapid social change in norms and values is *worsening* in America, the acting out of violence will continue.

It is possible that the new generation of young people will be less conflicted, such that the violence will decline. However, it seems that everyone in America is armed, and the guns are better than ever – even the pistols are now automatic weapons.

Our democracy is still functioning, but words are being replaced by violence – gun violence, bombings, and other forms of violence, are, unfortunately replacing words.

We need to look at one more factor affecting this move towards increasing violence: the *internet blogs*, which have been fomenting extremist views and making democratic discourse difficult.

---

[30] Emile Durkheim, *Suicide*, NY Free Press, 1950. (See the section on Anomic Suicide).

13.9   The Internet Age and Extremist Blogs

In ancient Greece, speakers debated face to face. In the British Parliament, representatives of the two parties debate face-to-face. But on the new computer internet media, individuals express their views on isolated, *extremist blogs*. Nobody debates their views, they state their views and are reinforced in their views by others with similar views. Rather than a logical interchange of views, and a rational debate, the individuals on these blogs incite each other to riot and kill, not to discuss.

Can democracy survive in this era of extremist blogs? Can democracy somehow adapt the blogosphere to democratic rules of procedure?

13.10   Pamphlets and Newspapers in the Era of the Printing Press

When the printing press was invented in Gutenberg, Germany, Luther was arguing for a complete break with the Roman Catholic Church, the end of celibacy, and other radical Christian ideas. At first, it was the Bible itself that was printed – in new more accurate Latin and then in German. Luther himself had translated the Bible into a very readable German, and thousands of copies of this German Bible were printed and sold. Soon, Dutch, English, Scandinavian, and other vernacular Bibles were printed and sold.

The Protestant Reformation generated varied and extremist views on the nature of Christianity and the structure of the Christian Church. The printers began to publish *pamphlets* stating the views of one reformer or another. Luther, Zwingli, *Luther vs. Erasmus, Erasmus vs. The Pope, Anabaptists vs. Lutherans, Lutherans vs. Calvinists,* and more.[31]

These pamphlets – printed by the thousands and inexpensive to buy – led to extremist acts of violence. People started killing each other, inflamed by the pamphlets of their sectarian views. This violence went on for more than a century.

Then, when the democratic revolutions occurred in Switzerland, the Netherlands, England, the USA, and France, the printers began printing political pamphlets. Monarchists versus Democrats, Oligarchs versus Democrats, Democrats versus Monarchists and Oligarchs.

The political pamphlets were extreme, and they began to get personal, as well. Individual leaders were praised or vilified, specific movements were targeted or encouraged. Political violence definitely escalated – in France, it led to "The Reign of Terror" and the Napoleonic dictatorship; in England to hangings, jailings, rioting, and emigration to America.

In the newly founded United States, political pamphlets inflamed the electorate and sometimes led to personal duels, such as Hamilton and Burr.

---

[31] Michael Massing, *Erasmus, Luther and the Fight for the Western Mind*, NY Harper, 2017.

As the Industrial Age modernized the economy, daily newspapers replaced the pamphlets. These newspapers were often biased for one party or another. In Europe, capitalist newspapers, socialist, communist, nationalist, militarist, and anarchist newspapers emerged.

All of these newspapers pushed the electorate toward extreme views. In the United States, where socialism, communism, anarchism, and militarism, had less of a hold, the newspapers still had biases – usually Republican Party oriented, from the 1890s onward, but others were union-oriented and favored the Democrats after the 1920s.

These newspapers, as a free press, not controlled by the government and able to criticize the government, represented a positive force for democracy. Even though they were extremist, in some case, as long as they were free from government control, they elevated *free speech* to a national level, and held governments accountable to the people. There is no doubt, however, that these newspapers could become too extremist. In France, Germany, Italy, and Spain, left and right wing newspapers inflamed the social divisions that destabilized the democratic regimes which had so recently been established.

In the Netherlands, Great Britain, and the USA, where democracy had become firmly accepted, newspapers presented less extremist views. So, on the one hand, the daily newspapers of the nineteenth and twentieth centuries enhanced democracy by reinforcing free speech with a free press which could and did actively criticize the government.

On the other hand, in nations where the democracies were weakened by extremist political parties, the newspapers reinforced the extremism: socialists read only socialist newspapers, communists only communist newspapers, nationalists only national newspapers, and so on. In those cases, the free press weakened democratic discourse and unwittingly encouraged political violence.

Today, in the twenty-first century, we are faced with a similar dilemma. The internet is the new medium of communication – the newspapers are being absorbed into the internet as online blogs of their own. And, as with the print newspapers, the blogosphere newspapers can enhance free speech and encourage civil debate, or, they can become extremist and encourage violent political activity. Both kinds of blogs exist: there are very well articulated, rational-intellectual blogs on the left and the right. They are a wonderful source of information to the electorate, and, they are good for democracies.

On the other hand, there are extremist blogs which present conspiracy theories and purvey "big lies."[32] Of course, these kinds of blogs are dangerous for democracy and engender anger, wild ideologies, and violent behavior.

For example, there was a man from the South who believed a blog which said that Hillary Clinton was running a child prostitution ring out of a pizzeria in Washington, DC. He went there armed with an assault weapon to save the children being trafficked. He believed the big lie. When he got to the pizzeria he found

---

[32] Goebbels put forth the theory of "the highlie" in the Nazi Era (1930s). Allegedly, Roy Cohen gave Donald Trump a copy of that book.

nothing but a family restaurant. Luckily, he killed no one, and surrendered himself. Here was a good person, a sane person, who was taken in by the extremist views on the blogosphere. Unfortunately, most of the individuals so taken in shout first, before they can be disabused of other wildest extremist views.

So, can Democracy survive the extremism of the blogosphere?

Let me put it this way: when newspapers were invented, both Democratic and despotic organizations used them. When microphones were invented both Hitler and Roosevelt spoke through them to great crowds of "charismaticized" listeners.[33] When radio was invented, both Churchill and Mussolini spoke through it to their nations. When television was invented both Kennedy and Khrushchev were visible to their nations during the Cuban Missile Crisis.

So now, we have the World Wide Web – a remarkable global communications network. We can speak to friends and family in California, New York, Germany, and Japan. Through Skype, we can see our family in Greece or Italy or Israel and they can see us, It's wonderful! The world is becoming a global village.

But, of course, dictatorial regimes will sensor the internet and use it for surveillance. The Chinese, the Russians, the North Koreans – they will use the internet for malicious purposes – hacking, interfering in democratic elections, stealing commercial technology, and more.

The internet and artificial intelligence in computer technologies that have not yet been invented will be used by despotic and democratic governments alike.

The dictatorial governments are not bothered by extremist blogs, only because they shut them down!

In democracies, there is free speech, freedom of the press, freedom of artistic expression. So we can't shut down the extremist blogs. We can, however, teach and encourage *civility* in political discourse. This can be taught, in the family, the schools, the universities, and on the mass media themselves.

It is possible to get to the point where the majority of the population in democratic societies, are socialized to democratic norms of behavior. Weber thought the Germans would never follow the "Anglo-Saxon Convention" of Great Britain. And Miguel de Unamuno believed that the Spaniards would never be able to institute a stable democratic government. And, Samuel Huntington[34] worried that the culture of Asia and other Third World regions was antithetical to democracy. Yet, there is democracy in Japan, Hong Kong, Taiwan, Kenya, Brazil, Argentina, Indonesia and other nation-states with differing cultures – and Germany and Spain have become stable democracies.

The internet and the blogosphere are very new. They present both great potential for human global interactions, and also a threat. Totalitarian use of the internet and the new technologies is as likely as is the expansion of democratic discourse. Humans always have the potential to create democracies or despotisms. And

---

[33] Max Weber, "Charismatic Leadership and Legitimacy," in *Economy and Society*, Trans. Guenther Roth and Claus Wittich. (Section on the forms of legitimacy – traditional, charismatic, and legal-national).

[34] Samuel Huntington. *Culture Against Democracy*, Amazon Paperback.

Aristotle tells us that humans can either be the most wonderful creatures on earth, or, worse than any animal imaginable.[35]

So, the blogosphere must be monitored in democratic nations to prevent *misinformation* from being blatantly put forth, and, to stop the *direct incitement to violent acts*.

Free speech must be protected, but incitement to violence can be constitutionally limited – by the courts. Misinformation must be monitored by the big internet companies, such as Google and Facebook. This is being done, and, of course, it must be constantly monitored by Congressional oversight committees.

The blogs are our new pamphlets – they engage the citizens, but they also inflame them. Democracies can be destabilized by these blogs, and yet, free speech and a free press must be protected.

What a balancing act for modern democracies!!!

We need to discuss one more factor in terms of "words versus violence": the power of the state.

13.11   State Monopoly of Violence and the Limitation and Separation of Powers

The state, according to Max Weber, is that institution which has a monopoly of violence.[36] The military, the police, and the courts are controlled by the state.

For a democracy to function properly, this state power must be limited and checked. The democratic citizen must be protected from state power. Free speech, free press, freedom of religion, and all the other freedoms articulated in various Bills of Rights that characterize modern democracies, must not be stifled by state violence.

In tribal society, there is no state. However, the functioning of the democracy had to be protected from the increasing power of the war chiefs and their loyal retinues Where warfare expanded dramatically, the war chiefs became "Kings" and overrode the democratic tribal council of clan elders, replacing democracy with tyranny based on the use of direct military violence against anyone *within* the society, as well as against enemies outside of the societies.[37]

When military kingship was reinforced with a priestly class convincing the people that the king was godly, and, when the divine king was assisted by hundreds of government officials loyal to him, the divine kingly state eliminated democracy

---

[35] Aristotle, *Politics*.

[36] Max Weber, *Economy and Society*. (Section on the state and its monopoly of violence.).

[37] In the Icelandic Sagas, the rise of the Norwegian Kingship is described – terrible violence was used to establish Kingly power. See also, Samuel's warning in *The Bible*, *Books of Judges*. (Samuel warns that Kingship will bring misery upon the Hebrew tribes.).

altogether, and used state violence against the people.[38] The people were no longer citizens, but subjects – slave-like in their fear and acquiescence to the state.

It is almost impossible to limit the power of the state in a divine monarchy.[39]

In the small city-states of ancient Greece it was possible to limit state power – the citizens organized themselves into hoplite-phalanx heavily armored regiments. The state had some policing power, but even the courts were in the control of the citizens. The only way an ambitious leader could gain power over the people was to bring in mercenaries from outside the city-state and gain their total loyalty. With such an armed regiment of mercenaries, a leader could become a dictator (tyrant) and use force to dominate society.

This did occur in ancient Greece, such that some city-states, such as Syracuse, relapsed into tyranny many times in their history.[40] In most Greek city-states, however, the citizens' regiments held more power than those of a potential tyrant.

When we evolved towards larger units of society, the problem of the power of the state emerged again. In the divine kingly empires, the power of the state was not challenged by the subjects therein, for the legitimacy of the Kings was accepted – this was an irrational legitimation, however, because the Kings, in reality, were not Gods.

With the Renaissance in Europe, and the reemergence of rational scientific thinking, both the godliness of the Kings and their absolute power, were challenged.

The Kings of Europe claimed to be divine, but the Pope claimed more of a share of that divinity. This unique "Caesaropapist," split[41] in divine authority weakened the claim of the Kings to divine right.

And, once trade-capitalism and later industrial-capitalism, emerged, parliaments of trade-merchants, who controlled the money-wealth of these newly emerging nation-states, held a power equal to the military power of the Kings.

The Kings had to call together the parliaments in order to gain access to the money-wealth generated by the capitalist economy, so that they could finance their armies and navies.

Once this new set of economic and political institutions emerged, the Kings no longer held a monopoly of state power, nor were they considered divine by the increasingly rational-scientific minded citizenry.

But, the Kings still had the army under their control, so how could their power be limited?

To understand the political theory and political practice that emerged during the Enlightenment, and that undergirds both our theory and practice today in all modern democracy, let us look into how the theory and practice of the limitations of the

---

[38] Henri Frankfort, *Kingship and the Gods*, Amazon Paperback.

[39] In China, Mencius warned that the Emperor could become murderous and tyrannical if not reigned in by the Mandarin officials; Xuu Xi argued that the emperor should use force against the people, because the people are untrustworthy and potentially violent.

[40] Aristotle, *Politics*. (On Tyranny).

[41] Max Weber, *Economy and Society*. (On Caesaropapism).

power of the state, and the checks and balances built into the modern democratic state, came about.

13.12 The Limitation of the Power of the State in Modern Liberal Democracies

Though the Greek city-states rarely fell to dictators (tyrants), both Plato and Aristotle warned that the *dictatorships were the worst form of government*. Once a dictator (tyrant) gained control of the violence in the state, he would turn that violence on the people – he would get worse than a beast – human despotism is much worse than animal alpha-dominance.

Plato says that once a dictator gains total power, it alters his behavior – he becomes like a man in a dream, wherein we kill our father or our best friend, and we have sex with our mother – no inhibition exists in a dream – and no inhibition exists in the reality of a tyrant. Tyranny – dictatorships – must be prevented at all costs.[42]

Plato spun utopian visions of the perfect polity, but Aristotle tried to suggest practical ways to stabilize democracy and prevent dictators from gaining power by using the poor as their mercenaries.

Aristotle created the theory of the "mixed polity," in which the rich, the poor, the middle class were all included, and in which the leadership positions of the assembly and the army were elective. He called this "polity" because it was composed of elements of democracy, oligarchy, and monarchy – but they all balanced each other.[43]

He warned that this balance could only be maintained if there was *a middle-class majority*. (I have described this earlier). If the poor predominate, then the mixed polity degenerates from democracy into tyranny (dictatorship), because the poor will turn to a dictator to force the redistribution of wealth from the rich. Similarly, if the rich gain control, they pay mercenaries and rule dictatorially to keep the poor and middle-class down.

So, the mixed polity must be kept in balance.

Further, Aristotle believed that the people could be socialized to follow *the law*. Constitutional law had to guide all actions, or the democratic assembly itself could vote to do violent things to minorities or specific individuals.

"When the law rules, God and reason rule; when a man rules, we add the character of the beast."[44]

Plato's last book was called, *The Laws*, and Aristotle believed that rational amendable law – constitutional law – should guide, and restrain, all political action.

---

[42] Plato, *The Republic*. (On the mind of the Tyrant.)

[43] Aristotle, *Politics*. (On "Polity" the best practical form of government.)

[44] Aristotle, *Politics*. (On Law.)

Centuries later, in the early Roman Era, Polybius, a Greek intellectual from Megalopolis, was taken hostage by the Romans. Polybius wrote a *History of Rome*, and in Book VI,[45] he described the Roman Republic as a *mixed polity*. He expanded upon Aristotle, explaining how the Romans divided state power between the Senate, an oligarchic body, and the plebeian assembly, a Democratic body, and, how the military leadership was split into two generalships – consuls – such that neither had complete power over the Roman army, and each had equal power when checking the power of the other.

Polybius believed the Roman mixed polity was wonderful, and held it up as a model for all future governments.

A Roman, Titus Livius, wrote his own *History of Rome*, adding a wide range of details which Polybius had glossed over.[46] When it came to the Roman government, however, "Livy" simply copied Polybius in his descriptions of the Roman mixed polity.

Centuries past. Then, during the Renaissance, Machiavelli revived the works of Livy and Polybius. In his *Discourses on the Work of Titus Livius*,[47] he described the mixed polity of Rome. And, though he could not read Greek, he had friends of his who could, read him parts of Polybius. The mixed polity became his ideal.

Most importantly, Machiavelli when he was Foreign Secretary of the Florentine Democracy, visited France. In France, the French King had called a parliament to gain money for his planned invasion of Italy. Machiavelli, saw the French King working with the parliament – in a lawful, procedural manner – sharing power and helping the French state function without the horrific violence and treachery he documented in his frightening book, *The Prince.*[48]

In *The Prince,* he described the use of unconstrained violence to gain and hold political power. But, in *The Discourses*, he held out the vision of lawful government with a separation of powers between the King and Parliament. And, France functioned well, and was stable at that time.

So, *the mixed polity*, consisting of an executive – a King – and a legislature – the parliament, constrained and guided by *constitutional, rational laws*, was described by Machiavelli as the best form of government. Florentine face-to-face democracy was unstable, Florentine oligarchy (The Medicis) was unfair, Italian dictatorships were hideously violent – as Plato had warned they would be – while the French mixed polity, as long as it was guided by the rule of law, was the best form of government.

---

[45] Polybius, *History of Rome*, Bk VI, NY, Penguin Classics, 1948.

[46] Titus Livius, *History of Rome*, London, Penguin Books, 1938.

[47] Niccolo Machiavelli, *The Discourses on the Work of Titus Livius*, NY, Penguin, 1953.

[48] Niccolo Machiavelli, *The Prince*, Amazon Paperback.

13.13   The Enlightenment Theorists Make Checks, Balances, and the Limitation of Power Central

Montesquieu,[49] continuing Machiavelli's extension of Polybius' work, outlined in greater detail, and in a newly rational-scientific context, the description of a mixed polity in the more developed era in which he lived.

Montesquieu divided government – the state – into three branches: the executive, the legislature, and the courts.

Significantly, for Montesquieu, the executive did not have to be a King – the European Kings continuing insistence on "divine right" to rule turned the French intellectuals towards the invention of a non-kingly executive: a president, or a prime minister, either chosen from the parliament or separately elected. Such an executive, since he was not a King, would have no claims to divinity.

And, such an executive could be constrained by a lawfully limited term of office, such that a president or prime minister could not attempt to exert dictatorial power.

Even if the executive was not term-limited, the legislature and the courts could check his power. Because, in Montesquieu's system of government, power was shared by the legislature, the courts, and the executive. No one branch of government could achieve dictatorial power, because it was *checked* by the other branches.

Finally, Montesquieu's treatise was called *The Spirit of the Laws*, for constitutional, rational, lawful, rules of procedure guided and restrained all political actions. This is right out of Aristotle, "when the law rules, God and *reason* rule...".

Montesquieu's model of checks and balances, the separations of powers between the executive, legislature, and courts, and constitutional law was replicated almost exactly by the American "Founding Fathers," for Jefferson, Madison, and most of the rest, were educated abroad in Paris, and learned their lessons well.

To this day, the American Constitution, with its separation of the branches of government, and its reliance on rational law, is the model for all modern democracies.

But why did we need a Bill of Rights, protecting the citizens from government violence?

To answer that question, let us cross the channel to England, and look at the work of John Locke.[50]

---

[49] Baron de Montesquieu, *The Spirit of the Laws*, NY, Penguin, 1952.

[50] John Locke, *The First Treatise on Civil Government*, Oxford, Oxford University Press, 1952.

13.14   John Locke on the Need to Limit the Power of the State, and to Prevent the Return of the Divine Kingship

Locke wrote during the period in England when Cromwell's parliamentary democracy had been replaced with an oligarchic parliament (1650–1680), and, where the heirs to the British throne were attempting to reestablish the divine Kingship.

The English Kings believed in their divine right to rule – Charles I had refused Cromwell's request that he become a limited monarch – faced with the choice of death or a power limitation, he chose death!

With Charles I beheaded, heirs kept attempting to restore *absolute monarchy*.

Locke saw the danger, and in his *First Treatise on Civil Government*[51] described how, once a King gains absolute power, he becomes a tyrant (dictator). He will abuse his subjects, enslave his subjects, violate his subjects. History, Locke tells us, demonstrates all too graphically the hideous acts committed by Kings who gain absolute power.

The example Herodotus gives us illustrates Locke's point.

The Persian King, Xerxes, while recruiting his massive army to invade Greece and avenge the loss at Marathon, announces that all the young men beyond a certain age had to be enrolled in the army. A man begged him to allow his youngest son to stay home to care for him in his old age. His three older sons, he said, had enrolled.

Xerxes told him to bring his whole family the next day and he would decide. The man came with his four sons and his wife. Xerxes ordered his guards to grab the youngest son and kill him on the spot. Then he ordered them to grab the wife – her breasts were cut off and her nose was cut off, but she was allowed to live. Xerxes told the man – who was now weeping and on his knees – when the King orders *all* sons for army, he means all sons. No one disobeyed Xerxes after that.[52]

In the Bible, Samuel warns the Jewish Elders that if they choose to have a King – Saul – the Kings will enslave them, use their daughters, get their sons killed in senseless wars. But, fearing the Philistines, the elders institutionalized a Kingship. Then, the Bible tells us in the Book of Prophets, that the Kings were worse than even Samuel thought they could be.[53]

Locke said that history tells us that Kings will become violent tyrants more often than not. For, as Lord Acton[54] would put it, "power corrupts, absolute power corrupts absolutely."

So, for Locke, the separation of powers was not enough. Specific measures had to be implemented to limit the power of the state, and the power of the executive especially. Regular elections of the parliament could constrain that bod's power.

---

[51] *Ibid.*

[52] Herodotus, *The Histories*, NY Penguin Classics, 1949. (The section on Xerxes and his army.)

[53] *The Bible, Book of Judges*, Samuel; also Isaiah, Book of Prophets. (Both Samuel and Isaiah condemn Kingship as despotic and immoral.)

[54] Lord Acton, a German, visiting England, famously stated, "power corrupts, absolutely."

For, they ruled with the *consent* of the people, and that consent could be withdrawn by electing new members to parliament, if the people disapproved of the old.

If the executive were a prime minister, he would be power limited through election as with the other members of Parliament. However, if the executive was separately elected, as with a Presidency, then that office, itself, had to have term limits on its tenure, and it had to be checked by the legislature and the courts.

As for the term limits on the presidency, these had to be written into law in the Constitution. The number of years and the number of terms in office could vary, but there had to be limits – although regularly called elections could be limit enough, in the sense that the people could vote the president out on any given election day.

The Founding Fathers of the American Constitution were so worried about state power and the repression of the people, that after they had written the Constitution – based on Montesquieu's checks and balances and separations of power within the state – they decided that Locke's warning about the power of the state and the tendencies of kings and tyrants to use that power to repress and harm the people, had to be addressed.

Under Madison's leadership, they wrote up the now famous Bill of Rights, an added these Ten Amendments to the Constitution.

They stated unequivocally that the people are empowered with *inalienable rights*: the right to free speech, free press, freedom of assembly, a fair and speedy trial, and more (we have already discussed the Second Amendment on the right to bear arms).

The citizens' rights in the Bill of Rights, could not be taken away or compromised by the government. The state and the executive could not use the monopoly of violence at their disposal to violate the rights guaranteed by the Bill of Rights, or repress the people.

The army, the police, and the courts are controlled by the chief executive of the state, and the power inherent in the state, as an institution, must be explicitly limited, or, state violence will override democratic, lawful, procedures.

With the institutionalization of the Bill of Rights, and the explicit limitations of power written into modern constitutions, we add a new set of processes to the Democratic processes of elections, discussion of policies, and majority voting on policies. *Power limitations* aimed at the state and the executive branch of government, are *something new* that did not exist in ancient Greek face-to-face democracy. The state was not yet fully institutionalized in ancient Greece, wherein official government positions were filled by "lot" and were *term limited*.

Once the modern state emerged, with its enormous military and police power potential, Lockean limits had to be institutionalized alongside democratic representation and regular elections to Parliament.

Political scientists refer to this combination as "liberal" democracy, because the limitation of the power of the state is specifically articulated in the modern constitutions, along with the lawful procedures for democratic elections to a representative legislative body. A Bill of Rights is almost always attached to modern democratic constitutions in most nations-states, and the limitation of the power of the executive is also explicitly articulated as embodied in term limits, regular elections, and the rights of the citizens that an executive cannot violate.

Liberal democracy works in the well-established nation-states of the modern world. In developing nations liberal democracy takes time to become institutionalized. There is a worrisome trend that has occurred in recent years that could override the balance of liberal democracy. Political scientists have been calling it, "illiberal" democracy.

Putin in Russia, Erdoğan in Turkey, Orbán in Hungary, Duterte in the Philippines, and others, have been using the powers of the state to do violence, to their citizens, and to violate the rights of their citizens.

Let us look at this disheartening trend.

13.15   Illiberal Democracy: A Twenty-First Century Trend

This new form of despotism has been dubbed "illiberal democracy" by political scientists. "Democracy," because the outward trappings of democracy are retained – there are elections, opposition parties, opposition leaders, oppositional journalists, and, the Constitutions are not changed radically. "Illiberal," because the democratically elected leader uses the power of the state – the military and the police – against any leader, any party, and journalist, who criticizes the regime or tries to defeat it electorally.

Putin, Erdoğan, Orbán, Duterte, others, have all used the violence inherent in the state to stifle opposition, and terrorize the population.

13.16   Russia

Russia had only had true democracy for a short moment in its history. Often centuries of tyrannical Czars and an era of Stalinist totalitarianism – a totalitarianism so violent and murderous that only Hitler's Nazism was worse – Russia had its moment of freedom and democracy with Gorbachev and Yeltsin.

When Putin was elected – and he was elected fairly – he secretly had his KGB friends take control of the economy. In a flash, the emerging capitalist economy, which should have been based on *contract law*, was subverted, and refashioned into a mafia-style economy, based on violence and threats – under the control of Putin's KGB friends. These economic managers came to be called "oligarchs." They are *not* actually oligarchs, however, because oligarchy means "rule by the rich." These KGB economic managers rule through the violent power of the state. KGB-style secret police threaten, frighten, and murder any banker or businessman who does not do what they want.

So Putin's despotism *is not undergirded by advanced capitalism*. The Russian polity is undergirded by an oil and natural gas export economy, run by KGB gangsters (who are called oligarchs).

Putin has used the army to: invade Georgia – he took a section of that country and made it part of Russia; invade Chechnya and prevent its independence; invade Crimea and take it away from the Ukraine; and invading the Ukraine and taking a section away and incorporating it into Russia.

The Russian people love Putin's aggressive foreign policy. They vote for him on "nationalist" grounds.

In terms of keeping the outward trappings of democracy, Putin does hold regular elections. If he did not win, he probably would have rigged the results. But, he does win.

Putin left the Constitution intact – and it is a good Constitution – but like all these new illiberal leaders, he got around the term limits. All these new despots attempt to rule for life, and utilize their control over state power to terrorize their citizens into compliance. The checks and balance and power limitations built into the constitutional systems are overridden.

If the military and the police remain lawfully committed to constitutional law and the separation of powers, then the parliamentary opposition could have such a despotic leader arrested, and, they could restore true democracy. If, however, the despotic leader gains the loyalty of the military and police, then democracy cannot function.

The Russian people do understand democracy. They understand elections, and free speech, and freedom of the press. But, they also have a cultural tradition of deeply despotic state power.

Thus, the emerging democracy was hijacked by the despots left over from the communist-Stalinist state.

The only hopeful condition in Russia is that the democratic institutions have been left in place. There are elections, Parliament does meet – though debate is inhibited – newspapers do print some oppositional articles, there are demonstrations in Moscow, St. Petersburg, and other large cities, demanding more democracy. The Russian economy, however, must become a lawful capitalist economy, in the hands of businessmen, not KGB gangsters.

Right now, Putin is a violent dictator, and the so-called oligarchs dominate the economy. Putin will remain in power for the foreseeable future. When he dies – at least the structure of democratic government remains intact. But one can see that without the limitations of the power of the state, democracy cannot function. Words are repressed by violence, and rational lawful actions are overwhelmed by bestial violence.

13.17   Turkey

Erdoğan in Turkey has done something similar to Putin. As in Russia, the democratic constitution and electoral process are still intact. Elections are held, and, so far Erdoğan does win – but by razor thin margins.

The democratic system in Turkey was first institutionalized under Kemal "Atatürk." Kemal grew up in Thessaloniki, in Turkish-dominated Greece. He admired the Greeks for their classical "golden age." And, he admired the Western democracies. After a bitter war with the Greeks – wherein both sides were betrayed by the British – Turkey became an independent nation.

Atatürk established a democratic lawful republic. But, he understood that the Turks in the countryside knew only the military traditions of the Ottomans and the despotic rule of the Sultans. He therefore created a modern military and empowered them to oversee the civilian democratic government – with its new capital at Ankara, rather than Istanbul.

The military intervened over and over again in Turkey's internal affairs. And it was only in the 1980s that the civilian democratic government gained enough legitimacy to keep the military at bay.

The Turkish democracy was going along well, until the Muslim nationalist movements – the *Islamicist Radical Muslim Movement* — destabilized it. Erdoğan was elected as the President of the Islamicist Party. Atatürk wisely sought to keep religion and politics separate, but Erdoğan fused them.

The better educated Turks of Istanbul, Izmir, and the Aegean Sea resort areas voted for secular parties. But, the less educated workers and farmers of Central Turkey outnumbered them such that Erdoğan and his Islamic Party won election after election.

We do not know exactly which groups were behind it, but a military coup was attempted. Erdoğan was almost overthrown. However, much of the military remained loyal to him.

The coup failed. Now Erdoğan has arrested all the coup leaders amongst the military, and, unfortunately he used the coup as an excuse to arrest *hundreds* of journalists, school teachers, and government officials whom he believed opposed him.

Erdoğan blamed the coup on a Muslim priest, living in exile in the USA, who had led a movement against him. This movement emphasized Islam, but as separate from politics. Whether this influential group was involved with the coup is not known at this time.

What is known, is that Erdoğan has set himself up as a dictator who uses the power of the state to jail and repress his critics.

It is a case of "illiberal" democracy, because Erdoğan holds elections, and may allow journalists to write again and free speech to return. Why? Because Turkey is part of the NATO alliance, and Turkey still wants – someday – to be accepted into the EU.

From Atatürk to Erdoğan Turkish leaders have looked to Europe for leadership. The Turkish economy is a real, growing capitalist economy. Businesses – small and giant – are regulated by Contract Law. As the economy grows, more Turks become educated and prosperous. The Turkish economy is integrated into global capitalism.

Yet, the Turks are grounded in their cultural traditions of military violence and centralized despotism. So, will Erdoğan's illiberal democracy evolve back to true democracy? There is a chance that it will. Erdoğan's last election was so close that he knows that he is *not popular* (the way Putin is). He has to be careful to make concessions to the middle classes in Istanbul and Izmir.

On the other side, the Islamic party it still radical and anti-democratic, and the Russians are gaining influence in Turkey.

13.18 Hungary and the Philippines

Here are two more examples of nations that have functioning democratic systems wherein a popular elected leader has been using the power of the state against the lawfully protected rights of the people.

Orbán in Hungary has used the immigration issue to rouse popular support for his blocking of all middle eastern immigration. He ginned up the Hungarian nationalism to near fascist levels, presently closing down an American-oriented university founded by George Soros, simply because it was not Hungarian and Soros was a Jew, not a Magyar.

Hungary is now an illiberal democracy. Will the immigration issue die down? Will the Hungarians restrain Orbán? Or, will he extend his dictatorial repression? We do not yet know, but, Hungary is part of the EU, and Hungary needs the EU economically. There is European pressure against Hungarian fascistic tendencies. Democracy may make a comeback in Hungary – but Orbán is popular, and like Putin, he will win elections and override democratic safeguards for the near future.

The Philippines, long in the Spanish mold as a colony, moved towards democracy after the Spanish-American War, when the USA took charge.

The Philippine democracy has been plagued with dictatorial takeovers and Spanish-style government corruption. However, the democracy has been running smoothly and lawfully for the last 20 years. The crisis that tipped the Philippines towards illiberal democracy has been the drug problem. Heroin, opioid, and other addictions had reached crisis levels. Therefore, the newly elected president Duterte, began utilizing state power to eradicate this problem. He literally ordered the army and police to *kill* the addicts and the drug dealers. Thousands have been killed!

Democratic and lawful government cannot be maintained if state power is unleashed on such a massive level – with no court trials, no pleas of innocence, no protections for citizens caught up in the government's net. Yet the Filipinos have supported Duterte, and he remains popular. Inevitably, he has extended his use of state violence against other groups – suspected terrorists, Islamicists, and more.

Will the Philippines move back towards lawful protections of its citizens? We cannot yet tell.

13.19   Conclusions on Illiberal Democracy

The fear is that more modern democracies will be overridden by elected leaders who are able to gain enough legitimacy to push the country in a despotic direction.

The hope is that, because the democratic institutions remain intact – the elections, the constitutions of laws and rights – when the charismatic despotic leader dies or is pushed out of power, the democratic apparatus will be revitalized. For, it is in place. The citizens see themselves as citizens – they participate in elections – they do gather and protest – they do speak out – they do not like it when journalists and opposition leaders are jailed and murdered.

So there is the hope, that after a crisis situation such as mass immigration eases up, and when the capitalist economy becomes sufficiently developed, and when an educated middle-class becomes dominant, then *liberal* democracy will be reinstitutionalized – with all the real power limitations and checks and balances functioning again.

One last comment.

President Trump is the first American President to actively oppose the press and to call for violent actions against demonstrators, and to assert the power of the Presidency beyond its constitutional limits.

This is not only bad for America, it is bad for the world. Numerous leaders in developing nations have been embolden to use state powers against their people by listening to Trump's rhetoric – the leaders of Nigeria and the Philippines have both quoted Trump to justify their actions. So, too, the Saudi Prince after the murder of a journalist.

America's democracy will eventually check Trump's power. The House of Representatives and the Special Counsel (Mueller) will prevent Trump from expanding his Executive Power. They must succeed if America's democracy is to be fully maintained. They will succeed when a new President is elected. That new President – whether democrat or republican – will have to restore the institution to its proper place, and lead the world, once again, in the democratic direction that America has always stood for.

Even President Reagan, a staunch conservative, gloried in American democracy, and held us out as a model for the world. This nation will return to its leadership role in the world democratic movement. But, the future of democracy is always in jeopardy, and without American leadership the world tilts towards despotism.

Part III
The Future of Democracy

Chapter 14
The Hope for Democracy in the Near Future

The hope for democracy is embodied in four global trends which push human beings towards *rational behavior in the political sphere*. They are: global high technology capitalism; global scientific cooperation; constitutional law and legal-rational authority; and the expansion of the middle class in many nations of the world.

I have discussed all of these factors, but let us focus on the factors in the modern context to make their link with democracy clear.

14.1   Global Capitalism, Law and Science

First, we must remind ourselves that world capitalism failed to prevent WWI and II. American, European and Japanese industrial-capitalism were interconnected—even though they were competitive. This did not prevent the wars, nor did it lead to democracy in Germany or Japan.

However, global industrial capitalism today is much more interconnected than it was back then. As Tom Friedman has described in his book, *The World is Flat,*[1] any given product is made with so many parts from different countries that it is difficult to tell where it is made. For instance, my bicycle has a frame designed and invented in the United States, but it is produced in Taiwan. The gears were invented and produced in Japan, the seat and seat post are made in Italy, the handlebars are made in France, the wheels are made in the US, and the tires were designed and produced in Germany. The bicycle is sold by an American company—Trek—but, where is it made?

Global capitalism, though it does not prevent wars, *does come with rules that are supportive of democracy.*

---

[1] Thomas Friedman, *The Earth is Flat*, Farrar, Strans, Giroux, N.Y. 2005.

© Springer Nature Switzerland AG 2019
R. M. Glassman, *The Future of Democracy*,
https://doi.org/10.1007/978-3-030-16111-8_14

That is, contract law, and patent law are at its core, as is the encouragement of science and its application to the production process and the products themselves.

Let us look at *contract law* first.

If you want to do business, you must abide by the law. If you refuse, as in Russia under Putin and his clique, the world's companies will not do business with you. Further, if you abide by contract law—the foundation for all business transactions since the days of Sumer, Phoenicia and Greece—and do business without violence and according to the contracted legally specified details, the world's companies will do business with you.

But, the law extends further. Contract law also delineates patent laws and copyright laws.

If you violate these laws, the world's business corporations will put pressure on your operation to comply—this is occurring in China today, where contract law is honored, but copyrights have been violated. Since the Chinese capitalist economy has been so successful, the Chinese businesses have been slowly complying with copyright and patent laws. Where they have not complied, companies have confiscated their products and ruined their profits. Therefore, the Chinese have increasingly been complying with all the details of contract law.

Why is this good for democracy? Because contract law, as secular business law, sets a framework in the economic sphere that can transcend into the political sphere. When contract law is firmly established, *constitution law* becomes easily understandable. And, constitutional law sets guidelines for governmental action, and, sets limits on governmental power.

Further, the limits on government power are eventually reinforced with the protection of individual rights in a "bill of rights." So, interconnected, global industrial-capitalism—especially in its new high technology iteration—does encourage lawful business behavior. And, this lawful business behavior can affect the political process in a democratic direction. Thus, an Apple I-phone, designed in California, assembled in China, with parts from Japan and Korea, could not come to the global market without carefully detailed legal contracts, with each subsidiary firm in each country. Since the people in every nation of the world want a "smart phone," the legal business contracts are honored. The global, high technology industrial-capitalist corporations are multi-national, and, *they follow the law*. If they break the law, they are prosecuted.

Along with the institutionalization of contract law, global *capitalism encourages* the pursuit of *science* and, the rapid *application of new scientific developments* to the production process and its products. In other words, both pure science and engineering technology are encouraged by industrial-capitalism.

The scientific method and scientific theorizing emerged from ancient Greece—from Thales to Pythagoras to Democritus. However, clever inventions and remarkable technology characterized the Great civilization, such as Egypt, Mesopotamia, China, and India.

The Greeks learned to apply their technology to military improvements, or architecture—so too the Romans. But, once the industrial system was invented, the technology was directed towards the improvement of machine-factory production, and to the products themselves.[2]

Because the industrial revolution was capitalist in its origins in England, Scotland, and the Low countries,[3] the profit motive drove the factory owners to try to out produce and out invent their competitors.[4]

Thus, it was that industrial-capitalism fostered the growth of science—which had already emerged from the Renaissance's rediscovery of Greek and Roman science—and applied every new scientific advance to the technology of machine-factory production, and to new high technology products, such as trains, cars, and mass-produced clothing.[5]

Why is this important for us in a treatise on democracy? Because modern industrial-capitalism, in its obsession to invent and produce new products that will sell to the global market, funds scientific "think tanks" and institutes for technological development.

Why is this good for democracy? Because it fosters the "rational-scientific world-view." When people become rational-minded, they tend to view politics in a rational way. That is, when a person with the rational scientific world-view looks up at the sky, they see galaxies of stars, supernovas, comets, planets, and the possibility to travel to Mars. This same person then observes the political system—is it rational and functional, or is it despotic, using repressive violence, where enforcement of the law would be enough to create "order".

Let us look more closely at the effect of the rational-scientific world-view on politics.

14.2 Global Science and the Spread of the Rational-Scientific World-View

In the era of fascism, Nazism and Communism, science had become international. Incredible scientific discoveries were made, and they did not generate a move towards democracy.

Today, however, there are many more cross-national projects going on. Medical research, space research, and atomic research have become truly international. Switzerland houses scientists from all over the world at their particle reactor project. And, the space program has Russians and Americans cooperating closely and the International Space Station program. Scientists and astronauts from the E.U., Japan, the U.K. and other nations are also deeply involved. China has its own competing

---

[2] Marx, *Das Capital.*

[3] Weber, *The Protestant Ethic and the Spirit of Capitalism.*

[4] Marx, *Das Capital.*

[5] Jeremy Bentham, *Collected Works.*

space program, but it is possible that China will eventually join in the quest to put people on Mars.

Cancer research, as another example, has become truly international, with Korean and Chinese researchers cooperating in the world-wide attempt to find a cure for cancer.

The hope here is that as science becomes an integral part of the educational curriculum world-wide, that it will provide two processes: first, a similarity in education which any student in any university in any nation can gain, such that he or she can communicate with any other student anywhere in the world.

As an example, a relative of my wife studied earthquakes in Greece, his home country, then went to Italy for a doctorate in seismology, and then to the United States for a post-doctorate. He can go anywhere in the world with this shared scientific expertise—as long as he learns the language—and he speaks many languages (and the journal articles are translated into many languages). And English has become the international language of science.

Second, the students of the world—and the new middle classes in general—view the world through the lens of the rational-scientific world-view. When a disease spreads, they look to a vaccine or antibiotic to cure it. There is a growing world population that shares this rational-scientific orientation to the world.

Why is this good for democracy? Because, as mentioned, rational thinking about the world and the universe, can lead to rational thinking about political policies and political systems. The spreading idea that being educated enough gains the new middle class the right to, at least, electoral participation in the political process, is enhanced by this rational world-view.

In another vein, and this could be a wonderful development, two scientific projects are lending some sense of unity to the world: one, the attempt to cure world diseases has gained universal approval, and the sciences connected to this project have become truly globally intertwined. A vaccine—like the flu vaccine—developed in one country, is quickly adopted in others. And, transnational health organizations facilitate, cooperate and monitor this scientific endeavor. Scientific cooperation has stamped out diseases like polio and measles that used to frighten the children of the world.

Two, the space program has already generated the International Space Station, where astronauts from all nations gather. And, once we humans are out in space, the awesomeness of the vastness of space—and the tiny trivialness of the "Big Blue Marble" that is Earth—are overwhelming.

So, there could be star wars as bad as our earth wars. But, it is not likely, given the difficulty of survival in space and the fragility of human life in that inhospitable environment. Space travel will demand total cooperation between the nations on Earth, with all our scientific acumen pooled.

`Now, the rational-scientific world-view may not lead to peace—China's competitiveness stands as a warning. But, it could lead to global cooperation in the near future.

Importantly, as we have emphasized, with a rational-scientific world-view, the new middle classes may see electoral participation as something they are equipped for. And with the rational-scientific world-view, rational, secular constitutional law becomes consistent with the world-orientation of the new middle classes.

Thus, rational-legal authority with electoral participation becomes the preferred set of political processes. Ruthless, dictatorial, repressive power seems *unnecessary* and *irrational*.

It must be mentioned before we proceed that science—in itself—embodies no moral or ethical values. It is a rational way of viewing the world but makes no moral judgments. There is no morality in the universe—stars explode, and others are formed out of the gases left behind. However, there is morality and ethics where humans are concerned—curing diseases is "good", poisoning people with the same drug is "bad".

We shall discuss *"humanistic ethics"* separately. Here, we wish to focus on the rational aspect of science alone.

14.3   Legal-Rational Authority

Max Weber developed the category, "legal-rational authority" as part of his typology of "legitimate domination."[6] "Traditional authority," he described as Kingship, with its bureaucratic state officials. Weber's third category of legitimate dominations, is "charismatic" authority, wherein an individual leader gains legitimacy through his or her "gift of grace," or social-psychological ability to instill in the charismatized populations a feeling of well-being that excites them to lend legitimacy to his or her rule.[7]

We will come back to charismatic authority—which arises during periods of rapid social change or serious crises—but here I wish to discuss legal-rational authority and its link to democracy.

Legal-rational authority emerged in ancient Greece, and I have already presented Aristotle's formulation of *government by law*. It is worth quoting Aristotle again: "when the law rules, God and reason rule: when a man rules we add the character of the beast."[8] He also said, and I shall paraphrase, "when men are constrained by the rule of law, they are the best of creatures; when they act above the law, they are the worst.[9]

Aristotle also predicted that once legal-rational authority is established, people no longer believe in divine Kings—traditional authority in Weber's typology, declines and disappears.

"Kingship has now gone out of fashion; and any government of that type which emerges today is a personal government or tyranny. Kingship is a government by consent with sovereign authority in matters of major importance—and *such a*

---

[6] Weber, *Economy & Society* (Legitimate domination).

[7] Glassman & Swatos, *Charisma, History and Social Structure*.

[8] Aristotle, *Politics* (on law) p 175–182.

[9] Ibid.

government is now an anachronism—For, equality is generally diffused, and there is nobody outstanding enough for the grandeur and the dignity of the office of *King*. *There is thus no basis of consent for such a form of government*, and when it is imposed by fraud or force, it is instantly regarded as a form of tyranny…

"Kings cease to be kings, when their subjects cease to be willing subjects, though tyrants can continue to be tyrants, whether their subjects are willing or not."[10]

Once the representative parliamentary state—with a civil service, meritocratic bureaucracy, and a constitution of laws limiting the power of the state and delineating a Bill of Rights for the citizens—becomes institutionalized, monarchy is no longer necessary to unify and maintain order in large-scale states.

And though tyranny—dictatorship—can arise and maintain its control through force, violence, and terror, such repressive military regimes become unnecessary where legal-rational authority is accepted.

Nobody from South Korea runs away to the North, while North Koreans—frightened, terrorized, and risking their lives, defect to the South (by way of the Chinese border) in a continuous stream.

However, where the majority of a given population are *not* university educated, and are linked into a religious or secular ideology, or a nationalist patriotic ideology, then legal-rational authority will not be accepted. In such cases, the people often reject secular constitutional law and legitimate ideologically driven despotic form of domination.

We saw this in Egypt, with the Muslim Brotherhood, and now—partially—in Turkey, with Erdogan gaining 51% of the vote to increase his powers to a dictatorial level and violate Ataturk's constitution. Erdogan got his votes from the less educated Muslims of the interior of Turkey. The educated Turks voted to retain the legal-rational constitutional limits on his powers.

The recent riots in Iran, emanating from the educated middle class in the cities, shows a similar pattern. The educated Persians want an end to the authoritarian theocracy of the Ayatollahs and the establishment of a legal-democratic system of government. They also want an expanded industrial-capitalist economy producing consumer goods, fashion, and high-tech products, while the Islamic theocracy is supported by the less educated working class and farmers in Iran. As long as the theocratic tyrants can count on the support of the working class, who make up the Iranian Guard militias, they can retain power. But, the pressure for legal-rational authority and electoral democracy is increasing in Iran, as the middle class increases in its percentage of the population.

These cases illustrate my point: the hope for democracy comes from the educated new middle classes—wherever they emerge—whether in Kenya, Indonesia, or South Korea—because these educated middle classes tend to be rational-minded.

---

[10] Ibid (on Kings & tyrants, p 241).

As a greater proportion of the population in each country gains a secular, rational-scientific education, the possibilities for democracy increase.

Let me add that I do not mean to denigrate religion as purely irrational and dangerously ideological—"the opiate of the people," as Marx called it. No, religion has a spiritual and moral-ethical role to play in society, so that sociopathic behavior does not become normative, and, Kierkegaardian despair does not overwhelm modern individuals and drive them towards depression, drugs and even suicide.

Where religion is separated from the state, as designated in the American Constitution, it can play an essential role in our moral-ethical- and spiritual quest for "meaning" and morality.

All the world's religions attempt to explain our life, our depth, our existence in the universe, and our moral-ethical standards of behavior. None of this is irrational. And, there has been a global revival of world religions in its spiritual and ethical form.

It is when religion is used to prevent a people from becoming educated, or religion is used to resist scientifically verified theories, that it is problematic. Finally, where religion is used to support and legitimate an authoritarian regime, it becomes irrational.

Legal-rational authority, with its constitutional law, allows for all religious beliefs to flourish—but keeps them out of the political realm.

All across the world, the religious revival has led fanatical religionists to try to violate the separation of religion from politics. Fundamentalist Christians in the USA have crossed the line, fanatical Hindus are trying to cross the line in India, and, of course, Islamist Muslims in the Middle East, Turkey, Indonesia and other nations, have crossed the line violently.

This world religious revival will be moderated as the world's populations absorb the rational-scientific world-view. Once this occurs, then the religious of the world will return to their spiritual and moral roles. These latter are rational, and do not conflict with science, because science is rational, but morally neutral.

To return to our mainline of reasoning, where the majority of the population gains enough education to absorb the rational-scientific world-view, legal-rational authority emerges. And, where legal-rational authority emerges, democracy replaces monarchy. Monarchies disappear where people become too rational to accept divine, or "royal" descent. But as Aristotle warned, tyrants will try to rule through force and violence anywhere they can gain control.

The cases of Turkey and Iran bring us to our next index of hope for modern democracy. In both these nations, the well-educated middle classes have demanded democracy and the rule of law. They are not yet a majority in either country, but they are expanding.

14.4   The Majority Middle Class as a Growing Global Phenomenon

There is a global middle class emerging, and, it is truly global in that the young people are becoming more alike, through university education and the mass media of entertainment.[11]

Not only do the students study many of the same subjects in the universities of the USA, the UK, the EU, Japan, Korea, India and China, but they also watch YouTube and stream videos, and go to the movies and watch television shows. Videos go "viral" from Korea to Canada, and the millennials respond to the same set of humorous or serious images.

In the opposite direction, increased nationalism and ethnic "tribalism" has accompanied the homogenization process. So, people cling to their ethnic identity precisely because it is being submerged in the new millennial middle class global identity.

The globalization of identity is wonderful in that students and scholars from all over the world can communicate with each other in a shared world culture. But, is this world culture democratic?

We have suggested—hopefully—that the inculation of the rational-scientific world-view, and the spread of capitalist contract law, have created a cultural milieu in which *rational-legal authority* can thrive, and in which *electoral participation becomes desired.*

The educated, prosperous middle class growing in any nations of the world has exhibited democratic proclivities. The problem is that in many developing nations, the middle class is not yet large enough.

Now, we have emphasized that *there is no mathematical formula for determining when a middle class is in the majority.* And, we have described how in differing cultural milieus, the influence of the middle class can be differently absorbed.

Thus, in India, though the middle class is *not* in the majority, it is very large, well-educated, and influenced by centuries of British legal-democratic tradition. It has also been pointed out that, in India, the masses of poor exist in the countryside, away from the centers of power, and tend towards passivity, because of millennia of Hindu caste denigration. So, the Indian middle class dominates the parliament and rules lawfully, though not very proactively.

In China, the middle class is growing rapidly, and becoming very rational-minded in its orientation. They would create a Hong Kong style legal-democratic system of government, but they cannot, because the authoritarian government in China draws from the billion-plus masses of poor and working class, recruiting them and training them as police and army forces.

The Chinese regime, can and does, use these police and military forces to repress any attempt at democratization. However, as the industrial-capitalist economy grows—and it is growing at a record rate—the regime has allowed more artistic

---

[11] Glassman, *The New Middle Class and Democracy in Global Perspective*, N.Y. MacMillan, 1996.

expression—as long as it is not anti-government—and it has encouraged the expansion of science in all its aspects.

Now, we know from Nazi Germany that science in itself does not create a democratic political culture. And, China has had millennia of Confucian political culture, based on the "benevolence"[12] of a supreme emperor and his wise, well-educated officials.[13] The Xi regime thinks of itself as "benevolent", and seeks to retain total power. *Maintaining order,* and *modernizing the economy* and infrastructure, are its goals. Democracy and legal authority are anathema to its goals, and they are sharply repressed.

So, where is the hope?

There is no hope until the next generation of communist party leaders takes control. If that generation is well-educated and rational-minded, then, like Gorbachev they might want a liberalization of the political system.

However, the Chinese leaders of today (2018) saw what happened when the Soviet Union broke up. They don't want Tibet or other ethnically different provinces to split off: These provinces contain valuable national resources that the Chinese now control and utilize for their expanding capitalist economy.

Nonetheless, the next generation of leaders may be different because of the indelible spread of "Western" style university education, which is becoming the norm for the new middle class in China. This new middle class is copying the fashion styles, consumer styles, and general lifestyle of its counterparts in America, Europe and Japan. The middle class in China is becoming more and more integrated into the intellectual, scientific, social and media world of the global economy. They know and love Confucius, but they want Gucci, Chanel, Cadillac, and Apple—look at the success of Ali Baba, the Chinese versions of Amazon. The Chinese new middle class is on an explosive buying spree. And, their children feel "entitled"—entitled to a modern career, a high-tech consumer lifestyle, and…electoral participations?

The future leaders of China *may* be drawn from this rapidly expanding, prosperous, well-educated middle class. If they are, Hong Kong, with its dynamic capitalist economy, excellent social welfare programs for the poor, and legal-democratic government could become the model for China—in the long run—but, the long run may be far away in the future.

If we look around the world, the developing nations have small middle classes. However, even in countries like Kenya and Nigeria, both of which had a smidgen of British legal-democratic tradition and education, democratic governance has been attempted.

Tribalism in these countries is still strong—as it was in Yugoslavia—and tribalism is hard to contain within a democratic framework. *Tribes are not political parties,* they are separate "nations" who usually want self-determination.

The hope is that university education and the rational-scientific world-view will override tribalism and ethnic divisions. It is a weak hope, but a hope nonetheless.

---

[12] Confucius, *Analects.*

[13] Weber, *The Religion of China.*

Obviously, many of the developing nations have a long way to go before an educated, prosperous, majority middle class can militate for, and stabilize, a legal-democratic political system.

14.5   The Rich and the Poor Can Destabilize Democracy

The rich, emerging with the global high tech industrial-capitalist economy, can help stabilize democracy by re-investing in their nations capitalist economy. When they do this, the economy may grow, and with its growth, expand the middle class and increase its prosperity.

In many instances around the world however, the rich have acted selfishly, aggrandizing themselves with a grandiose lifestyle, and worse, stashing their money in secret Swiss bank accounts or offshore tax havens, like The Cayman Islands, Cyprus and Panama.

When the rich pull their money out of their national economy, it obviously is not being invested in the growth of that economy. The attempt to avoid taxes and use the skimmed money for an "aristocratic" lifestyle, is a world-wide problem.

In order for a capitalist economy to expand and provide the base for a majority middle class, national and global policies to encourage the rich to reinvest their wealth must be established.

First, tax shelters, such as those of the Cayman Islands and Panama, must be made illegal. And longtime banking shelters, such as that of Switzerland, must be forced to open their books. The Swiss have been reluctantly cooperating with the EU and the USA to make their accounts open to scrutiny, but more pressure must be brought on them.

The rich, in the burgeoning global capitalist economy, will continue to try to find ways to avoid paying their fair share of taxes. So, this will be a continuing struggle. The progressive taxation of the E.U. is currently the best model for global capitalism, in terms of taxation of the individual rich. Corporate taxation is different, and can be kept lower *if, if*, the corporations use their lower tax status to reinvest in the growth of their corporation and their national economy.

Since most rich individuals keep their wealth in stocks and bonds, the taxation rate of this financial income should be set at no lower than 25%. Otherwise, the rich will not pay their fair share of the progressive income tax system.[14]

Further, as suggested, a Financial Transaction Tax—FTT—a *miniscule tax on every financial transaction*—would bring in billions of dollars in tax revenue without hurting the rich or the upper middle class at all—they would barely notice this tiny tax on their computer trading and where it has been established, it has not discouraged trading in any way.

---

[14] Gerald Scorce, (Raise the rate of taxation on stock market income) in the Los Angeles Times, 2017.

The billions in revenue that would be generated by an FTT could be utilized to fund colleges and universities to make them free—as in the E.U.—and to support the healthcare system, which has become incredibly expensive due to the marvelous new technologies and pharmaceuticals utilized to save people's lives.[15]

Utilizing the FTT to support free universities and healthcare could reduce the burden on the middle class in every high tech industrial-capitalist nation. In this way, it would strengthen the idle class, allowing for its increased prosperity and, expanding the middle class through the free tuition program for the young people. The new university graduates, entering the high-tech industries, will expand the numbers of the middle class wherever such an economy is growing.

So, the rich in all the nations must be encouraged, as Aristotle put it, by "wise legislation", to contribute their wealth to the civic good.[16] In most cases, the new rich are so wealthy that progressive taxation and the FTT still allows them enough wealth for a fabulous lifestyle. Where the rich hide their wealth in offshore tax shelters and do not invest it in economic growth, they not only stunt the growth of their nations' economies, but they tend to live such a lavish lifestyle as to cause jealousy and rage in their lower classes. Such extremes of wealth and poverty, of course, lead to the destabilization of democracy—or the prevention of the establishment of democracy.

14.5.1   The Poor

The existence of a vast population of uneducated poor makes the establishment and stabilization of democracy very difficult indeed. As discussed, there are countries like India, where the poor are passive—in the countryside, and even in the city-slums—because of centuries of the Hindu caste system—and they are passive because the rate of upward mobility into the middle class is increasing. In most countries, masses of poor, uneducated people create a situation of volatility for democracy.

Again, however, I must point out that any generalizations made about human society, must be tempered by the specific social and cultural conditions in the country in question.

Nonetheless, a nation made up of a majority poor will have difficulty in establishing and maintaining democracy.

The examples of Venezuela and Hong Kong show two differing programs for including the poor in the political system. I will argue that Hong Kong's system is the better way.

In Hong Kong, with the withdrawal of the British, a legal-democratic government was established by a large, well-educated Chinese middle class. Hundreds of

---

[15] Ronald M. Glassman and Gerald Scorce, "The Financial Transaction Tax and Free College Tuition," Los Angeles Times, 2017.

[16] Aristotle, *Politics* (wise tax legislation concerning the rich).

thousands of poor Chinese from the mainland were drawn to Hong Kong during the period of transition away from Britain. The Hong Kong Chinese consciously crafted a set of programs designed to improve the lifestyle of the poor, and, to integrate them into the industrial-capitalist economy that was rapidly emerging.

The Hong Kong Chinese were blessed by the fact that the mainland Chinese allowed them to establish a capitalist style industrial factory economy in the mainland territories near Hong Kong. These "new territories" were owned by China but managed by the Hong Kong businessmen and bankers. Thousands of the new poor were, thus, easily employed in these New Territory factories.

But, the workers could have been left in slums and hovels—as they were in England at the time of the industrial revolution there. Hong Kong could have become "Dickensesque." However, the Hong Kong Chinese had read Dickens, and they also knew that the Beijing communists were looking to take control. So, to show Beijing and London that they could create a new high tech industrial capitalist economy without engendering hideous poverty and wretched slums, they made sure that the masses of poor received decent housing and that their children were educated in good schools.

The program worked. The children of the poor factory workers have begun to be upwardly mobile into the middle class. And, as the middle class expanded, became well-educated and prosperous, their identification with constitutional law and electoral democracy became ever stronger.

The Beijing government has taken control of Hong Kong and the New Territories and are actively attempting to repress the democratic system. Resistance against the despotic Beijing government is continuing. Whatever the final result, in this treatise we wish to emphasize that the Hong Kong program for absorbing the poor into the economy, the education system and the polity, was the right program. Aristotle had said in ancient Greece, that the poor must be trained in craft workshops or cash-crops farms so that they would not be angry and jealous, but rather could become stable democratic citizens. He also said that just giving money to the poor is "like pouring water into a leaky jar."[17] This latter statement brings us to the case of Venezuela.

I once met Romulo Betancourt. He told me that the newly productive oil wealth of Venezuela could be invested in the nation to create a modern, democratic country. As president, he helped facilitate that.

Venezuela was a successfully modernizing country. The vast oil wealth was being used to build modern cities, a functioning infrastructure, a tourist economy, and an industrial-capitalist economy—with American corporations employing thousands of Venezuelans.

The middle class grew large, and it was well-educated and prosperous.

As in many developing nations, there was a large population of poor people in the countryside, and gathering in the cities, creating vast slums, with terrible conditions.

---

[17] Aristotle, *Politics* (the poor- "leaky jar").

Venezuelan democracy was slow in developing. Before Betancourt there had been a series of military dictators, as in most of Latin America. But, after Betancourt, Venezuelan democracy did stabilize, and the regime was relatively progressive in its policies. The education and absorption into the modern capitalist economy of the Venezuelan poor was horribly slow.

Venezuela like most of Latin America, is a mixed society made up of Spaniards, Native Americans and African-decent Venezuelans—and every mixture thereof— but the majority of the poor were Native American, who came to the cities from their villages.

Many of these Native American poor could barely speak Spanish and they were slow to assimilate in the schools. Lacking an education and with poor language skills, they were not quickly absorbed into the modern capitalist economy. The slums degenerated, crime increased, and anger spilled over into the political arena.

14.5.2   Enter Hugo Chavez

Hugo Chavez, a charismatic leader, became champion of the poor. He organized them into a voting bloc. Since they outnumbered the middle class, Hugo Chavez won election after election. He meant well but his program of redistributing the wealth of the nation towards the poor was unwise in the Aristotelian sense. Because, if you give the poor money, but you do not give them job-training, and you do not absorb them into the modern economy, you end up having to give them money over and over again.

Hugo Chavez bankrupted Venezuela. He helped the poor for a while, but he also ruined the economy of Venezuela. The middle class has taken to the streets in an effort to overthrow the government of the poor—whom they cannot outvote. Hugo Chavez died of cancer and his protégé is not charismatic and increasingly ruling through violence. Venezuela's democracy has been ruined and its capitalist economy has now collapsed.

Chavez, though well-intentioned, did the wrong thing. The poor of Venezuela needed education and job-training—this is a slow process and needs to be carefully nurtured by any regime seeking to maintain a stable democracy in a country with a majority poor. There are no shortcuts. The poor cannot be empowered and showered with money. This leads to economic collapse and demagogic dictatorship.

Given the fact that many developing nations in Africa, Latin America, and South East Asia have a large majority, uneducated poor, it will be difficult for these nations to absorb the poor into a stabilizing educated middle class. The process is slow, as I have emphasized, but it is the proper policy.

There are nations in Africa, like Kenya, Nigeria, Ghana and a few others where this process of education and absorption of the poor is going well. Yes, tribal divisions will continue to destabilize the politics – as in Kenya after the 2017 election. But, as the middle class increases, and the economy modernizes, there is still hope for the future of law and electoral democracy.

Thailand, Vietnam, Indonesia and yes, the Philippines, are also fitfully educated and absorbing their vast populations of poor, into a slowly growing new middle class.

The problem of the majority poor, and their tendency to follow charismatic demagogues and dictators is a continuing problem. The case of Venezuela shows that this political choice does not necessarily benefit the poor, and does, in fact, slow the progress of the entire society.

Chapter 15
High Technology Mass Media as Strengthening Democracy: Immediacy and Community in the Blogosphere – Extremism Plus Increased Citizens' Involvement

It is easy to revive *Orwell*[1] and project a future of *high technology totalitarianism*. Big Brother is already watching us through our smartphones, Amazon deliveries, credit cards, and computers. The Chinese and the Russians are already using Cyber surveillance and, in the USA, Amazon, Apple and Google know where I am, and what I like to buy, watch and listen to. *Dystopias abound*: every movie about the future seems to be dystopian—combination of high technology totalitarianism and medieval monarchy.

Further, the recent Russia hacking into the American presidential election, and, the European elections as well—even the "Brexit" vote in Britain—have furthered our pessimism about the future of politics.

Further yet, those negative television ads and robocalls denigrated the character of anyone who runs for office—these certainly do not increase our optimism on the future of democracy!

However, I wish to point out that there are some *positive* effects that have occurred regarding the new technology.

Jean Jacques Rousseau, in the heady days leading up to the French revolution, contrasted the *face to face democracy* of the ancient Greek city states—and his adopted city of Geneva, in Switzerland—with the representative democracy being established in France (and already established in the Dutch Republic and England). Rousseau believed that *representative democracy becomes too distant from the citizens*, that the face to face democracy of the smaller city-states was the only real democracy.[2]

Now, Rousseau was behind the times, for representative democracy was needed to integrate large scale nation-states into functioning political entities, and, to replace the monarchies as a new and viable form of government for large-scale

---

[1] George Orwell, *1984,* any edition.

[2] Jean Jacques Rousseau, *The Social Contract*, NY: Cosimo Books, 2008, Originally published 1762.

© Springer Nature Switzerland AG 2019
R. M. Glassman, *The Future of Democracy*,
https://doi.org/10.1007/978-3-030-16111-8_15

political entities. The other French "philosophe" like Voltaire[3] and Condorcet,[4] thought Rosseau was either joking or misguided. But, he was neither. His position that face to face democracy creates more immediacy and more of a feeling of genuine participation in government for the citizens, is correct. He was misguided, though in two ways: one, as mentioned, because the representative system was absolutely necessary in order to replace absolute Kingship as a unifying political institution; and two, he was misguided because he failed to highlight the fact that face to face democracy was more volatile, more likely to get caught up in "mob' psychology—as Polybius called it, "ochlocracy"—rule by the mob.[5]

Rousseau failed to realize what Locke,[6] Montesquieu,[7] Madison, Hamilton[8] and Jefferson[9] understood: that representative democracy—because it creates a distance between the citizens and their representatives, allows the representation to debate issues with a cooler head—*there is no mob psychology in a small group of representatives debating an issue.*

Further, the representatives are limited, guided, and bound by checks and balances, constitutionally institutionalized. These checks and balances are lacking in a face to face democracy, even though constitutional guidelines may exist.

There is no doubt that the representative democracies of the Netherlands, Britain and the USA were more stable than the face to face democracies of the ancient Greeks.

So, what is my point here? Representative democracy has proven to be stable and deliberative in a good way. However, Rousseau was correct that the mass of citizens does feel a certain alienation from the democratic process. In the USA, our citizens often complain about "Washington"—the representatives are characterized as far away from "main street" and "out of touch" with the citizens. Just this week (January 2018) the German millennials (younger voters) complained that the "politicians" in Berlin were too willing to make compromises and unwilling to stand up for their party's principles—they were "out of touch."

Why am I describing this citizens' alienation from their representatives?

Because, *the new mass media have created a new sense of immediacy and political community* that had been lacking in the representative-democratic system.

Yes, this new "blogosphere" and "Twittersphere" and Facebook sphere does cause greater volatility and increased extremism—*there is the danger of regenerating mob psychology in the cyberworld.*

This new mass mediated "intimacy" does cause extremes, and it can lead to mob-like actions in the real world: marches, demonstrations, online money-raising directed at local elections far away from the blog-incited contributors.

---

[3] Voltaire—writings, Google Books.

[4] Condorcet—*writings*, Google Books, 2008.

[5] Polybius, Bk VI, *Roman History*, "mob rule".

[6] John Locke, *Second Treatise on Civil Government*, London, Penguin, 1950.

[7] Montesquieu, *Spirit of the Laws*.

[8] Hamilton Madison, Jay, *The Federalist Papers*.

[9] Jefferson – helped write the USA Constitution.

But, look at the excitement this has engendered in terms of *democratic participation*! During the 1950s and then again in the 1970s, voter apathy was considered a major problem. Low voter turnout was worrisome, not only in the USA, but also in Italy and France.

With the introduction of political blogs on the right, the left, and center, citizen participation has gone way up. Voter turnout is higher, voter involvement is more passionate, citizens' participation is more enthusiastic Is this frightening? You bet it is. But is it creating a more vibrant democracy? Yes. Our representatives don't seem so far away anymore, because—through the blogosphere—we can petition them, urge them, or challenge them (in a primary). If they are not doing what their constituents want, their constituents let them know it in no uncertain terms.

This whole new technological world of the mass media, linked to computers, tablets, and smart phones, has created a political reality that allows the modern citizen to actively participate in the political process. The modern citizen does not feel alienated anymore. Not only have they become much more active in the computer world, but many more of the modern citizens are running for office.

Hence, we should be worried about the increasing polarization of opinions engendered by the rigidly ideological blogs, while at the same time, we should be celebrating the new vitality of political process in modern high technology democracy.

More:

Television coverage of primary and general elections—in all the modern democratic nations—has created a familiarity between the candidates and the viewers. The viewer feels like they are really seeing the candidate face to face. Of course, they are not, but since television presents the candidates in many venues: debates, stump speeches, informal talk shows, interviews and more, the citizens do get a chance to judge the candidates more closely than in the days when a stump speech was all you could get.

Thus, the television coverage of elections has created a heightened immediacy between the candidate and the citizen. The citizens feel like they are really seeing the candidate face to face. Of course, they are not, but they are seeing the candidate more intimately than in a large hall, or by way of a newspaper article. With all this election coverage, voters definitely feel more connected to, and less alienated from, the participating process. People watch carefully; they have gatherings at their houses and apartments; they hold fundraisers while watching the debates.

This is all good for democracy—it brings the citizens closer to the political process, and replicates—in a mass-mediated way—the face to face democracy of ancient Greece or eighteenth century Geneva.

Though this process is, of course, not actually face to face, it is better than the very distant process we used to have wherein the majority of voters just voted along party lines and barely knew the candidates.

Of course, demagogues have learned to use television and other mass media to their advantage. However, Hitler and Mussolini, as dictators, and Roosevelt and Churchill, democratically elected leaders, had already learned how to use the mass media available to them to the maximum advantage.

15.1   Blogs

Then there are the blogs. The blogs definitely add to the extremism in democratic policy positions. Voters tend to read and write on the blogs which represent their views. Since the blogs are hotly partisan, their policy positions tend toward extremism.

Extremism is not good for democracy. It destabilizes democracy. It discourages lawful compromises and encourages volatile political action.

How can this be positive for democracy?

The blogs, because they are partisan, encourage political activism—rallies, marches, fundraisers, policy research centers and more. This kind of activism makes democracy more vibrant, if more volatile.

The blogs raise the participation level of citizens. Far from feeling alienated from the electoral process, the citizens feel energized and "engaged,"[10] to use Jean Paul Sartre's term. I know this seems foolish, and I know that extreme partisanship makes lawful compromise more difficult, but there is no doubt that the blogs have energized the electorate—and electoral participation and enthusiasm have increased. This is true in pre and post "Brexit" Britain, in "immigration-crisis." The Netherlands, France, and Germany, as well as in "financial crisis" Spain and Greece.

Both extremism and electoral participation have increased in all the European democracies and in the "culture-war" problematical USA. Old party lines are blurring, and new interest groups are forming. For better or for worse, *there is increased electoral participation because of the new blogosphere and intense television coverage of elections.*

15.2   Referenda

Benjamin Barber, in his book, *Strong Democracy*[11] describes the Swiss systems of referenda. In the Swiss system, policy decisions are put to the vote through a series of referenda. These referenda by-pass the legislature, which is very weak in Switzerland (on the national level).

Barber believed the referenda systems could be brought to the USA and the EU, and, that it would enhance democracy.

Referenda, however, have proven to be *too volatile*. The "Brexit" vote in Great Britain is a perfect example, or, the California vote on the proposition that set a limit on taxation. *Referenda bring out the irrational and ideological* in the electorate. This is why the system of parliamentary representations and constitutional law was put in place—precisely to control debates within a framework of law, and to keep debates in a rational context.

---

[10] Jean Paul Sartre, *Existentialism*, (engage in politics) Britannica.com-Existentialism.

[11] Benjamin Barber, *Strong Democracy*, Rutgers, Rutgers, Univ. Press, 1990.

So, why discuss referenda at all?

Because referenda will be used from time to time to test the opinions of the electorate. As long as they are *non-binding referenda*, and they are repeated a number of months apart, the representatives can gain a sense of where the electorate stands on current policy issues.

In fairness to Switzerland, they run three referenda in a given issue, months a part. The first referenda and non-binding, so that the final vote can be taken when the issue is less volatile.

Still, the Brexit vote, and the Catalan separatist vote in Spain show us that referenda should only be used for polling reasons and never for binding votes that bypass the legislature.

The checks and balances of the Enlightenment theorists are necessary to the stability of modern democracy and must not be sidestepped through the use of "instant referenda."[12]

15.3   Computer Voting

Computer voting should have been the wave of the future. Citizens could have voted right from their own living rooms, using computers set for local and national elections. However, computer-hacking has destroyed this possibility—the enemies of democracy, mischievous geniuses and criminals have successfully hacked into the computer systems containing voter registration rolls, party affiliation rolls and voting machines (that had been computerized).[13]

This computer hacking has occurred in the UK, the EU and the USA. The Russians have been the most malevolent of the hackers in attempting to discredit and disrupt the electoral democracies of Europe and America. But there have been North Korean, African and Eastern European hackers as well. All those hackers, national or criminal, have created mischief in the voting process, and made the use of computer voting unwise.

Will computer voting in some protected form become part of the modern voting process? Only if a fail-safe system can be invented. The hackers, however, always seem to learn to override every new safety system.

15.4   The New High-Tech Communication Devices & Systems

Computers, tablets, smartphones and other new communication devices have created the most wonderful system of global interconnectedness. I still remember my amazement at sitting with my German friend, at a Canadian University, while he

---

[12] USA Constitution.

[13] Glassman & Swatos, *Charisma, History, and Society Structure.*

"skyped" with his wife in Munich. They chatted with each other as if they were together—and they were together "virtually".

Wherever we go in the world, we can connect with our family and friends. This does create a "global citizen" potential.

Already, there is a global middle class, who communicate easily with each other—using English or Spanish, and interacting through email, Facebook, Google, Skype or cellphone.[14]

This could, someday, reduce world tensions and lead to a world-wide model of democratic electoral processes constrained by constitutional law. The United Nations already exists as a world forum, with instant translating (and bilingualism with English). The United Nations, at this point in the twenty-first century, is made up of a majority of developing nations, which are not yet exhibiting a majority middle class which is well-educated and prosperous. When and if, the UN reaches the point where the majority of the nations of the world *are* developed—economically, educationally and politically—then the UN itself could become a democratic, lawful world government. It is not that now.

Let us return to the new communications systems.

I have waxed eloquent about the spectacular new avenues of communications which are interconnecting the peoples of the world in a positive way. We can and do talk to our families and friends in distant cities and far away nations and, they feel close to us, and this is nice. So too is the democratic potential of the new communications networks.[15]

15.5 High Technology Totalitarianism

The totalitarian potential of the new communications devices is even more obvious than their democratic potential. The totalitarian impulses jump out at us. It is so much easier to be dystopian than utopian on this global phenomenon. "Big Brother" is, as mentioned, already watching us.

Facial recognition technology is on the way from Apple. Amazon is watching your living room and your packages in your doorway. Your smartphone knows where you are and where you have been. Your Apps know what products you want, what music you play, what art excites you. Your websites tell you whom you should date and what kind of person you should marry. And, so much more. The computer surveillance systems already know who you are, where you are and what you like and dislike. They know your political opinions, too, from the blogs that you favor.

High technology totalitarianism is a real and horrifying possibility. Right now (2018) if you are sitting in a café in Beijing and you try to bring up the Tiananmen Square uprising on your computer, the Chinese police will be alerted to this on their computer surveillance system and they will detain you.

---

[14] Movie: Triumph of the Will, (woman director), Leni Riefenstahl, available on Google.

[15] Aristotle, *Politics* (Kings, p. 241).

Yes, high tech surveillance can lead to the worst form of totalitarian domination that has ever existed. Hitler, Stalin and now Kim Jung Un, have already created totalitarian regimes that were, and still are, overwhelming with their mass mobilizations and continuous terrorizations of the populations living within them.

Now, aided by the new communications surveillance devices, totalitarian control can become even more total. Let us look at a few of the hideous possibilities.

Chapter 16
High Technology Totalitarianism: The Ultimate Dystopia; Manufactured Charisma in the Cyberworld

Just as Kings magnified their charisma with very successful manufactured effects[1], so too, dictators could do so using the new high technology mass media.

Kings used magnificent clothing, golden crowns, scepters, and thrones and surrounded themselves with "royal" officials and regiments of soldiers—all splendidly dressed and regally arranged accompanying the King. Palaces with impressive architecture and gilded interiors enhanced the charisma of the King, the royals, and the state officials. The total effect was to make the Kings and the royals seem more than human—Godlike in their appearance—and therefore above the ordinary people.[2]

Dictators, like Hitler, used such effects quite as successfully as the traditional Kings. In the movie, *The Triumph of the Will*, the Nazis showed the world that they were superior to all other peoples—the "master race." They used mass demonstrations of soldiers and well-organized civilian "regiments". And, they surrounded these demonstrations of power with gigantic Nazi symbols—swastikas, flags, uniforms, salutes. It all worked. The German people became caught up in the frenzy of totalitarian control, regimentation and symbolic identification with the regime. The Nazis and Hitler created a set of manufactured charismatic effects, that rivaled the ancient Kings.[3]

And, these manufactured charismatic effects worked. The German people lent their consent to the Nazi regime and its leader, such that a form of legitimate domination did occur. It certainly was not rational or legal authority. But it was legitimate to its subjects.[4]

This is the fear for the future of the modern world. The Nazis have shown us that manufactured charismatic effects can work on modern populations. Aristotle has told us that Kingship has gone out of fashion, because humans have become

---

[1] Karl Jaspers, *The Axial Age of Human History*. Google Books, Originally published 1953.

[2] Confucius, *Analects*.

[3] Plato, *The Republic*; *The Laws*.

[4] Confucius, *Analects*.

© Springer Nature Switzerland AG 2019
R. M. Glassman, *The Future of Democracy*,
https://doi.org/10.1007/978-3-030-16111-8_16

rational-minded and egalitarian. No one, he said, could be looked upon as so special—divine—as to be a King.[5]

But, Aristotle also warned, that though Kingship has gone out of fashion, tyrants will continue to rule through force. And, tyrants—dictators—in many nations of the world are ruling through force.[6]

This is obvious. But, what if a dictatorial regime, using the new mass media communications technology, not only increases its surveillance capacity, but also creates manufactured charismatic effects on the mass media, which enhance the legitimacy of the regime? The Nazi example haunts our imaginations and stand as an example that the irrational legitimation of traditional Kings and royals could possibly be recreated through the new communications media, which are becoming ubiquitous in the global economy.[7]

Thus, high tech dictators could present themselves on television and computer venues, as bigger than life—Big Brother—the Hollywood movies and televisions series already show us these dystopian, totalitarian, high tech societies. The *Star Wars* movies exhibit a form of government that is a combination of high tech dictatorship and ancient monarchy. The "Emperor" is evil, and in complete control of most of the galaxy. Dozens of other futuristic films, like *The Hunger Games*, show us similar images.[8]

However, the heroes and heroines in these movies are somehow broken out of the manufactured, high technology legitimation system. They come to *hate* the "charismatized" leader, and *they see through* the regime's benevolent façade.[9]

They are fully well-aware of the regime's power and terroristic tactics, and they are afraid that they may be discovered and killed. However, they are willing to take the chance and defy death, because they perceive the regime *rationally* and wish to reestablish a *humanistic* regime, with some sort of high technology representative democracy.[10]

So, in most of these films and television shows—and in Orwell's *1984*—the original high-tech dystopia—a group of "rebels" risks their lives to overthrow the high-tech dictatorship.[11]

Of course, all of this is fiction. What would happen in the real world is unclear. The Germans did not revolt against the Nazis, although General Rommel and a clique of German Generals, did try to assassinate Hitler. They failed, of course. And in the case of Stalin, who did much of what Hitler did (but less successfully—Stalin never became legitimated as a great charismatic leader), when Stalin was dying of a stroke, Khrushchev and the other communist party leaders, did not call in the doctors. They waited until Stalin died, because they not only hated him, but feared for

---

[5] Weber, *Religion of China.*

[6] Locke, *First Treatise on Civil Government.*

[7] Lord Acton, Power Corrupts, Absolute power corrupts absolutely.

[8] Plato, *Republic* (women as "guardians").

[9] Bella Vivante, *Daughters or Gaia.*

[10] Aristotle, *Politics* (critique of Utopian political schemes).

[11] Marx-Engels, *Communist Manifesto.*

their own lives. After Stalin died, the totalitarian dictatorship was scaled back and eventually dismantled, until Putin came along.[12]

And, it must be understood that the Germans *are ashamed* of their past, and they are happy with new legal-democratic government—at least for now.[13]

It is possible, therefore, that as the population of the world becomes more science-oriented and rational-minded, the kinds of manufactured charismatic effects that appealed to the Germans might not be so easily accepted anymore. In the film, *I am a Camera*, and the musical version, *Cabaret*, the British observer who happens to be in Berlin at the time of the Nazi ascendency, thinks Hitler is a madman, and the Nazis are racist and misguided. He is not "charismatized". He sees through the grandiose effects. So did General Rommel in the real situation.[14]

We must remember the paradox of human political interaction: we have the capacity to be rational and to utilize our conscious awareness of the world and our language capabilities to create a truly democratic political process and a legal-rational authority system We can also become irrational and succumb to domination, submission and territoriality—mass "patriotic" dictatorship. We humans alternate between "humanistic" caring and terroristic rejection of the "other".

So, with the possibility of high technology totalitarianism hovering over us, like a surveillance drone, let us take the positive side for a moment—if you can.

16.1   Utopian Visions and Practical Programs for the Near Future

Democratic societies with legal-rational authority may—may—have the capacity to regulate and control the new communications networks and devices. Democratic nation-states are already attempting to limit and regulate Google, Apple, Facebook, Instagram, Amazon and other giant communications networks.[15]

The new technology, however, improves and changes so quickly and in such unexpected ways—who thought your telephone could be miniaturized, carried anywhere, made wireless, and hold more information than the house-sized computers of the 1960s? – that is difficult to regulate, much less control, the world of high tech communications.

The democracies of the E.U., the U.K. and the USA and Japan are attempting to successfully regulate these new systems. And, if they can, modern democracy may be *enhanced* by the new technology, rather than destroyed. I have discussed the "immediacy" of the political interaction as enhanced through television and the blogosphere, such that the representatives do not seem so distant as they used to be.

---

[12] Abraham Maslow, *Self-Actualization.*

[13] Karl Marx, *The Woman Question*, collected works-International Publishers.

[14] Thomas More, *Utopia*, London Penguin Classics, 1947.

[15] Jonathan Swift, *Gulliver's Travels*, London, Penguin Classics, 1948.

This is good, in that it reduces the alienation inherent in the electoral-representative process. Yes, extremism is increased—and worrisome—but so is participation increased—and this is good for democracy.[16]

I know that the dystopias are so much easier to imagine—new dystopian movies, television series, and novels seem to flow out every year. Therefore, it is important that we try to think in a more positive fashion, so that we can imagine—and make actual—ways in which the new high technology communications networks and devices can be utilized to improve the processes of modern democracy.

For, as the new technology pours forth at a mind-blowing pace, democracy and legal-rational authority still exist and still function well. And, the new middle class—globally expanding—seems to appreciate electoral participation and the legal protection of citizens' rights—even in this mass mediated world of global political processes.

---

[16] Max Weber, *Economy and Society,* Roth & Wittich, section on "unintended effects"' see also, Weber, *The Methodology of the Social Sciences.*

Chapter 17
Utopian Visions Produce Both Good & Bad Political Policies

If we look back at the "axial age" of 600–400 BCE, we find two of the greatest utopian thinkers of all time: Confucius and Plato.[1] Confucius knew nothing of democracy, as Chinese tribalism had been left behind for village agriculturalism centuries earlier. China had local war—Kings—violent and ruthless like all war-kings. And, of course, these local Kings engaged in endless war with each other.

Confucius envisioned a unified Kingdom, wherein one Emperor had absolute authority so that local wars could be eliminated. And, this unifying monarch would be surrounded by government officials, who, because of their excellent education, would encourage the supreme King to rule "benevolently" for the people.[2]

The very good "utopian" portion of Confucius political program focuses on the creation of a high level educational system, and, the selection of the officials based on *merit* with every boy-child given an equal chance to excel. This did create a mar-velous set of state officials who administered China brilliantly for millenia.[3]

The bad portion of this utopian system was the granting to the King absolute power. He ruled with the "Mandate from Heaven." But as Locke would theorize, centuries later, if you give a King absolute power, he will become a tyrant and enslave his subjects.[4] whether surrounded by well-educated officials or not as Lord Acton put it "power corrupts, absolute power corrupts absolutely."[5]

The Emperors were often tyrants, having people killed on the spot for violating the simplest protocol, and murdering whole families—clans of a hundred or more—because one member offended him.

So, the Confucian utopic did create a peaceful, well-run society in China. But, the price the Chinese paid was slave-like prostration in the presence of the King or his educated officials.

---

[1] Karl Jaspers, The Axial Age of Human History, *Commentary*, 1948.

[2] Aristotle, *Politics* (on law).

[3] Locke, *Second Treatise* on Civil Government.

[4] Aristotle, *Politics* (on "distributive justice," and "proportional equality").

[5] Locke, *Second Treatise*.

© Springer Nature Switzerland AG 2019   161
R. M. Glassman, *The Future of Democracy*,
https://doi.org/10.1007/978-3-030-16111-8_17

And, of course, only boys could qualify for the merit-based officialdom.

When we come to Plato and his mentor, Socrates—perhaps the greatest philosophers the world has ever known—their utopian vision was even more detailed than that of Confucius, and, even more flawed. Nor was Plato's *Republic* ever really institutionalized anywhere, though Plato tried, in his lifetime, to institute it in various city-states.

Plato, like Confucius, wanted a political system dominated by the smartest and best educated individuals. He describes a program of education similar to that of Confucius, except for two factors: one, Plato includes physical education—Olympic-style training and military training—for all the individuals competing in this merit-based education system; and two, Plato included girls in his merit-based education program.[6] Plato said, "are not women equal to men in one important way, their intellect." And, he said, "is not my female guard dog as good as my male guard dog in keeping strangers at bay?"

Plato had the example of Sparta, wherein the women ran the economy and controlled the family (while the men only trained for war). The Spartan women were famous for their success in economic matters. Confucius had no such model of female excellence in China. Also, Plato's mother was a Pythagorean philosopher,[7] and he knew Aspasia, a sophist in her own right, and Pericles' consort. We know nothing of Confucius' mother, and he had no women as disciples.

So, in his utopia, Plato liberated women. And, he suggested the creation of state-run nurseries, so that women could do all the work that men do, while their children were cared for in the nurseries. This is wonderful utopian thinking, in that, in today's world of women's liberation, child care is one of the biggest stumbling blocks to women's career aspirations.

So, what is the problem with having a society run by the smartest, and best educated as "Guardians."?

The well-educated "guardians," as Aristotle warned, would begin by governing for the good of all the people—as Plato would—but eventually, power would corrupt them. The guardians would rule for themselves, as well-educated oligarchs.[8]

Plato is so wonderful, but in his utopia, he could also be terrible. For, he advocated *censorship* of the playwrights and poets, with state control over literary and artistic production. And, even worse, he advocated *"eugenic"* breeding, wherein the intelligent guardians would only breed with each other—during festival sexual orgies—in order to "improve the herd." "We breed horses for speed, don't we," said Plato, "so why not breed people for intelligence?"

Centuries later, in the nineteenth and twentieth century, dictators like Hitler took seriously both eugenic breeding—of the "master race," and state censorship of all literary and artistic productions.

So, utopian thinking can produce both good and bad programs as models for future societies.

---

[6] Montesquieu, *Spirit of the Laws.*

[7] USA Contributions.

[8] Hamilton, Madison, Jay, *Federalist Papers.*

Marx, following Plato in many ways—and Marx was deeply familiar with Plato—envisioned a utopia of his own—a communist utopia, wherein humans could reach their complete potential—"species being"[9]—they could be "a farmer in the morning, a poet in the afternoon, and a violinist at night." "Self-actualization," as we now call it following Maslow,[10] was a good factor emanating from Marx's utopias thinking.

So, too, was Marx's complete liberation of women. Following Plato, Marx suggested the establishment of state nurseries, so that women could work alongside men in every vocation. Definitely a good thing.

And, unlike Plato, who was an elitist, Marx advocated full equality for all citizens within his communist utopia. An excellent educational system would be used to bring all citizens—no matter what their vocation—up to a high enough standard, that equality could be achieved. This is very different from Plato's or Confucius's system, wherein only the smartest could gain high status and power.

All this utopian thinking in Marx is good. But, then he insisted that this communist utopia of the future could only be ushered in by a "temporary dictatorship" of the communist party intellectuals, acting as temporary guardians of the working class, until they were educated enough to rule themselves. Then, "the state would wither away," and true peoples' democracy would emerge. And, because there would be *no class distinctions*, it would be true democracy—no oligarchy in disguise, as in capitalist class-based societies. Remember that in Marx's time in England (1850s–70s), England had restrictions on voting rights—it was an oligarchy.

Of course, the utopian idea of a temporary dictatorship that would wither away of its own accord was tragically mistaken. Stalin turned the Soviet dictatorship into a totalitarian tyranny, only outmatched for its murder and terror by Hitler's Nazi Germany.

Utopianism, then can be dangerous, as well as, enlightening. That is why I will advocate for *practical programs* to engender support and stabilize democracy.

Before we discuss the *practical programs*, we have been describing throughout this treatise let us mention Thomas More, who coined the term "utopia" and who made utopian thinking popular.

More, with his classical education and strange sense of humor, titled his book, *Utopia*, inventing a Greek word which mean "no place".

In this island paradise, he advocated religious tolerance of all beliefs—except atheism, which he thought would lead to sociopathic behavior. Given the religious disputes of his time, the religious tolerance in utopia was, at least, a good start. (Modern atheists, who are also "humanists", hotly dispute More on his belief that atheists, not fearing the punishment of hell in the afterlife, would become sociopathic).

Along with religious freedom, of a sort, More also advocated the liberation of women—he says at the beginning of utopia, that "he will out-Plato Plato"—but he

---

[9] *Magha Gessen, The Future is History*, Amazon Books, 2017.

[10] Abraham Maslow, *A Theory of Human Motivation. Google Books. First published 1943.*

can't really do it. He says women are liberated, but, they didn't do any of the heavy work, and, they must make all he communal meals, and take care of all the children, and they don't really want to participate in the polity, nor do they want to be priests. Then he jokes that "each night the wife must apologize to her husband, on her knees, for what she did during the day to aggravate him."

It is a joke, but it's not funny, because More just cannot liberate women in his utopia, or in his own life.

Finally, after opposing the death penalty for poor people, who steal out of need, and after advocating a wonderful job-training program to absorb the poor—out Aristotling Aristotle, so to speak, More advocates a prison system so harsh that it is akin to slavery—he calls it slavery. He allows for the rehabilitation of these thieving slaves, but the harsh conditions, override his rehabilitation intent.

More revised Plato's utopianism—giving it its permanent name—but he also made fun of utopianizing at the same time. After More, humorous, but biting, utopias were written, bordering on dystopias—Jonathan Swift, with *Gulliver's Travels*, comes to mind.

But, it was Marx, who really out-Plato'd Plato, and we have already described what mixed bag Marx's communist utopia was, and still is.

To conclude on utopian thinking, just as dystopias stand as a warning for a future with no freedom and no democracy, utopias stand as a warning that human societies do not always turn out as the utopian theorist expected. There are "unintended effects" that occur in human societies, that are both fully understandable, and at the same time, defy logic. Humans are neither electrons nor bees. There is change in human societies, and change is very difficult to predict, because we humans can act rationally and willfully, or we can act irrationally and emotionally. Also, we are very inventive creatures—we continually invent things that change society in ways we do not expect.

For instance, scientists invent the birth control pill, and it liberates women's sexuality, and, it also allows women to postpone childbearing. Thus, family and gender roles become altered. No one expected this. Or, we invent computers and smartphones and the whole world is connected to the internet—you can talk to anyone, anywhere, and you can "Google" anything—information on all things is omnipresent.

Keeping this problem in mind, let us look at some practical programs that can support democracy in the near future.

Chapter 18
Education for Democracy in the Twenty-First Century

I have mentioned that the British educational system seems to have had a positive influence on the English colonies attempting to set up democracies. India, Hong Kong, Singapore, Kenya Nigeria, Cyprus and other English colonies—though sometimes brutalized by the British or subjected to racism, nonetheless were successful when establishing their legal-rational democratic political institutions.

British education is a "classical" education. It focuses on the great classics of philosophy, literature and art. The ancient Greek classics are studied from Thales and Pythagoras to Herodotus and Thucydides; from Plato and Aristotle, to all the playwrights and poets, and sculptors and architects. The classics of the Renaissance and the Enlightenment are also studied, from Dante to Shakespeare, from Michelangelo to Handel from Galileo to Newton, including all the philosophers, artists, poets, scientists and more.

This classical British educational system contains a great deal of political theory and encourages an attitude of rationality in its approach to politics. Of course, the history of Kings and battles is there—and somewhat glorified—but a basically rational-minded approach is encouraged. And, in terms of politics, itself, the authority of "*the law*" is emphasized very strongly.

Given the fact that this kind of classical British education has had a positive effect in terms of inculcating a belief in democracy and constitutional law, we should think about teaching this "core curriculum" as it has become known, in all the colleges and universities of the world.

I am focusing on this, because I know that the trend is going in the other direction—this *classical core curriculum* is being de-emphasized, in favor of scientific, technological, or career-oriented curricula.

Now, I have made it clear that science and technology can be good for democracy because science encourages rational thinking, and rational thinking is necessary in a democracy, so that the citizenry can analyze and vote on policy matters.

But, I have also emphasized that science, in itself, is amoral. Science does not make ethnical decisions. The Atomic Bomb is invented, but so is the polio vaccine.

© Springer Nature Switzerland AG 2019
R. M. Glassman, *The Future of Democracy*,
https://doi.org/10.1007/978-3-030-16111-8_18

Whether to use these becomes a moral decision not inherent to the scientific quest of understanding the "laws of nature."

Therefore, teaching science and technology, in themselves, does not insure that the student will come away with a democratic mentality.

So, the *classical curriculum must be maintained*, and *required*, such that the modern new middle-class students will come to grips with all the arguments for and against democracy and dictatorship, presented in the classics.

The emphasis in today's universities is to go technological—in terms of online teaching, exams, lecture notes, and student-faculty interactions. This is fine—progress in technology cannot be ignored. However, the technology in itself—has *no* academic content. Whether one teaches in-person, or online is *not* the key question. The key question is: what are you teaching?

What should be taught—along with the technological and scientific studies necessary for the high technology economy that we all desire and depend on—is the classical curriculum that has been shown in recent history to foster a legal-democratic mentality.

I know that Germany had this same curriculum, but went unlawful, undemocratic and totalitarian. However, after WWII, Germany did go democratic and lawful with little difficulty.

18.1   The Global World, the P.C. Movement and the Trend Away from the Classics

Given that this is a global world now, and all the nations are interconnected by computers, capitalism, and air-travel, it is natural and good that the great thinkers of all the civilizations are included in the core curriculum.

Of course, we should study Confucius, Mencius and Xunzi. And yes, to the Rig Veda and Upanishads and to the books of the Buddha. African and Latin American art and literature should be studied, as should the contributions of the Arabic Golden Age—I have already mentioned that without Ibn Sina and Ibn Rushd there would have been no Aquinas and no Maimonides.[1] So, of course, the greatness of all civilizations should be studied.[1]

However, the study of Buddha and Confucius should *not* displace Herodotus and Thucydides. For, nowhere in Buddhism or Confucianism can we find reference to democracy. While in Herodotus we get the first defense and critique of democracy (and monarchy). And in Thucydides we watch as decisions are made in the Athenian Assembly—both wise and unwise—but democratic to the core.

So, globalize the curriculum, but make the Greek, Renaissance, and Enlightenment classics, mandatory. Yes, *required*.

---

[1] Moses Maimonides, *The Guide for the Perplexed*, N.Y. Oxford Univ. Press, 1956. First written 1190.

Thousands of students from Eastern Europe, China, Korea, India, France, African nations and Latin American nations and South East Asian nations, come to the USA and UK and EU to study. We should make sure that these students are exposed to the ideas of the "Western Classics". Otherwise, how can their cultures change in a democratic direction? The contrast between Hong Kong and Beijing should convince the reader that the British classical education had a positive influence on the Chinese in terms of politics. This is not to condemn Chinese culture, only to add a democratic element to it—similarly with Iran or Turkey or any other culture.

Let me add that American students, too, must be nurtured with a democratic education, or they too will lose their cultural proclivity for it.

Why do I mention this? Because today, in 2018, the American students—pushed by "politically correct" ideas on women, gays, abortion, race, Native Americans, and more, have begun to forget our lawful and democratic traditions.

Now let me make clear that I agree with the P.C. movement on these issues. Women have been liberated and the process is by no means complete. Gays and lesbians have "come out", and gay marriage surprised the world as a new institutionalized happening that seems to have a very positive effect—on gays, and on marriage. Racism, sexism and prejudice against immigrant groups must be ended. All the P.C. goals are good.

The problems are that the P.C. people are so committed to their program and to righting the wrongs of society, that they won't allow speakers with opposing views a platform and have been acting "fascistically" against free speech and open dialogue.

Why discuss this?

Because the P.C. radicals do not want to teach the works of "dead white men" or the classics of "western society".

Just as it was necessary to include the great books of all civilizations in the curriculum—"the globalization of the curriculum"—it is necessary to include the works of women and to "out" the works of men and women who were gay.

From Aspasia to Hypatia the works of classical Greek women should be included in academic study—the poetry of Sappho along with Pindar. Christine de Pizen wrote the *City of Ladies*, defending the great women of history who have been defamed by men. From Eve in the Bible to *Medea* in Greece and Cleopatra in the Hellenistic and Roman Eras, Christine de Pizen defends their integrity.

And Mary Wollstonecraft wrote in defense of the rights of women, at the time of the French Revolution, though her work was not appreciated until modern feminists revived it.

So, from Sappho to Simone de Beauvoir the works of women had to be rediscovered and studied seriously.

Does this mean that the works of Plato and Aristotle should not be taught—they are "dead white men"!? Plato was the world's first women's liberationist, though most of the philosophers were misogynistic, like Aristotle.

Whatever, their views on women—and like Thomas More—in *Utopia*, most of their views on women are negative—they still are great. And, their works must be taught if democracy and legal-authority are to be preserved. As for gays, Greek culture was bisexual in its orientation. Socrates asks in one of Plato's dialogues, "Is the love between men and men more beautiful than the love between men and women?"[2] And, this question is not purely philosophical. Socrates was teased for being excited by the masculine beauty of Alcibiades. "Alcibiades, every man and every woman in Greece, was in love with him."[3]

And, Sappho loved her girls, but also loved her male lover so much, she contemplated suicide on his death.[4]

Yes, the works of gays and lesbians should be openly discussed. The trend in today's universities is away from the classics. The success of the high technology economic system is overwhelming, we want everything the high-tech economy produces, we can't live without these things. But, the technology, in itself, as we have emphasized, is value neutral.

If we want democracy to remain in our future, we must *teach democracy* and the reverence for lawful behavior, in our schools.

The classical core curriculum should be retained and made mandatory—although it should be amended by global great works, and by the works of women and gays who have been ignored historically.

18.2   Education for Democracy in Our High Schools: "Civics"

There was once a course called "civics", in which students were instructed in how to be a good citizen. The course included information on: the voting process, on the different branches of government on constitutional law, on the Bill of Rights, and, on the process by which laws were passed.

In Great Britain, these civics courses included *debating*. Students were taught how to debate effectively and argue for the policy one preferred. This, of course, was part of classical education, since the Greeks taught "rhetoric" which included speechmaking and debating techniques.

In the United States, the private prep schools continued this British tradition, and many of the public schools also offered civics courses and even had debating societies.

It is important to note that even though the German universities offered an excellent classical education, the high schools—gymnasia—did *not* offer civics. Einstein, who went to high school in Germany, characterized them as run as if they were a Prussian military regiment![5] They discouraged free speech and debate and encouraged rigid obedience and the absolute authority of the teacher. Einstein hated these

---

[2] Plato, *Symposium - Dialogues*, Benjamin Jowett, translator. Amazon Books.

[3] Thucydides, *Peloponnesian War* (on Alcibiades-the handsome traitor). Richard Crawley, translator.

[4] *Poems of Sappho*, University of Houston Press.

[5] *Walter Isaacson*, Einstein Biography, Amazon Books.

German high schools so much, that when his family moved to Italy and left him behind to finish his schooling, he ran away to Switzerland.[6]

So, teaching students to become good democratic citizens at a young age may be part of the reason that British education has been so successful in inculcating a democratic and lawful mentality.

Now, in this era of high technology mass media, it is necessary to include the use of television and blogs in the debating and policy-pushing process.

We can still teach citizenship, the Constitution, and the Bill of Rights, but we do have to include this new context in which political debates play out.

Young people love the new media, but they still need to be taught the old—and successful—structure and procedures of legal-rational authority and democratic law-making.

Freedom of speech, religion, press, and demonstrations are not changed by the blogosphere, even though debating techniques have been adapted to television and computer outlets.

So, given the intrusion of the new technology into the democratic political process, the question remains: can democracy be taught?

The answer is *yes*. In every democratic nation, just as rhetoric was taught in ancient Greece, an updated version of *civics* should be taught at the high school (gymnasium) level. Young students are very impressionable, and they will participate in modern forms of debate on the controversial topics of the day.

This is one way to establish cultural change where it is needed, and to maintain a culture of democracy where it is already established.

Earlier, I highlighted the culture of Spain to show that culture can change, and democracy can be taught, such that citizens can re-evaluate their attitudes towards it.

In nations unfamiliar with democracy, it is imperative that civics be taught. And, given the pace of social and technological change, it is all the more imperative that democracy and the reverence for law be taught in the modern democratic nations, as well. Given the fragility of democracy, civics—education for democracy—should be taught to all high school students.

Students can be taught to get their message across to other citizens—using the media or in face to face gatherings—in a lawful manner and within the guidelines of a bill of rights.

Hotly debated issues, such as immigration policy, abortion, gay marriage, racism and more bring out the irrational "passions" in us. But, citizens can be taught to rationally evaluate such issues. In a civics course, students can be asked to debate one side of an issue, and then later, to take the other side. This produces empathy for the opposing view and encourages moderation and compromise. The ancient Greek rhetoricians used this trick, and the British debating societies were famous for it.

Even though the new mass media have encouraged extremism, if this extremism plays out within constitutional guidelines and Bill of Rights protections, it can be contained as "political activism".

---

[6] Ibid.

Therefore, the young people of every generation have to be taught the principles of democracy and law. If they are not taught these principles, democracy and legal authority will slowly slip away.

Chapter 19
Climate Change as a Challenge to the Legitimacy of Advanced Capitalist Democracies

19.1   Introduction

Naomi Klein wrote a best-selling book, published in 2014, called, *This Changes Everything: Capitalism vs. the Climate.*[1] In this book, and some of her previous books,[2] she warns that advanced capitalism, because it is driven by the mass production of commodities and the continuous need to sell new commodities, demands so much energy in both the industrial production process and the fueling of the products themselves, that the environment is overwhelmingly damaged.

The mass production, mass advertising, mass consumption, and technologically innovative economy is amazing in its creativity and productive capacities, but this economic system demands so much energy utilization that it has totally altered the climate and threatens our precious atmosphere.

Klein warns that if we do not scale down our desire for these ever-changing commodities, and scale back the over-production and over-selling, the climate will be irrevocably changed and the atmosphere unrecoverable. If we do not alter the economy, the earth will be uninhabitable. We will all die – with all the "toys" we thought we needed.

Klein points out, what psychologists have long known: "things" do not bring us happiness, human relationships bring us happiness.

The "fetish of commodities"[3] that capitalism engenders, inculcates within us a desire for new "things" – the latest cell phone, the newest car, the trendiest videogame, the latest fashion style, the newest technological marvel (like a robot with artificial intelligence (A.I.), that not only talks to us, but anticipates our needs.

---

[1] Naomi Klein, *This Changes Everything: Capitalism vs. the Climate*, NY 2014, Simon & Shuster.

[2] Naomi Klein, *No Logo*, Toronto, Canada, 1999, Random House of Canada (first published by Knopf of Canada).

[3] Karl Marx, on "the fetish of commodities" in Marx and Engels, *Collected Works*, NY, 1948, International Press.

© Springer Nature Switzerland AG 2019
R. M. Glassman, *The Future of Democracy*,
https://doi.org/10.1007/978-3-030-16111-8_19

All these "things" are wonderful, but they become obsolete quickly, and then we want the newer, better version of that commodity.

A spiraling cycle of: buy it, use it, then get bored with it, and buy a new one, keeps spinning us towards more and more commodity consumption. This drives the economy to produce more and better "things," and does lead to remarkable creativity and technological development.[4]

However, it is a "fetish," because no matter how many "things" we buy, we want more.

The commodities we continually buy do not bring us the happiness we thought we would get from them. Yet, we keep on buying and we keep on hoping that these commodities will bring us joy and well-being.

Happiness or unhappiness is no longer the issue. The focus now is, can we – homo sapiens and all the other creatures – survive the dramatic climate change that the onslaught of the advancing capitalist economies have wrought. Carbon and other deadly emissions that emanate from the advanced capitalist economies are polluting the air and water and earth; the pollution is warming the ocean waters and thinning the atmosphere.

And so, "This changes everything," as Klein warns us. For her, this is a crisis in advanced capitalism – it is the economic system that must be changed.

For us, in this volume on the future of democracy, climate change creates a crisis for democracy, as well as capitalism, because it is the democratic political systems that will have to legislate to roll back and reverse carbon and other poisonous emissions, and, it is the democracies which will have to fund the scientific think tanks and universities such that non-polluting sources of energy can be developed and implemented, and it is the democracies that will have to legislate to give tax credits to new energy companies and the consumer public.

The legitimacy of democracy itself is in jeopardy if modern democracies cannot rise to the occasion and help humankind survive the negative consequences of climate change.[5]

However, and this returns us to Klein's thesis, modern democracy is based on advanced capitalism. And, advanced capitalism is based on the continuous overproduction of commodities, the continuous technological improvement of commodities, and the mass consumption of commodities. The "fetish" of commodities is ingrained in the system.

So, combating climate change looks hopeless unless the advanced capitalist system is changed. And, modern democracies, it seems, will be helpless to change the system they are grounded in.

In this book, I wish to project a different approach.

---

[4] Thorstein Veblen, *The Theory of Business Enterprise*, NY, Mentor Books, 1952.

[5] Nico Stehr, "Exceptional Circumstances: Does Climate Change Trump Democracy?" *Issues in Science and Technology, 32(2)* Winter 2016.

I agree that *commodities do not bring us happiness.* Human relationships – marriage, family, friendship, workgroups – bring us happiness. And, "self-actualization"[6] brings us happiness. For some individuals, spiritual connections with God and a congregation bring happiness.[7]

"Things," commodities, in themselves just bring us the desire to want more and better things – no matter how much we have.

So, the accumulation of commodities does not improve "the human condition" – human happiness is based on other factors.[8]

Yet, there is something that the advanced capitalist economies have improved – that is, the advancement of technology has cured many diseases, cools us in the summer and keeps us warm in the winter. We are living longer, and starvation is being replaced by an expanding food supply – the problem now is obesity, not starvation, but most of us in the advanced capitalist world are well fed.

No one wants to go back to the days when people trembled with fear at the outburst of plagues and other contagious illnesses. And most of us want the newest cell phones and computers which connect us to friends and family all over the world, and are creating a global village culture of shared values and lifestyles from New York to Hong Kong.

Let us be honest, our modern lifestyle is dependent on the technological innovations that the advanced capitalist democracies are the best at producing.

So, how do we survive climate change and its devastating effects? Can we develop new, alternative, nonpolluting sources of energy that will allow the advanced capitalist economies to continue to innovate new and better technologies and products, without the devastating pollution of coal, oil, natural gas, and ethanol?

If modern democracies can legislate for, fund, and implement alternative energy sources, and, if the democracies can legislate to inhibit and reverse industrial pollution, and if the scientists of the world can invent and implement nonpolluting energy sources, then we will survive. We may not be happy, but we will survive – and we will live longer – whether we are happy or not.

It may be that Klein is correct, and we will die off, as a species, with the latest iPhone in our pockets. But, it is also possible that the incredible scientific and technological creativity inherent in the advanced capitalist democratic societies will save us, with our iPhones intact and our vaccinations up to date.

Let us look more closely at the *crisis of legitimacy facing the advanced capitalist democracies.*

---

[6] Abraham Maslow, Hierarchy of Needs (The Psychology of Self-Actualization), 2018, Amazon Paperback; also, The Path to Self-Actualization, Amazon, 2018. See also Psychology Today, 2013, The Theory of Self-Actualization of Abraham Maslow.

[7] Martin Buber, *I and Thou,* originally published 1923, now in Amazon Paperback, 2018. See also, Joseph B. Soloveitchik, *The Lonely Man of Faith,* first published in 1965, now in Amazon Paperback, 2018.

[8] At Yale University in 2017–2018, a class on "Happiness" was offered by a psychologist, and enrolled over 1000 students!.

19.2   Climate Change as a Challenge to Democratic Legitimacy

Modern advanced, or high technology, capitalism is the base upon which contemporary democracy is built.

I have emphasized that both the separation of the economy from direct political control, and the necessity of contract law and patent law, undergird and reinforce modern representative democracy.

However, advanced, high technology industrial capitalism is characterized by mass production, mass advertising, and mass consumption.[9] Sell, sell, sell, and buy, buy, buy.

Furthermore, the application of scientific discoveries to both the production process and the products themselves, creates a situation of continuous obsolescence in the products owned. So, the consumer must continuously purchase new products.

This is wonderful in terms of the creative development of new technologies and improved products – this is why high-tech capitalism is so creative and so much more productive than state-run economies.

However, the mass production – mass consumption economy of advanced capitalism is dependent upon an *enormous use of energy*.[10]

This was not a major problem until the middle of the twentieth century, because the resulting pollution of the air and water was local. In fact, though pollution was recognized as a potential problem, the search for more and better energy sources was the main problem of the nineteenth and twentieth centuries. The search for coal, oil, and natural gas became the focus of the capitalist–democratic nation–states of that era. (The discovery of oil in the Middle East drew the British, French and Germans into that region and after World War II the Americans rushed in.)

Now, however, we know that the pollution from the global, high-tech industrial capitalist economy is polluting the entire globe. Such pollution must be contained and reversed, or all of us will die.

The climate scientists are clear on this – the most recent report from the United Nations scientific committee in 2018 warns that *we have 12 years* to reverse this pollution, or it will be too late to save the planet.

There is no scientific controversy on this. It is only the big oil, gas, and coal companies who deny the scientific consensus. We will come back to these giant corporations and their influence on the electorate in the United States shortly. First, we wish to describe the problem facing all advanced capitalist corporations, and every nation in the world.

The problem for advanced, high-technology, industrial capitalism is: How can they sustain the mass production, mass advertising, mass consumption, ever-improving technological economic systems?

---

[9] Thorstein Veblen, *The Theory of Business Enterprise*, NY, Mentor Books, 1952.

[10] Naomi Klein, *This Changes Everything: Capitalism vs. the Climate*, NY 2014, Simon & Shuster.

Can *new sources of energy* be found, vast enough and usable enough to replace coal, oil, and natural gas? And will these new sources of energy *pollute* sufficiently *less*, such that the planet will not be destroyed?

And – this is where democratic legitimacy comes in – can modern democracies legislate controls on the polluting energy sources while legislating to encourage the development of non-polluting alternative sources of energy?[11]

Given that the modern democracies are based on advanced capitalism, and that these corporations have enormous power within the democracies, can democracies legislate effectively to avoid the calamity of global destruction?

First, can the capitalist democracies legislate to fund the scientists and engineers such that they are able to develop the alternative energy sources that will not pollute, or, pollute much less? We shall discuss solar, wind, water, liquid hydrogen, and atomic energy sources shortly.

Second, can the capitalist democracies do anything to inhibit current levels of pollution, when the giant coal, oil, and gas companies have so much influence and power over them?

Let us look at the second problem first.

In those nations which have advanced capitalist production, the nations with the most coal, oil, and gas have the greatest problem, because legislation to control and reverse pollution is actively inhibited by these big energy corporations. In this regard, the United States has the worst problem, because we have the most powerful energy corporations.

Donald Trump and the Republican Party are so linked in with the big energy companies, like Exxon-Mobil, and Koch Industries that they have been actively inhibiting the development and deployment of solar, wind, water, and other sources of non-polluting energy. This administration and its Republican allies in Congress have reversed the Obama administration's attempts to limit carbon emissions and to develop solar and wind power. I will come back to the USA, for the Obama administration and the Democratic Party *were* able to begin the process of converting to new energy sources.

But first we wish to point out that those nations which do not have coal, oil, or natural gas – or have very little – have been able to move more rapidly to new energy sources.

So, Germany, France, Spain, Denmark, Norway, Sweden, Japan and others, since they do not have powerful coal, oil and gas corporations, have been able to legislate for a more rapid changeover to less polluting energy sources. Thus, electric cars, hybrid cars, wind and solar energy have been pushed, and, at the same time, the electric generating companies and the electric grid have been targeted to create a system that is less polluting – it makes no sense to have electric cars unless the electric charging system does not pollute.

This brings us to a discussion on nuclear power plants.

---

[11] Nico Stehr, Op. Cit.

19.3   Nuclear Power: Great Promise, Greater Danger

It was believed, a few short years ago, that nuclear power would save us from carbon pollution, and provide us with an unlimited source of energy. Nuclear power plants produce an enormous amount of power with little carbon pollution.

However, two factors emerged that make nuclear power unusable: one, the danger of their imploding and polluting an entire region with atomic radiation so deadly that no one can live there, or even near there. This occurred at Chernobyl, in the Ukraine, near Kiev, wherein a systems-failure destroyed the plant and killed thousands. A similar meltdown occurred at Three Mile Island in the New Jersey–Pennsylvania area, but was closed off before a mass death toll occurred. And, most recently in Japan, a massive earthquake and tsunami destroyed a huge nuclear power plant complex, such that no one can live in that area anymore, and the brave men who went in and shut down the nuclear reactor before it could implode, will surely die young of radiation poisoning.

So, because nuclear power plants are unsafe, nations such as Germany, the USA, Canada and others, have decided not to expand nuclear power usage.

Someday, perhaps, nuclear power plants will be developed – and nuclear *fusion* power is still being researched. However, so far, no safe nuclear power plants have been developed.

In fact, even the plants that were thought to be safe, have been shown to pollute: strontium 90 and other cancer-producing nuclear substances are found in high concentrations in the water used to cool such plants and this water seeps into the groundwater, the rivers, and the ocean surrounding the nuclear plants.

So, the advanced capitalist democracies without powerful coal, oil, and gas companies, have been actively legislating for alternative energy use, since the recent decline in dependence on nuclear energy.

19.4   Nuclear Power as a Bridge Between Carbon Polluting Energy and Renewable Energy

Although nuclear power plants are inherently dangerous, and although their spent fuel poses a threat to the environment, we may have to utilize them during the transition to renewable energy sources.

In France, a nation with little coal and no oil or natural gas, nuclear power plants have been successfully deployed. The French design is considered a state-of-the-art design in terms of safety and efficiency. The French nuclear plants have never had an accident – so far. Given their success, Canada has deployed similar nuclear power plants and is expanding their usage.

China and India must follow the French lead. With over a billion people each, these two mega-nations will pollute all of us to death, as they expand their advanced capitalist economies – unless, they go over to hundreds of nuclear power plants, while at the same time transitioning to electric cars.

China has already mandated that all car companies must convert over to electric vehicles in the next 5 years – the Chinese already buy more Teslas than any other country. If the Chinese do convert to electric cars, and if they do build hundreds of nuclear power plants, then the world may survive carbon pollution.

The Chinese have bought the French patent, and are now actively building their own version of the French-style nuclear power plant. In terms of the reduction of carbon pollution worldwide, this is great, but will the Chinese nuclear plant be safe?

Chinese products have been notoriously shoddy. Chinese cars are poorly made. Chinese manufacturers rush their products out, and they are often unsafe and inferior in quality. Knowing this, it is still critical for the Chinese to go over to nuclear energy. It is hoped that French inspectors could be deployed, or Americans, to ensure that the Chinese nuclear power plants are properly built and maintained. The risks are great in this, but these risks are worth taking during the transition between the use of carbon-based fuels and renewables.

The electric cars will get better and better – especially their batteries – and the nuclear power plants will also improve if we allow our scientists to do research and development on them.

India will have to follow the Chinese lead. Tata Motors and the German, Japanese and American automakers, will produce electric cars for India.

What of nuclear power plants? India will have to buy them from the French, the Canadians, or the Russians. Whoever India buys them from, with a billion people and an expanding capitalist economy, India must temporarily institute nuclear power plants.

Russia, though it is the world's largest producer of natural gas, also builds nuclear power plants. After Chernobyl, the Russians adopted the much safer American and French models of nuclear power plants. But, the Russians have gone further. They have built some state-of-the-art nuclear power plants that they claim are even better than the French model. Furthermore, they have built the world's first Breeder Reactor, which consumes its own wasted fuel.

We do not know whether this Russian Breeder Reactor really works. And we do not know if it is safe. We must be aware that, of the dozens of nuclear submarines built by the USA and Russia, the only three deadly accidents occurred on the Russian subs.

Nonetheless, the Russians are building nuclear power plants, and offering them for sale to India.

As for the USA, since the Japanese accident, we have stopped building nuclear power plants – and so has Germany. But, what is the alternative? In the USA, natural gas – which is actually methane – is replacing nuclear expansion. This is not good, for it expands carbon pollution and worse, methane pollution – to say nothing of the increasing number of explosions when natural gas lines are hit by construction crews.

In Germany, the nuclear plants have been replaced by coal plants – the worst polluters of all. Should Germany be doing this, or should they keep their nuclear plants online?

To sum up: nuclear power plants are scary and potentially dangerous. And, their spent fuel presents a terrible problem for the earth. Nonetheless, it may be necessary to expand and deploy nuclear power as we are making our transition to renewable energy sources. This is debatable, but should not be eliminated as an option – we may only have 12 years to reverse the carbon pollution before disaster hits the earth.

19.5   India, Brazil, China

These nations are increasingly linked into the global capitalist economy. They are also attempting to develop their own advanced capitalistic economic systems. Since they are still "developing," their economies are not sophisticated enough to attempt a conversion to new, less polluting energy sources. Therefore, they pollute at a very high level.

These nations, especially India and Brazil, have asked for more time to slowly make the transition to less polluting sources of energy. This was given to them in the Paris Accords on world energy use. The trouble is, we do not have that kind of time to give – the scientists have estimated that 12 years is all we have.

India has a democracy, but it is not the democracy that is slow to react to climate change – India has always been a loosely held together subcontinent, wherein no central government has ever held strict power. India is still a nation loosely held together. The democracy functions, but mass mobilizations have never occurred in India (as they did in Ancient Egypt and China). Therefore, programs to convert two new energy sources will be slow in their implementation in India.

This is not meant as a criticism of India, but rather a description of the difficulties facing the world.

Brazil also has a democracy – though it is plagued by corruption on a deeply cultural level. Again, this is not meant as a criticism, just a description.

On the positive side, Brazil's capitalist economy is the fastest growing in Latin America. And, Brazil has vast energy resources, such as Sawgrass and other vegetable sources of ethanol. This is what Brazilians use to power their electric grid and their cars. The problem is that the energy from plants pollutes as much as that from oil. Ethanol and other vegetable and grain sources of energy are renewable but they pollute terribly. But since Brazil has so much plant energy, the Brazilian government has no incentive to convert to solar, wind, or other non-polluting sources of energy.

Further, and this is critical, the Brazilians are actively logging the Amazon rainforest and depleting one of the world's greatest anti-pollution agents. The Amazon rainforest absorbs more carbon dioxide than any other forest in the world. Thus, preserving the Amazon rainforest is critical for global survival.

We can barely prevent USA loggers from denuding our forests, and at this moment, the Brazilians are actively promoting logging in their forests. Brazil's democratic government has caved into its huge logging industry.

19.6 China

Here is a case of a non-Democratic, authoritarian, strongly centralized government attempting to control pollution, while rapidly expanding its advanced capitalist economy.

The case of China is important because it is not a democracy. Can a nondemocratic nation do a better job of controlling and reversing pollution – given that their economy is the fastest growing *capitalist* economy in the world?

The Chinese economy is based on mass production, mass consumption, and rapid technological innovation – just like the American, Japanese, or European economies.

So, is the despotic Chinese government better than the democratic governments of the Western World and Japan?

The answer is mixed: the Chinese government, under Xi Jinping, is attempting to cope with the terrible air, water, and earth pollution that their industrial-capitalist economy is generating, and, they are making some progress. But, China is more polluted than Japan or Europe or the USA.

In fairness, the Chinese government has just begun to attempt to reduce carbon and other emissions. One problem is that China has coal – the most polluting of all the fossil fuels and, it is importing enormous amounts of oil.

Will China go nuclear, Ukraine and Japan notwithstanding? Will they deploy solar panels – they are among the world leaders in solar panel production? Will they use wind and water power? We do not yet know.

Significantly, *American scientists* have been working with Chinese scientists to try to evaluate and reduce the air pollution in Beijing – the pollution is horrendous. I mention this because I do not think that democratic legitimacy alone will be destroyed by failure to deal with climate change. *All* the countries of the world – whether democratic or nondemocratic – will be working on this problem. The scientists of the world will work together on this – and they will be funded by the democracies and some of the dictatorships (such as China).

I will come back to this. First a word about Russia.

19.7 Russia

Russia has reverted to an authoritarian government. Putin is a dictator – not a totalitarian like Stalin – but a tyrannical dictator nonetheless.

So, why am I mentioning Russia? Because Russia has a great scientific community – it is an advanced scientific nation-state, but without an advanced capitalist democratic economic system.

Putin and his tyrannical KGB "oligarchic" henchmen have pushed their scientists toward computer hacking – and space exploration weapons development – but not towards any program of pollution control or alternative energy development.

Russia has seemingly unlimited supplies of oil and natural gas, and is surviving economically as a supplier of these polluting energy sources to Europe, China, and Japan.

Given their economic dependence on oil and gas, the Russian government has done nothing to develop alternative energy, nor has it done anything to prevent or reverse pollution. And because Russia is a vast underpopulated country, with a cold climate, the air pollution in the big cities, such as Moscow and St. Petersburg, has been less problematic than such cities as Beijing or Los Angeles.

So, here we have a case of a non-democratic country doing nothing to prevent climate change, whereas the EU democracies are actively legislating for change.

Having establish this, let us look at the USA. *Here we do have a real legitimation crisis* – especially since the Trump election to the presidency.

19.8   The USA

Given the fact that America's corporations are the most mass production, mass advertising, mass consumption in the world, and, that America has big oil, gas, and coal companies, American democracy should be the least active in the alternative energy development field.

However, America's economy is enormous and diverse. Therefore, there are giant, billion-dollar corporations which favor alternative energy development and pollution controls.

The Silicon Valley high-tech corporations, like Google, Apple and Facebook, and Amazon and Microsoft in Seattle, along with Tesla Motors and SpaceX – and Hollywood moguls too – actively finance the scientific development of solar, wind, water, and other nonpolluting energy sources (such as liquid hydrogen auto engines).

These corporations have also funded the Democratic Party, which encouraged the Obama administration to regulate and reverse carbon pollution and fund the development of solar and wind projects.

So, the American democracy may fail in its attempt to stop pollution and convert to non-polluting energy, but it also may succeed.

Trump was not elected because of his stance on coal, oil, and natural gas – yes, these giant corporations funded him – but except in West Virginia, the issues that elected Trump were immigration, abortion, gay marriage, women's liberation and various other religious issues.

It was Christian fundamentalists, and, white male workers – who lost their jobs to outsourcing to China, and to automation, and the women entering the workforce – who backed Trump. We discussed these factors in our chapter on the rise of neo-fascism.

While Trump and the Republicans remain in power, no pollution controls, and no alternative energy sources will be introduced.

In America, however, the scientific community is actively working on new energy sources. And, they are funded by universities, and high-tech corporations, such that they are continuing their efforts to avert the disasters of climate change.

Since the Democrats have won the House of Representatives in November 2018, climate change will be addressed as an urgent issue.

19.9   Can the Scientists Save Us?

In order to understand this question, let us first look at nuclear power again.

The nuclear physicists who developed the atomic bomb felt some guilt about having developed such a monstrous weapon of mass destruction. Attempting to give something good back to humankind, they developed the nuclear power plant. These physicists and engineers believed that the nuclear power plants would be able to produce an unlimited supply of energy to fuel the mass production economy forever. And, they believed that these plants would not pollute and would not be dangerous.

Well, nuclear power plants can produce an unlimited amount of energy, but, unfortunately, they do pollute and they are dangerous. The pollution – of strontium 90 and other radiation factors – was bad enough, but the Three Mile Island collapse in New Jersey–Pennsylvania, the Chernobyl disaster near Kiev in the Ukraine, and then the Japanese implosion, caused, not by a plant malfunction, but by an earthquake and tsunami, warned the world that nuclear power plants were too dangerous.

Maybe they can be perfected such that plant malfunctions and natural disasters will not cause them to erupt with horrifying radiation. More likely, they will have to be abandoned.

Having warned of the scientists' fallibility, let us be more hopeful.

19.10   Solar Energy

Solar energy could, in theory, produce enough energy for the needs of the high-technology mass production economy – and without polluting the earth.

In reality, the technology of solar panels, storage batteries, and other solar driven devices (such as that in Spain which I will describe), is not yet well developed enough to produce even a fraction of the energy needs of the advanced capitalist economies.

However, solar panels and storage batteries have barely been deployed. For instance, in Greece, Italy and Spain, with sunshine nearly 300 days a year, and little cloud cover and rain, millions of solar panels could be deployed on rooftops, in arid fields, along the mountainsides where very little grows (and the sheep and goat herds can still be managed).

So why don't they do it? In Greece and Italy solar panels were being deployed, until the economic crisis hit. So now, these nations need to be subsidized to do so. In Spain, where the economy has improved, solar panels are being deployed. Also, the Spanish scientists developed a mirror technology, wherein giant mirrors target a water tower which produces steam energy from the sun's rays. Technology like this is barely in its infancy – and it does not pollute.

Solar panels and solar devices could be deployed in all of the North Africa countries, which are also sunny and dry and need little battery backup. In fact, many years ago, a team of British scientists studying the Sahara Desert near Egypt, suggested that solar panels could be used to generate electricity, which would then be used to run water de-salinization plants – combined, these technologies could irrigate the Sahara and reverse the expansion of that desert. This could be done in many drought areas, such as the disastrously drought stricken East African region.

Thus, solar panels, storage batteries, and solar devices could be installed worldwide. In Germany, where it is usually cloudy, solar panels plus storage batteries still work to produce energy, and the Germans, Dutch and Scandinavians are beginning to deploy more and more of those solar units.

In China, where it is very polluted, due to the use of coal and oil, solar panel production has become a major industry. And, the Chinese are deploying them, although at present, most are exported.

The case of Florida in the USA (and Texas) shows us the dilemma of modern democracies. Florida is the most vulnerable state to climate change – ocean levels are rising, hurricanes are increasing in strength as the waters warm, and, the coastline is flooding at an increasing rate. Yet, the Floridians (and Texans) vote conservative Republican, and refuse to acknowledge climate change, and do not deploy solar panels.

So, *here you have the legitimation crisis of modern democracy*. It is based on the mass production economy of advanced high-tech capitalism, which will not reduce the use of oil and natural gas or install solar and wind devices.

Florida and Texas have bright sunny climates, where solar energy could easily be utilized, and the winds off the ocean and the Gulf could produce enormous amounts of energy. But in a democracy, the people vote. And, in Florida and Texas: many people are fundamentalist Protestants and do not believe climate change is manmade, and, oil and natural gas companies dominate the politics of the arena. Even with the recent 2018 devastating storms and flooding in both states, they are continuing to vote in anti-climate change candidates.

Can the scientists save us? Maybe. Can democracy answer the call and mobilize? Maybe. Let us look a little further.

19.11   Wind Energy and Water Energy

As with solar energy, the scientists tell us that wind and water energy can produce a great deal of non-polluting energy.

Giant windmills are appearing all over the world. In Greece, on the mountains around Megalopolis giant windmills have been built. Greece is mountainous, and windmills could be deployed by the thousands on the unpopulated mountain ridges. Also, in Greece, the infamous "Meltemi" winds, that blew Odysseus off course and lost him and his crew in an Odyssey of endless adventures – these winds still blow relentlessly across the Cycladic Island region and along the Turkish coast. Windmills could be deployed on the Islands and offshore along the coasts.

In Northwest Europe, the Dutch, Danes, Germans, Norwegians and Swedes have placed enormous fields of windmills out in the North Sea and Baltic Sea. The winds that blew the Vikings' ships to Iceland, Greenland and the New World, are powering electric plants all across Northwest Europe.

Do these windmill fields produce enough energy to power the mass production economies of the northern section of the EU? No. But, they are generating an increasing percentage of such energy. And, combined with solar power, that percentage will increase.

There is a problem with bird migration that must be addressed, but otherwise there is no pollution in wind power. There could be noise pollution, but only if the windmills are near residential areas – this is usually avoided.

Finally, the potential for water power electricity is enormous. Already waterfalls like Niagara are being utilized to generate pollution-free electricity. Now, scientists tell us that the ocean times – regular and and powerful – could be utilized. Underwater "waterwheels" can generate electricity in every ocean on the planet. This source of energy has not even been tapped yet.

So, again, can science engender non-polluting sources of energy that produce enough energy to drive our relentless mass production advanced capitalist economies?

Again, we answer, maybe. There are many more sources of energy – from algae, bacteria, grasses, grains – that have barely been developed. Some pollute, some do not. Liquid hydrogen is another nonpolluting source of energy. Hydrogen is everywhere and superabundant. But, the process of creating liquid hydrogen takes energy – polluting energy at present. And, the liquid hydrogen auto engines are not yet perfected.

The world's alternative energy sphere is in its infancy. But, it had better mature fast.

19.12   The Legitimation Crisis for Modern Democracy is Very Real[12]

Since modern democracy is linked with mass production, mass consumption high-technology capitalism as its economic engine: can modern democracies (1) mobilize the scientific community to develop and deploy nonpolluting energy sources, (2) contain and reduce coal, oil, natural gas, and ethanol production, such that pollution is reduced, and (3) can modern democracies mobilize massive population shifts away from the coastlines?

The answer to all of these questions is unclear – and we do not have much time.

In Northwest Europe – including the UK and France – the EU democracies have moved towards the increasing deployment of solar panels and storage batteries, the deployment of windmill fields, and the conversion to electric car production in the near future.

But, look at what Volkswagen Corporation did: they cheated on diesel emissions standards. However, they were caught and fined. And now, electric vehicles are being developed. Can the Northwest European countries utilize solar and wind to energize their mass production economies? Not yet, and maybe they will need a nuclear powerplant boost to really do away with oil and natural gas pollution.

The Southern European and North African countries could probably generate enough solar and wind power to fuel at least half of their energy needs – but what about the other half?

In nations such as the USA, Venezuela, and Brazil, the existence of powerful giant corporations can and has reduced the ability of these democracies (Venezuela *was* a democracy, but, of course, now is not) to act to convert to non-polluting energy sources.

The USA under Obama and the Democrats versus the USA under Trump and the Republicans gives us a picture of both the possibilities and the barriers to reacting pro-actively to climate change in capitalist democracies.

Under Obama and the Democrats, scientists from MIT to Caltech were funded generously to study climate change and develop non-polluting energy sources. Solar panel and windmill companies were subsidized and encouraged to deploy their products. Tax credits were offered to consumers and electric companies to help the deployment of solar panels and windmills. And, carbon emissions levels were mandated by law to come down in cars and in power plants and industrial plants.

Things looked good in the American Democracy in terms of its response to the climate change crisis.

As mentioned, Trump and the Republicans were elected over issues like: immigration from Mexico and Central America, abortion, gay marriage, women's liberation from the family and the outsourcing of jobs to the developing nations. We discussed all of this in our chapter on the rise of neo-fascism.

---

[12] Naomi Klein, *This Changes Everything: Capitalism vs. the Climate*, NY 2014, Simon & Shuster.

In terms of climate change, Trump and the Republicans are funded by big oil, big coal, and big natural gas. They have undone Obama's initiatives, they have created disbelief in the sciences, and they have inhibited the deployment of solar and windmill sources of energy.

Will the Democrats win in 2020? We will find out. But one thing we know is that the blocking of new energy initiatives shows us that *in advanced capitalist nations, democracies can fail in their attempts to deal with the coming disasters of climate change.*

In the United States, Brazil, and other modern democratic nations, if the governments fail to act, the legitimacy of democracy itself could collapse, as the world collapses into an epic of natural disasters of an unprecedented level.

19.13   Do Dictatorships do a Better Job of Mobilizing the Population in terms of Climate Change?

Even though some of the leading democracies, like that of the USA, may not respond fast enough to the threats of climate change, it is also true that the dictatorships may also fail.

As discussed, Russia, under Putin, is a perfect example. The Russians have a marvelous scientific establishment – they are leading in the space exploration field – they run the International Space Station – American astronauts go up in Russian Rockets. Yet, the Russian scientists are barely involved in the study of new energy sources. The Russian economy exports oil and natural gas, and pollutes – look at the Caspian Sea and other of the great inland lakes of Russia – they are hopelessly polluted.

So, here is a dictatorial nation where the government does not care about climate change. Putin's Russia is worse than Trump's America.

19.14   What about Xi's China?

China is responding quite well in terms of its very dangerous pollution levels. China's cities are horribly polluted. Beijing, is perhaps, the worst. But let me emphasize this: *China's government is responding* to the pollution and climate change problem, not because it is a dictatorship, but *because it has a Confucian tradition.*[13]

That is, Xi is a Maoist – his family was personally involved in the Communist Revolution and its aftermath. But, at its core, his regime espouses the Confucian model of governance: an authoritarian ruler, aided by an educated officialdom,

---

[13] Confucius, *The Analects*, NY Penguin Classics, 1958. (Also, Amazon Paperback.).

whose job it is to rule "*benevolently*." The government must make sure the economy is running well, and the people are protected from outside invasion.

Xi Jinping is an authoritarian – the secret police are everywhere and the military arrest and harass anyone who speaks or acts against the government. Look at what the Chinese government is doing to the Uygers – the Muslim minority group, who did act and speak against the government.

Xi Jinping declared himself president for life: dictator.

However, because the tradition in *China is Confucian*,[14] Xi and the government and the scientific community have been mobilized to try to reduce pollution. Solar and wind energy are being utilized, and coal is being slowly phased out.

Because China is a dictatorship, the government can act without interference from capitalist corporations. But, but, but, since China has the fastest-growing advanced capitalist economy in the world, and mass consumption is a growing fact of Chinese economic life – look at Ali Baba, China's Amazon – the pollution problems and the energy problem is multiplying faster than Xi's government can control it.

So, China though authoritarian, is not doing a bit better than the USA – though the government is trying.

Thus, though climate change challenges the legitimacy of capitalist democracies, it also threatens the existence of the nations under dictatorships.

19.15   Two Examples of Hope: The Hudson River Clean-up and The Pooper Scooper

In the 1950s in New York State, the condition of the Hudson River, after a century of industrial pollution, was horrendous. That beautiful river that had inspired the Hudson River School of Art and had been a highway for the Tappan Indians and other Native American Tribes, had become so polluted that no fish lived in it, no people dared swim in it, and it smelled of sewage and chemical waste.

In the seventies and eighties a movement emerged to clean up the river. It was led by Pete Seeger, the folksinger, who had retired to a home near the Hudson above New York City.

Most New Yorkers believed the river could not be cleaned up. However, after years of protests, the New York State legislature passed laws and enacted fines such that sewage plants were built and corporations were forced to fund cleanups.

Today, the fish run again – not the great salmon that once dominated the river, but many smaller fish species – and people do swim up river from New York. Pleasure boats and kayaks abound, and the river smells fresh from the George Washington Bridge and North.

The Hudson River is not the magnificent model that the artists painted before the industrial revolution. But, it is at least acceptable in its level of pollution. The

---

[14] *Ibid.*

increasing number of ferries running between New York and New Jersey has recently created pollution in the form of boat exhaust and emissions. This is a new problem which has not yet been addressed. Still, the river is acceptable above the George Washington Bridge and up to Albany.

The second example might seem silly, but I mention it because no one believed anything could be done – but they got it done.

I am discussing the problem of the dog poop that really troubled New Yorkers. Many people have dogs in New York City and the dogs dropped their poop on the sidewalks all over Manhattan – the streets stank.

A group of liberal reformers from the West Side of Manhattan came up with a solution: the "Pooper Scooper": a plastic bag that seals tightly and a plastic scooper to pick up the dog poop and put it in the bag.

New Yorkers laughed and said no one would pick up dog shit! The law was passed, fines were enforced, Pooper Scooper's were sold everywhere, and, low and behold, people scooped and the sealed bags hid the smell, and the Sanitation Department picked up the trash, and, the city no longer smells – even though New Yorkers still have their thousands of dogs.

The pollution problem from fossil fuels looks hopeless. But, it is not hopeless. Democratic governments and the scientific world community *may*, succeed before it is too late. We shall know in the next 12 years. We have been warned, and, we may act.

19.16   Should We Get Rid of the Mass Production, High-Technology Industrial Capitalist Economy?[15]

There are many social theorists that believe we should find a new paradigm for the economy. For, not only has advanced capitalism *exacerbated economic inequality*[16] and failed to redistribute wealth more fairly, but it has created a lemming-like mass production, mass consumption, mass advertising economy that will drive us over the cliff (like lemmings) of climate change, such that we will all die of pollution, flooding, droughts, fires, and the loss of our entire atmosphere.

The problem with the idea of a new paradigm is that it is the advanced capitalist economies that generate the scientific and technological creativity that makes capitalism the most creative and productive economy the world has ever seen.

Given the fact of the link between science and the application of scientific advances in technology to production processes and new products, it would probably be counter-productive to get rid of advanced capitalism.

On the other hand, advanced capitalism may kill us, before it has a chance to save us!

Will the world's scientists be prevented from developing alternative energy sources by the big energy companies?

---

[15] Naomi Klein, *This Changes Everything: Capitalism vs. the Climate*, NY 2014, Simon & Shuster.
[16] Thomas Piketty, *Capital and Inequality*, Cambridge, Mass, Harvard University Press, 2014.

Will the deployment of solar, wind, water, and other non-polluting sources of energy be deployed too slowly to save us from the mass production, mass polluting capitalist economies?

Are the modern democracies unable to act because of their capitalist underpinnings?

The problem with an alternative paradigm to mass production and mass consumption is that *the world's peoples want the high-technology products being produced by the capitalist economies.* From New York to Hong Kong, Buenos Aires to Tokyo and London to Moscow, people want: cell phones, computers, televisions, high-tech cars, high-fashion clothing – the world's population want the cornucopia of remarkable products that the advanced capitalist economies churn out – communism fell, in part, because communist economies could not produce such goods!

This technological revolution is very new. The world of the Internet and Skype and self-driving cars, and artificial intelligence – this is all so new that we do not even know its effect on society as yet.

And, all of it is linked to the advanced high-tech capital economies. These economies – *global capitalism* – are going to continue. We can only hope that the science and technology connected to global capitalism will outrun the negative effects this economy has on our climate and our atmosphere.

It may be, that the *democracies will take the lead in funding and encouraging the scientific development of new, non-polluting energy sources* sufficient to power the ever hungrier needs of the mass production capitalist economy.

And it may be, that the democracies take the lead in fining any big corporations – like Volkswagen and Exxon-Mobil – who lie and cheat about their products' pollution value.

This is the hope: the legitimacy of modern democracies can be upheld if they become proactive in the struggle to contain the horrific results of climate change, and if they can control the advanced capitalist corporations upon which they are based. Remember, the corporate executives – as amoral and profit oriented as they are – have to breathe the air and drink the water, like everyone else.

So, just as the tobacco companies were slowly brought to task, so, too, coal, oil, and natural gas companies can be reined in. And, in a free market economy, aggressive alternative energy companies can come to compete with the old energy companies, and, can fund Democratic politicians who favor them. *In the USA the Democratic Party is funded by billionaire capitalists who favor alternative energy and who believe that climate change is real.*

The response of the American Democratic Party, and all the parties of the EU and the UK towards proactive programs to combat the negative effects of climate change, show us that democracies can act against climate change, even though they are linked with advanced capitalism. Because of this, the legitimacy of modern democracy will be upheld.

Whether *all the world's nations* – Democratic or despotic – *can work together* to prevent the disasters inherent in climate change, is another question.

We have 12 years to act.

Chapter 20
Will Artificial Intelligence (AI) Make Democracy Irrelevant?

20.1 The Exciting and Frightening New World of Artificial Intelligence (AI), Robots, and Biotechnology

Yuval Noah Harari, in his new book, *Homo Deus*[1] describes a new world dominated by AI machines – a world in which humans are either gods – homo deus – or irrelevant. Humans become irrelevant because the AI machines are more intelligent than homo sapiens.

It is always easier to imagine a dystopia than a utopia. However, the future, when it arrives, usually looks like neither. We humans do not create perfect societies – neither perfectly wonderful nor perfectly terrible. And new technologies usually become integrated into our societies as morally neutral.

We – homo sapiens – have to add the morality and ethics to the technology. For, the technology in itself has no ethical content. Science is also ethically neutral. Scientists can create atomic bombs or atomic energy power plants, passenger airplanes or fighter planes.

Think back to 1492 A.D. in Spain: Columbus excited the world by crossing the Atlantic Ocean with a group of small sailing ships. What if you told the Medieval Europeans that someday we would be able to fly across the ocean and go anywhere in the world by airplane – and even fly off the Earth to the Moon and Mars. The Medieval Europeans would be dazzled and confused. What would the world be like with such marvelous technology?

Well, we have it now, and it is wonderful and the world is becoming a "global village," but the social issues are still with us: should our politics be democratic or despotic? Air travel does not answer that question. The USA and Russia both have airplanes and space rockets; and, should a society have a free market capitalist economy, or a government managed economy? Airplanes don't answer that question either.

Is AI different because the AI machines can *think* and airplanes cannot?

---

[1]Yuval Noah Harari, *Homo Deus*, Amazon Paperback, 2018.

© Springer Nature Switzerland AG 2019
R. M. Glassman, *The Future of Democracy*,
https://doi.org/10.1007/978-3-030-16111-8_20

20.2   Can AI Machines Think?

Contemporary intellectuals, such as Harari, are dazzling us with examples of what the AI machines can do.

First of all, they are *supercomputers* that can out calculate us. So, Watson, the IBM supercomputer, can defeat the greatest chess champions. Yes, Watson has done this, and Watson can defeat any human at any game with set rules and moves.

And, Harari also tells us that a musicologist spent 7 years programming an AI machine with algorithms that instructed the machine to compose Bach concertos. It took 7 years, but finally, the musicologist created a successful set of algorithms (step-by-step instructions) that successfully instructed the AI machine to pump out hundreds of Bach concertos. These AI created concertos were so Bach-like, that no one could tell the real Bach from the AI Bach.

The AI machine, however, could only create Bach-like concertos. So, the musicologist created another set of algorithms that instructed the machine to create Chopin piano pieces, and then, another set instructing the machine to create Mozart symphonies.

However, look carefully: the AI machine did not make the decision to create Bach or Chopin or Mozart. The musicologist – the human – made the decisions. And, furthermore, the AI machine did not experience any pleasure from listening to the classical music – the machine did not "feel" anything, nor did it "know," it was creating anything. The AI machine was dependent on the human to give it the algorithms that allowed it to create.

Look further: the musicologist realized that the AI machine could be used to create more than classical music. He – the human – decided to program the machine to create Haiku poetry. So he developed an algorithm for that, and the machine began cranking out hundreds of Haiku poems – again, indistinguishable from the human-created Haiku poems.

But, again, the AI machine did not enjoy or understand the rhyme and rhythm or meaning of the Haiku poems it had churned out.

The AI machines can *simulate thinking*, and can create new music and poetry never seen before. However, *the AI machines cannot simulate consciousness*. The machines do not "know" what they have created – they, did not ask "Why not Mahler symphonies?" or "Why not Homeric poetry?"

At this moment in history, the AI machines do not operate like the human brain. Supercomputers operate differently from the human brain. Scientists have not yet been able to fully understand the millions of brain neurons and electrical and chemical circuits of the human brain. In the future, scientists may be able to better understand the brain, and, create AI machines more like the human brain.

Now, the AI machines have a different operating system than our brain. They are much better at calculations, but they are dependent upon humans to direct them in their tasks. Watson does not *want* to play chess, or, help a factory produce cars faster. But, Watson is doing both when we set it up to do so.

Therefore, since the AI machines *lack consciousness*, they do not have the aware-ness – or the "desire," or the "will" – to take over the world. Someday they may acquire this ability, but right now homo sapiens is still the unique creature that has *conscious awareness of itself and the world* – "I think, therefore I am" – the Cartesian conundrum – still puts us at centerstage.

20.3   The AI Machines Cannot Think, but They Can Make Decisions

Watson does not want to play chess, but it can make chess moves that out think the best human Chessmaster's mind. All the chess choices – moves – are programmed into the machine by humans at IBM. But the machine can out calculate the humans – it can make the right move at the right time.

If AI machines are connected to factory production, electrical grids, internet communications networks, and all other modern technological systems, these AI machines will make decisions that will determine what happens within the system in question. This is both good and bad, because the AI machines can out calculate humans, but have no idea what the resulting calculations are for. Remember that Watson can win the chess match, but has no idea why it is playing chess, or what chess is.

So, look at the stock market right now (2018/2019). With the introduction of AI machines, "indexed funds" have absorbed a large portion of human investments in the market. The indexed funds are programmed with algorithms that instruct these funds to buy or sell, depending on certain market conditions.

In a steady market, they are excellent: as the market goes up, the indexed funds go up; as the market goes down, they go down. However, when the market gets erratic – due to data not included in the algorithms of the AI machines – such as a USA president who decides to have a trade war with China and Canada, or, the British Brexit from the EU – then the decisions made by the AI machines can be disastrous. Hence, the stock market suddenly drops by 2000 points because the indexed funds all sell. While, the next week, when the trade war is eased the market gains a thousand points.

Those wild fluctuations in the stock market have been exacerbated by the AI machines, and, *there is no algorithm* that can take into account *events that have never happened before,* or, events based on the irrational greed or fear of the humans involved in the stock market.

Therefore, humans must watch over the machines, because the machines can never be perfectly programmed. Human society is not like a chess game. Human society is always changing and evolving, so the AI machines always will have to be reprogrammed to include the new directions of human history.

Not only can the AI machines not be perfectly programmed, but they cannot know what we humans may want them to do. The AI machines do not want to go to Mars. We humans want to go to Mars. Yes, the AI machine will help us get to Mars and sustain life on Mars. But, we humans have to tell them – provide them with the algorithms that tell them – what we want them to do.

20.4   Artificial Intelligence Machines and Totalitarianism

In the near future, AI machines will not become the rulers of a high tech totalitarianism state. Why? Because these machines do not want to become dictators – they have no will of their own, they have no consciousness of "self" – they do not covet power or revel in the adulation gained by charismatic dictators. "They are, because we program them with specific algorithms." This will be the case until scientists are able to construct them like the human brain. When that happens, if they do gain consciousness of themselves as existing entities, then a machine takeover of the world could be possible.

In the near future, this will not happen. And, it is the near future that we must attempt to analyze.

20.5   The Near Future and AI Machines

In the near future, in the advanced capitalist countries (including China and South Korea), AI systems are going to be increasingly utilized in the production process. Combined with robots, they will produce everything from cars to electric shavers. And, they will produce them faster and more efficiently than our current factory system.

Already, if you Google AI, you will find advertisements for competing AI systems that are being applied to various industries. Many different companies are developing AI systems and creating algorithms that will instruct the machines to produce certain products, and produce them in the most efficient way.

If more and more factories are staffed with AI machines and robots, the human workforce will not be needed. So what will the human labor force be like? Will humans be irrelevant in the new AI-robotized economy?

Humans will be needed, but in different tasks.

20.6   The Workforce in the Near Future: Low-Tech Low Paid Workers and High-Tech High Paid Workers

As we described in our chapter on the revival of fascism, global capitalism has already been eliminating the factory workforce in the advanced capitalist countries by outsourcing the factories to the developing nations where the wages are much lower. So, the factories were moved to China, India, Mexico, Brazil and other low wage nations.

The industrial working class in the USA, the EU and the UK has already been cut substantially. This has altered the political party system in the advanced capitalist countries in that the Social Democrats (the New Deal left-leaning Democrats in the USA) have lost their voting base.

Many of the working-class voters have turned in anger to the right wing neo-fascist parties. I have discussed this in the chapter on Neo-Fascism in this volume.

With the working class in decline, what jobs will be available when the economy becomes more fully automated?

With the advent of AI machines running factories of robots – that is full-scale _automation – will humans be needed? The case of Philips–Norelco in The Netherlands is illustrative. Philips–Norelco moved its factories overseas – "out-sourced" the factory jobs to the developing nations.

However, with the advent of AI and robots, Philips–Norelco moved its factories back to The Netherlands. Most of their electric shavers are now made in The Netherlands. The unskilled factory workers did not get their jobs back. But Philips–Norelco does need workers: technically skilled workers are needed to monitor the automated production process, and unskilled workers are needed to help ship and deliver the electric shavers to distributors worldwide.

Far fewer workers are needed, but human workers have not been fully eliminated.

The near future workforce will be divided into two groups: *unskilled* workers for the delivery system – Amazon, for instance, hires thousands of such workers in the delivery process for millions of different products. And, these unskilled workers get paid *substantially less* than the factory workers in unionized shops. These workers do not make a middle-class wage, and this is definitely problematic.

Second, high-tech workers are needed – workers who have the scientific skill to oversee the automation process, to make sure it is functioning well, and to implement the latest technological advances in AI, robots, and assembly-line logistics.

These highly skilled workers – these scientifically trained "engineers" and "techies" – are being well-paid.

However, these high tech workers do not make millions unless they are the founders or top managers of the companies in question. Yes, Steve Jobs, Bill Gates, and Jeff Bezos made billions. But the high-tech engineers receive a salary of upper-middle-class value – not millions.

Thorstein Veblen, back in the 1920s, wrote a book called, *The Engineers and the Price Systems*,[2] in which he predicted that the high-tech engineers would run the factory system, rather than the capitalist managers or financiers. Veblen called the managers, "captains of industry" and the bankers, "captains of finance."

Veblen was correct in his prediction that scientifically trained engineers would come to hold a critical position in the future factory production system. But he was incorrect that they would come to control and direct the companies themselves.

Rather, advanced, high-tech, capitalism has remained capitalist. That is, financiers still control the funding, through venture capitalism and bank loans, and, the corporate managers (as Berle and Means[3] pointed out) still control the pricing, profits and losses, and salary scale of the advanced high-tech capitalist corporations – and these top managers determine their own salaries and stock options, giving themselves huge salaries and bonuses in most cases. (In Japan, managerial salaries are limited, elsewhere, they are not.)

So, the near future workforce will consist of low wage workers at the bottom end of the automated system, and high paid tech workers attached to the overseeing of the automated system itself. These workers – both the high-tech and the low-tech – will be controlled by the top managers of the companies and their Wall Street financiers.

More:

Workers Will Still Be Needed in the Non-automated Sectors of the Economy.

20.7   The Continuing Need for Human Workers in the Non-automated Sectors of the Advanced Capitalist Economy

I will begin with a strange category of workers that will be increasingly needed.

We have discussed *climate change* and the devastating effect it will increasingly have on the world nations. Storms, flooding, fires, coastal flooding – all these natural disasters demand a large workforce of skilled workers. Every country affected needs: firefighters, electrical grid repair workers, construction workers to remove debris and rebuild hard-hit areas.

Since climate change will worsen the national disasters in the near future, we will need more of these disaster relief workers. It is bizarre, but "nature" is creating work for thousands of humans worldwide.

Climate change has also forced the advanced capitalist nations to develop alternative energy sources. Therefore, we will need a growing workforce of technically trained workers to: scientifically develop the solar panels, windmills, tidal mills, and other alternative energy sources and devices; we will then need workers to

---

[2] Thorstein Veblen, *The Engineers and the Price System*, Amazon Paperback, 2015.
[3] A.A. Berle and Gardiner Means, *The Managerial Revolution*, Amazon Paperback, 2015.

install, tend, fix, and improve the solar panels, battery packs, windmills, tidal mills, etc.

These workers will be well-paid at a middle-class wage and salary level.

Also, along with electrical grid workers, we already need cable TV installers and maintenance workers; smart phone workers, who sell, activate, upgrade, and fix the billions of cell phones used worldwide. There are telephone company stores on every corner, in every mall, in every country in the world – there are human jobs therein. There are also Apple stores and Google stores, and Microsoft stores and other computer stores springing up in all the world's nations. These computer servicing stores and their online and telephone support centers also are creating jobs – high-tech, low-tech, and in between.

All these jobs are here to stay in the near future.

Further, anyone who owns a house or condominium knows that we still need plumbers, electricians, carpenters, flooring installers, furniture movers, and more. These skilled jobs pay well and a continuing workforce of such workers will continue into the near future.

We should not forget that the food industry – farming and meat production – still need an army of low-paid workers – so badly paid, that immigrants often do such work in the advanced capitalist countries. These food industry jobs have not declined, even though much has been automated. Since these workers are underpaid, they can become problematic in terms of the lack of education and upward mobility for their children. So the working poor will be with us into the near future.

Finally, with the biotech and medical revolution that is taking place – and it is astonishing – a massive workforce is needed in the expanding *healthcare* industry.

The work is becoming more and more high-tech at the level of medical procedures and pharmaceuticals, such that robotic operations, high-tech diagnostic machines, and computers are playing an ever increasing role. And chemists, biochemists, and other scientifically trained workers are needed in the expanding pharmaceutical corporations.

The high-tech workers, such as specialized doctors, engineers, tech workers, specialized nurses, and physical rehabilitation workers are highly paid and in growing demand.

There is also, however, an expanding workforce of lower-level hospital workers and caregivers who are moderately paid.

Both sets of healthcare workers are expanding, as the biotech revolution keeps people alive longer, as women have children later in life (and need fertility treatment), and as our ability to treat heart disease, cancer, and infectious diseases improves.

Having established that there will still be a need for *human* workers in the near future – even after AI and robotized automation takes charge of factory production and healthcare operating systems – let us now turn to the effect AI will have on Democracy.

20.8   Will Democracy Become Irrelevant when AI Machines Make Policy Decisions?

AI machines are supercomputers. They can out calculate humans. They will win at chess and produce cars more quickly on an assembly line. They can out diagnose most doctors.

However, we have also established that the AI machines do not know what chess is, nor why they are playing it. The AI machines have to be programmed by humans. The machines do not determine what algorithms they have been programmed to follow. The AI machines, as we have made central, do not have consciousness; they do not have a "self"; they do not want to do anything they have not been programmed to do, nor do they want to do what they have been programmed to do.

Therefore, though the AI machines will play an ever increasing role in the technical decision-making process – as supercomputers – the final decisions have to be made by humans.

Yes, it is true that atomic energy power plants were not implemented by Democratic vote. But, Congressional (Parliamentary) Oversight Committees did supervise these plans as problems were discovered with them. Once it was determined that atomic energy plants do pollute with strontium 90 in the water and soil, and that they could implode – as in Chernobyl and in Northern Japan – then Democratic decision-making determined that they should not be used anymore.

Remember that technology is morally and ethically neutral, and, so is science in general. Once a scientific discovery or new technology is implemented in society and begins to have profound effects – both intended and unintended – then it is up to the Democratic processes of government to engage: expert witnesses, and rational-scientific information are presented, and then partisan debate occurs. Hopefully the correct decision is made concerning the new technological and scientific advances.

Neither democracies nor dictatorships always get decisions right. But AI machines cannot make a decision based on human ethics. They can provide all the data needed to make a moral choice, but they cannot make a moral choice.

So, AI, like every other technology, will be used by both democratic and despotic regimes. And, until AI machines develop self-consciousness, they will be like any other technology.

20.9   Conclusions on AI and Democracy

If you tell people that they are going to be like *gods* – ruling the universe with machines and robots – they love it! And, if you tell people that they are going to be irrelevant – that the universe is going to be ruled by AI machines and robots, and they will be nothings – they also love it!

20.10   Both Utopias and Dystopias Excite the Imagination

Neither utopia nor dystopia is in the near future. Humans will have to oversee the new exciting and frightening technologies that we produce. And remember that new technologies allow us to fly around the world and into space, and to live longer, but the new technologies do not increase human happiness. Human happiness is still dependent upon human relationships and human self-fulfillment. And, even though we are better able to treat depression and illnesses, we are not going to find a happiness pill.

Just as the new technologies do not produce increased happiness, so too, the new technologies do not create a perfect polity. We will still have to choose between democracy and despotism. And, if we choose democracy, we will still have to work hard to maintain it.

In regard to maintaining democracy, the wisdom of the great thinkers of the past will still be very relevant in the near future: Aristotle's wisdom[4] on *"the middle class majority,"* and *"the rule of law"* – "When the law rules, God and reason rule, when a man rules, we add the characters of the beast" – is still to be heeded, for it becomes the basis for Max Weber's *legal-rational authority*, in the modern world,[5] and, a middle class majority is still needed for democratic stability.

Montesquieu's[6] ideas on the *separation of powers*, and Locke's[7] on *the limitations of power* – these are still to be heeded – look at what is happening with Donald Trump's excessive use of executive power in the USA, or Erdoğan's in Turkey.

And, J.S. Mills,[8] Jefferson,[9] Hamilton, and Madison,[10] on free, civil debate, and the *inalienable rights of citizens* – all this wisdom should not be lost because we *think* that AI machines can *think*.

AI machines can compute and follow algorithms that we humans put into them. They cannot think consciously, but we can. So, we must make a conscious decision to establish and maintain Democratic forms of government. After all, it was the advent of our new found species characteristic to become consciously aware of ourselves that gave homo sapiens the ability to expand and become the dominant creatures on earth. And, do not forget, that this remarkable species' characteristic – conscious awareness of self in the universe – not only enabled us to take charge of the earth, but it enabled us to create a *non-animal political structure*. A political

---

[4] Aristotle, *Politics*, Barker Translation, Oxford, Oxford University Press, 1961.

[5] Max Weber, *Economy and Society*, section on "Legitimate Domination" – Legal-Rational vs. Traditional Legitimization, Claus Wittich and Guenther Roth Translation, NY, Bedminster Press, 1968.

[6] Baron de Montesquieu, *The Spirit of the Laws*, Amazon Paperback, 2014.

[7] John Locke, *Second Treatise on Civil Government*, Amazon Paperback, 2014.

[8] J.S. Mill, *On Liberty*, Amazon Paperback, 2015.

[9] Thomas Jefferson, *The Declaration of Independence*, Google.

[10] Alexander Hamilton and James Madison, *The Federalist Papers*, Amazon Paperback, 2015.

structure based on the unique human ability to consciously interact with one another, and *discuss decisions*, rather than fighting over decisions.[11]

Animals fight, dominate and submit. Humans do too, for, we are animals. But, as homo sapiens, we can talk, discuss, debate, and come to a non-violent decision. And, we can be led, not by the strongest and most aggressive, but by the smartest and most capable.

As homo sapiens, our key species characteristic allows us to interact politically in a democratic manner. But since we are both animal and human, our politics can be democratic or despotic. Our history shows this: yet, it is the democratic form of politics that brings out the humanity in us. We are neither gods, nor irrelevant. We are homo sapiens, but, we must emphasize the sapiens – "We think, therefore we are democratic."

---

[11] Ronald M. Glassman, *The Origins of Democracy in Tribes, City-States and Nation-States*, The Netherlands, Springer International Publishers, 2017.

Printed by Printforce, the Netherlands